Nutrient	Functions	Food Sources
ASCORBIC ACID	1. Helps hold body cells together and strengthens walls of blood vessels. 2. Helps in healing wounds. 3. Helps tooth and bone formation.	Cantaloupe, grapefruit, oranges, strawberries, broccoli, Brussels sprouts, raw cabbage, collards, green and sweet red peppers, mustard and turnip greens, potatoes cooked in jacket, and tomatoes.
RIBOFLAVIN	1. Helps cells use oxygen to release energy from food. 2. Helps keep eyes healthy. 3. Helps keep skin around mouth and nose smooth.	Milk, liver, kidney, heart, lean meat, eggs, and dark leafy greens.
NIACIN	1. Helps the cells of the body use oxygen to produce energy. 2. Helps to maintain health of skin, tongue, digestive tract, and nervous system.	Liver, yeast, lean meat, poultry, fish, leafy greens, peanuts and peanut butter, beans and peas, and whole grain and enriched breads and cereals.
VITAMIN D	1. Helps body use calcium and phosphorus to build strong bones and teeth, important in growing children and during pregnancy and lactation.	...ds fortified with vitamin D, such as milk. ...duces vitamin D from cholesterol in the
CARBOHYDRATES	1. Supply food energy. 2. Help body use fat efficiently. 3. Spare protein for purposes of body building and repair.	... cereals, corn, grits, potatoes, rice, ... noodles. Sugars: Honey, molasses, ... er sweets.
FATS	1. Supply food energy in compact form (weight for weight supplies twice as much energy as carbohydrates). 2. Some supply essential fatty acids. 3. Help body use certain other nutrients.	Co... ...g butter, margarine, salad dressings, anc ...
WATER	1. Important part of all cells and fluids in body. 2. Carrier of nutrients to and waste from cells in the body. 3. Aids in digestion and absorption of food. 4. Helps to regulate body temperature.	Water, beverages, soup, fruits, and vegetables. Most foods contain some water.

D0938489

The Thrifty Cook

TASTY BUDGET RECIPES

Other Cookbooks by Farm Journal

FARM JOURNAL'S COUNTRY COOKBOOK

FREEZING & CANNING COOKBOOK

FARM JOURNAL'S COMPLETE PIE COOKBOOK

AMERICA'S BEST VEGETABLE RECIPES

BUSY WOMAN'S COOKBOOK

LET'S START TO COOK

HOMEMADE BREAD

HOMEMADE CANDY

HOMEMADE COOKIES

HOMEMADE ICE CREAM AND CAKE

INFORMAL ENTERTAINING COUNTRY STYLE

FAMILY FAVORITES FROM COUNTRY KITCHENS

EVERYDAY COOKING WITH HERBS

The Thrifty Cook

TASTY BUDGET RECIPES

Edited by

Nell B. Nichols

Farm Journal FIELD FOOD EDITOR

Doubleday & Company, Inc.

GARDEN CITY, NEW YORK

Library of Congress Cataloging in Publication Data

Main entry under title:

The Thrifty cook; tasty budget recipes.

1. Cookery. I. Nichols, Nell Beaubien, ed.
II. Farm journal and country gentleman.
TX715.T25   641.5'52
ISBN *0-385-05496-3*
Library of Congress Catalog Card Number 73–20524

Contents

CHAPTER 1

Cooking with Taste and Thrift

Step into a country kitchen on a rainy evening and you may find golden-crusted loaves of bread baking in the oven and ham-and-bean soup bubbling in the kettle ready to ladle into bowls. Such renowned, tasty dishes exemplify thrifty country cooking at its best.

The place to find economical recipes that don't sacrifice good eating is in farm kitchens. That's where cost-conscious homemakers have for generations cooked three square meals a day, plus in-between lunches, for hard-working, active families. So it was natural for us to go to the country and collect recipes and menus that would help meet the higher cost of living.

The first rule in farm kitchens is, as it always has been, "waste not." This means making the most of what you have. If you grow some of your own food or buy foods when they are plentiful (and thus lower in price), you will have seasonal surplus and need creative ways to serve the same food often in different ways. Farm women are good at this and we share their best recipes.

In developing this cookbook, we took particular pains to consider the nutritional content of recipes. The supply of body-building protein along with a good balance of valuable vitamins and minerals enters into the selection of foods as well as their cost. Inside the front cover of this book, you will find a chart listing nutrients needed by the body and important food sources.

Because most women appreciate the value to health of an adequate supply of protein, this cookbook devotes three chapters to recipes featuring foods that are rich sources of top quality protein. These are the animal foods—meats, fish, poultry, eggs and cheese (milk protein). Most of our main-dish recipes provide enough protein to meet the accepted daily needs. With those that may be a little short, we suggest in a "Memo to Meal Planner" foods to accompany them that boost the protein. This might simply be a salad containing cottage cheese, for example.

The "Memo to Meal Planner" follows most of the recipes. It is a convenient place for you to obtain suggestions for what to serve with the particular recipe you are considering, and other helpful tips.

Notice throughout this cookbook the return to old-time thrifty favorites, adapted to today. Many of them contain valuable vegetable protein—dry beans, peas and lentils, for instance. Teamed with some meat or chicken, as they are in soup kettles and casseroles, they provide a tasty main dish high in protein.

A few special recipes include textured vegetable protein in the ingredient list. These manufactured food products contribute low-cost protein and are often used to stretch the meat supply. Soybeans that grow on American farms are important in their manufacture.

Since seasonings can do so much to lift economy dishes above the commonplace, we developed recipes for inexpensive seasoning mixes to make up and have on hand. You will find these and also mixes for cookies, pancakes, biscuits, puddings and sauces in the chapter "Homemade Mixes Save Time and Money."

One of the key secrets to the success of thrifty country cooking is to include in a meal something the family especially likes. This might be money-saving Hamburger Soup—many mothers tell us their children prefer ground beef above all other meats. We have a great collection of family-favorite dishes made with ground beef. Or it might be homemade yeast breads or hot quick breads that make a simple meal special.

In a special section which follows, we answer typical questions about how to shop wisely for food. You also will find a section describing some of the pet economies of country women.

As for the recipes, we guarantee that they are so good you would want to make them even if they weren't thrifty. Each one has been tested and perfected by home economists in our Test Kitchens.

How to Get the Most Food Value for Your Money

Here are some common questions homemakers ask with answers from FARM JOURNAL food editors, based on the latest research.

Q. I'm not the best food shopper in the world, and I need to do a better job. How do I go about it?

A. To become a really good shopper takes consciously trying to select food that (1) will provide nutritious meals that will keep your family healthy and feeling good, and (2) to do so at a reasonable cost. This means *planning* meals ahead and shopping from a list.

Q. Since I'm not a dietitian, how can I be sure I plan well-balanced meals?

A. It is not as difficult as it seems. The U. S. Department of Agriculture has worked out a "Daily Food Guide." Until a few years ago, nutritionists recommended following the Basic Seven groups in order to maintain nutritionally balanced diets. The seven groups were: deep green and yellow vegetables, citrus fruits, potatoes and other vegetables and fruits, milk and milk products, meat and meat substitutes, bran and cereal products and butter or margarine.

Then the Basic Seven was simplified to the Basic Four. This is a good guide to follow, although it is somewhat oversimplified. For example, there are valuable protein foods outside of the meat group, such as milk and cereal products.

Q. I get confused when I try to follow charts. Can you explain the Basic Four group in more detail?

A. Start with the meat group, since this can end up taking the largest share of your grocery money.

Meat Group:

Everyone needs protein for the growth—and repair—of body tissues and also to provide iron, thiamine, niacin, riboflavin and other nutrients. One serving consists of 2 to 3 ounces *cooked lean* meat, poultry or fish; 2 eggs; 1 cup of alternates such as dry beans or lentils, and ¼ cup peanut butter. The adult daily requirement is two servings per day.

Vegetable and Fruit Group:

Four or more ½-cup daily servings are needed to provide the essential amounts of vitamins A and C.

Every day choose one main top source of vitamin C, such as grapefruit or grapefruit juice, orange or orange juice. Other sources are tomatoes or tomato juice, cantaloupe, broccoli, Brussels sprouts, green pepper, sweet pepper, fresh strawberries, honeydew melon, lemons, watermelon, cabbage, cauliflower, potatoes and sweet potatoes cooked in their jackets, rutabagas and turnip greens.

Every other day serve a top source of vitamin A, such as a dark green or deep yellow vegetable. Vegetables rich in vitamin A are carrots, collards, spinach and other vegetables with dark green leaves, sweet potatoes, winter squash and pumpkin. Among the fruits with considerable amounts of vitamin A are apricots, cantaloupe and persimmons.

Milk Group:

Milk—whole, skim and buttermilk, or evaporated and reconstituted nonfat dry milk—is the major source of calcium needed for strong teeth and bones. It also contains protein, riboflavin, phosphorous and vitamins A and C. Daily needs are as follows: adults, 2 cups; children under nine, 2 to 3 cups; teen-agers, 4 cups.

Substitutions you can make are: 1″ cube Cheddar-type cheese for ⅔ cup milk; ½ cup cottage cheese for ⅓ cup milk; ½ cup ice cream or ice milk for ¼ cup milk.

Bread and Cereal Group:

Whole grain and enriched breads or cereals give you valuable sources of thiamine, niacin, riboflavin and other nutrients. Always read labels to make sure your selection has been enriched.

Select four or more servings daily from whole grain or enriched breads, cereals, cornmeal, grits, macaroni, spaghetti, noodles, rice and quick breads. One slice of bread, or a similar serving of baked goods made with enriched flour, makes one serving, so does 1 ounce of ready-to-serve cereal, ½ to ¾ cup cooked cereal, rice, macaroni, spaghetti or grits.

Q. Is it really important to plan this carefully?

A. With the wide variety of foods you probably will serve your family, they are not likely to have any of the *serious* deficiency diseases (like scurvy and beriberi) that are found in many parts of the world. But nutritional carelessness is potentially dangerous. It can inhibit both the mental and physical growth of children, cause fatigue and anemia in women and lower the resistance of everyone in the family to colds and flu, add difficulty in handling emotional distress and lay the groundwork for diseases later in life.

Q. What is the best (and easiest) way to plan a shopping list?

A. It is helpful and desirable to make out menus for a week, or at least for a few days. Check a few of your meal plans with the Basic Four group to see if they meet the day's requirements.

Incorporate as many of the weekly advertised specials in your meals as possible. Try to work at least one third of your meals around advertised meat specials. Buy favorite cuts of meat for freezing when they are on sale.

Keep a memo pad or slate on the kitchen wall to jot down remember-to-buy items. If you have ample storage space, buy staple foods when they are "on special."

Q. Figuring out menus may help me get nutritious meals, but can they save me money?

A. Yes, if you look at each food critically. Ask yourself how its price compares with another food that could replace it nutritionally. For example, carrots are likely to provide your vitamin A needs at a lower cost than broccoli. Frozen orange juice may be a more economical choice for vitamin C than strawberries, at least in most seasons. Chuck steak is just as nutritious as porterhouse.

As the Basic Four group indicates, meat alternates such as eggs, dry beans and peas and peanut butter can substitute for meat part of the time. Research has shown that while cereals do not themselves supply the top quality protein your body needs, combining them with foods from vegetable sources can provide the type of protein required for good health. Soybeans combine with wheat, corn and rye to make complete protein. Peanuts supplement the protein in wheat, oats, corn and rice. A combination of soybean and sesame proteins compares favorably with milk protein.

Q. What can I do to make a shopping list that simplifies shopping?

A. Learn the order items appear in the aisles of the supermarket. Make out your shopping list in the same order. You will avoid backtracking which will save time and exposure to tempting foods. Try to avoid impulse buying—it can wreck the budget. But keep an open mind for genuine specials.

Q. How can I tell what is a good buy?

A. Brush up on your mathematics so you can buy on a price per ounce basis. Divide the price of a food by the number of ounces and you have the cost per ounce. If a 16-ounce can of peaches sells for 31 cents, the cost per ounce is about 2 cents. The value per ounce of a 29-ounce can of peaches at 43 cents is about 1½ cents. Remember that a bargain is a bargain only if your family likes the food and it can be used in a reasonable length of time.

Q. Isn't the largest can or package cheaper?

A. Usually it is, but there are exceptions. Don't be fooled by box sizes labeled Giant, Economy or King size. Check the cost per ounce. A large size never is cheaper if part of the contents goes stale and is thrown out.

Q. What besides ounces is important to check on labels?

A. Inspection marks or grades—they show quality—and contents are listed in order of their proportions. For example, noodles with chicken indicates the product contains more noodles than chicken.

Q. Is it a good idea to buy the least expensive canned goods?

A. Not necessarily. Buy foods best suited to their use. A less expensive vegetable may be perfectly all right to use in a casserole while you may prefer a higher-priced version to serve by itself. Cut vegetables usually cost less than whole and are a better buy unless you are preparing a dish where appearance is important. Supermarkets' own brands usually are cheaper. Compare them with national brands to find out which one you prefer.

Q. How can I get the best buys in meat?

A. Don't look at just the cost per pound, but at the servings of lean meat in a cut. The proportions of fat, bone and gristle vary. One pound of cuts with a medium amount of bone provides three or four servings compared with only one or two servings if cuts have much bone, gristle or fat.

Q. What grade of meat is the best buy?

A. The U. S. Department of Agriculture grades of beef most commonly sold are, starting at the top, Prime, Choice and Good. Common lamb grades are Prime and Choice. *Prime* beef is the most expensive, and Choice is perfectly adequate. Choose Choice beef for cuts you plan to broil or roast. The grade of beef labeled *Good* is an economical buy when you can use less tender cuts, such as for pot roasts and stews. Choose meat of a good red color with little fat around the edge. Pork usually is not graded. The federal or state inspection seal on meat insures your quality.

Q. What about poultry grades?

A. Again, look for the U. S. Department of Agriculture grade shield. Most poultry is grade A. However, grade B is acceptable when you are not interested in appearance, such as for use as cubed chicken. Choose a firm, plump chicken with white or yellow skin (not gray) and a soft breastbone. Large birds, especially turkeys, generally yield more meat per pound than small ones.

Although stewing hens traditionally have been a thrifty buy for stewing, modern poultry growing methods have made broiler-fryers frequently the better buy. They also are an inexpensive choice for roasting. Whole chickens usually are cheaper than chicken parts, so if you do not know how to cut them up, it will pay you to learn how (see Index for "How to Cut Up a Chicken").

Q. How can I select the best buy of ground beef?

A. Starting with the lowest to the highest priced, you probably will have a choice of ground beef, ground chuck, ground round and ground sirloin. A federal law now restricts the fat content of ground beef to no more than 30 per cent. So for meat loaves and casseroles, ground beef is acceptable, but you may prefer a better quality for casseroles. Buy ground beef when it is on sale. Divide it into patties for hamburgers and recipe-size portions for casseroles and other dishes before wrapping and freezing.

Q. Are luncheon meats economical?

A. Sometimes they are because there is no waste. You may find unsliced varieties, such as bologna, thriftier than the sliced.

Q. Is a boneless ham a better buy than a bone-in ham?

A. A whole ham with bone in is worth 75 per cent as much as a boneless ham. If you use the bone for seasoning, consider the ham with bone worth 80 per cent of a boneless ham. You are justified in paying up to 15 cents per pound for the butt half of a ham over the shank half because it contains more meat.

Q. What is an economy choice in pork?

A. Pork shoulder cuts, such as pork steak, cost less than leg and loin cuts. End-cut loin roasts and pork chops are as tender as the more expensive center cuts, but they may contain slightly more fat and bone.

Q. Would I be money ahead to buy a side or quarter of beef for my freezer?

A. It depends partly on whether your family likes all the cuts from the portion of beef you buy. Some women prefer to buy their favorite cuts of meat when on sale at the supermarket, and to wrap, label, date and freeze at home.

Before you try to compare prices of meat you buy from the supermarket and freeze with a whole side or quarter of beef you buy for freezing, you need to know how much usable meat you will get and which cuts. A choice steer that weighs 1,000 pounds will dress out to about 590 pounds. This provides about 465 pounds of retail cuts because there are about 125 pounds of unusable bones, fat and waste. The 465 pounds include 110 pounds of ground beef, 105 pounds of chuck roasts, 65 pounds round steak, 45 pounds stew meat and miscellaneous cuts, 45 pounds rib roasts, 20 pounds boneless rump roast, 40 pounds sirloin steak and 35 pounds porterhouse, club and T-bone steaks.

Q. I have seen "vegetable protein" in my supermarket—what is this?

A. Yes, you probably will see and hear more about these proteins. They are manufactured from plant sources, such as the legumes—particularly soybeans. Some scientists believe they may provide 10 per cent of the "meat" supply by 1985. Versatile spun soybean and textured soybean products can be made with any level of protein, fat or carbohydrate desired. Some soybean products are meat-flavored and resemble meat. No doubt you are familiar with bacon-flavored textured vegetable protein now on the market.

Textured vegetable protein is not new, but gets more attention in a protein-hungry world than it formerly did. The U. S. Department of Agriculture in 1971 approved its use in school lunch programs. Vegetarians have used it for years. Recipes in this cookbook that call for textured vegetable protein are: Barbecued Meat Balls, Twin Meat Loaves, Oatmeal Drop Cookies, Exceptional Tuna Patties and Bacon Flavor Dip Mix (see Index for these recipes).

Q.   What is the best buy in eggs?

A.   Look for both grade and size when you make your decision. Buy grade AA or grade A for use where appearance is important, as in fried eggs. Grade B eggs are perfectly satisfactory to use in baking and for scrambled eggs. Generally, if there is less than 7 cents per dozen price spread between one egg size and the next smaller one, you get more for the money by buying the larger size.

Q.   How can I cut my milk bill?

A.   You can save a few cents by buying milk at the store rather than having home delivery. Buying larger cartons or bottles provides additional savings. Skim milk is less expensive than homogenized, but check to make sure it is fortified with vitamins A and D. Nonfat dry milk can be a real budget stretcher. If your family objects to drinking it when reconstituted try mixing it with an equal amount of fresh milk. Or use it in baking, soups, sauces, desserts and other cooked dishes. Buy as large a package of nonfat dry milk as you can store without waste. Be sure to select the pasteurized grade A and U.S. extra grade of nonfat dry milk. Evaporated milk also is a good buy for cooking. You can get part of your milk via ice cream, but 1 cup of ice cream used to replace ½ cup milk may cost three times more!

Q.   Should I use fresh, canned or frozen vegetables and fruits?

A.   Fresh vegetables in season in your area often are top quality and real bargains. Fresh produce shipped considerable distance does not always provide food value equal to vegetables straight from the garden. Seasonal changes can affect the price of canned and frozen fruit, too. Frequently there is a drop in prices in late spring or early summer when the new crops are being packed. This is a good time to stock up if you have the space. With improved canning and freezing techniques, there is little difference nutritionally between fresh, canned and frozen fruits and vegetables. So make your choice on personal preferences and current prices.

Q. What is the best buy in frozen vegetables?

A. Loose-packed vegetables in clear plastic bags can save you as much as 40 per cent over smaller packages. You can see what you are buying and use exactly the amount you need. If you have time, you will save money by seasoning and preparing your own sauces for frozen vegetables (see Index for frozen Sauce Cubes). Frozen vegetables with sauces and seasonings carry a premium price over plain frozen vegetables. Avoid buying frozen foods in stained containers which may indicate that the contents were accidentally defrosted. Buy from freezer cases that register a temperature no higher than 0°.

Q. What about all the quick-fix and convenience foods on the market—are any of them economical?

A. Unless time is money to you, generally your best bet is to start cooking "from scratch." However, some quick-fix items actually cost less or no more than home-prepared versions. Frozen orange juice concentrate, instant coffee, canned spaghetti and some cake and biscuit mixes compare favorably in cost with homemade kinds. Packaged seasoning mixes, seasoned rice and pasta mixes, frozen main dishes and specialty items cost more than "from scratch" versions.

Q. Any way to save on bread cost?

A. Take advantage of the day-old bread counter if your supermarket has one. Some areas have day-old shops. Doughnuts and sweet rolls are just as good as they were the first day if you give them a quick warm-up in the oven, and the price is often as much as one third to one half less. Buy day-old bread and buns too if you can use them right away, or freeze them.

Choose breads that are either whole grain, enriched or fortified. Check the weight of the bread, not merely the size of the loaf or package. Compare prices of equal weights of bread to determine which is the better buy.

Most breads are enriched, but specialty breads, such as French, Italian and raisin loaves, and other bakery products often are not. Check the wrapper or ask the baker whether enriched flour is used. Breads baked at home usually cost less than ready-baked. If made with enriched flour, they may be more nutritious. Compare the cost of the ingredients used in one of your favorite recipes and the price of an equal weight of a similar bakery product your family enjoys. Then you can decide whether it is worth while to make your own.

Q. My children like presugared cereals for breakfast. Am I wasting my money buying them?

A. You may not be wasting money when you purchase them even though they cost more, considering their nutritive properties. Family preference should be an important factor in all food plans. But you should realize that they cost more per ounce than many unsweetened cereals and furnish more calories and less food value than cereals you sweeten yourself. Ready-to-serve cereals in multipacks of individual boxes may cost two or three times as much per ounce as the same cereals in large boxes.

Q. What should I look for at the cheese counter?

A. You usually will find that cheese cut and wrapped in the supermarket costs less per pound than prepackaged cheeses. Sliced, cubed and shredded cheese is more expensive than when you fix them in your kitchen. Mild Cheddar cheese is more economical than sharp, process cheese is cheaper than Cheddar. Pasteurized process cheese has more of the cheese flavor than pasteurized cheese foods and spreads. Cheese in large boxes and jars and cottage cheese in large cartons cost less per pound than in smaller containers. Cottage cheese is comparatively low in cost and calories, but high in top-quality protein.

Buy and Cook the Right Amounts

To make good use of your food dollar, you'll want to avoid both skimpy servings and also the waste of throwing unused food away. Here is a guide for planning how much to purchase and some tips on how much to cook. It's based on average servings, so take that into account if you have a hearty eater in the family.

How Much to Buy

Meat, Poultry, Fish, Cheese	Servings per pound
Meat	
Large amount of bone (ribs)	1 to 2
Medium amount of bone (chuck roast) . .	2 to 3
Minimum amount of bone (steaks, roasts) . .	3 to 4
Boneless (ground meat, rump roast, liver) . .	4
Luncheon Meat	5

Poultry   *Servings per pound*

Chicken
  Broiling 1¼
  Frying, roasting, stewing 2
Duck 1
Turkey
  Whole 2
  Rolled turkey roast 3

Fish
Whole 1
Dressed, large 2
Steaks and fillets 3
Canned (tuna, salmon, sardines) 5

Cheese
Natural and process 8
Cottage cheese 8

Vegetables, Fruits
Fresh Vegetables
Asparagus . . . . 3 or 4
Beans
  Lima (in pods) 2
  Snap . . . . 5 or 6
Beets, diced (without tops) . . . . 3 or 4
Broccoli . . . . 3 or 4
Brussels sprouts . . . . . . 4 or 5
Cabbage
  Raw, shredded . . . . 9 or 10
  Cooked . . . . 4 or 5
Carrots
  Raw, diced or shredded . . . . . 5 or 6
  Cooked 4
Cauliflower 3
Kale (untrimmed) . . . . . . 5 or 6
Okra . . . . 4 or 5
Onions, cooked . . . . 3 or 4
Parsnips 4
Peas (in pods) 2
Potatoes 4
Spinach 4

Fresh Vegetables   *Servings per pound*
  Squash
    Summer .   .   .   .   3 or 4
    Winter .   .   .   .   2 or 3
  Sweet Potatoes .   .   .   .   3 or 4
  Tomatoes, raw, sliced   5
Frozen Vegetables   *Servings per 9- or 10-ounce package*
  Asparagus .   .   .   .   2 or 3
  Beans
    Lima .   .   .   .   3 or 4
    Snap .   .   .   .   3 or 4
  Broccoli   3
  Brussels sprouts   3
  Cauliflower   3
  Corn, whole kernel   3
  Kale .   .   .   .   2 or 3
  Peas   3
  Spinach .   .   .   .   2 or 3
Canned Vegetables   *Servings per 1-pound can*
  Most vegetables .   .   .   .   .   .   3 or 4
  Greens (kale or spinach) .   .   .   .   .   2 or 3
Dry Vegetables   *Servings per pound*
  Beans   11
  Peas, lentils .   .   .   .   10 or 11
Fresh Fruit   *Servings per market unit*
  Apples, bananas, peaches, pears, plums .   .   3 or 4 per pound
  Apricots, sweet cherries, seedless grapes .   .   5 or 6 per pound
  Blueberries, raspberries .   .   .   .   .   4 or 5 per pint
  Strawberries .   .   .   .   8 or 9 per quart
Frozen Fruit   *Servings per 10- or 12-ounce package*
  Blueberries .   .   .   .   3 or 4
  Peaches .   .   .   .   2 or 3
  Raspberries .   .   .   .   2 or 3
  Strawberries .   .   .   .   2 or 3
Canned Fruit   *Servings per 1-pound can*
  Served with liquid   4
  Drained .   .   .   .   2 or 3
Dried Fruit   *Servings per 8-ounce package*
  Apples   8
  Apricots   6
  Mixed fruits   6

Dried Fruit	*Servings per 8-ounce package*
Peaches	7
Pears	4
Prunes	4 or 5

How Much to Cook

	Amount Before Cooking	*Measure After Cooking*
Cornmeal	1 c.	5½ c.
Macaroni	1 c. (3½ oz.)	2 c.
Noodles	3 c. (4 oz.)	3 c.
Quick-cooking Oats	1 c.	3 c.
Rice		
Long grain	1 c.	3 c.
Packaged precooked	1 c.	2 c.
Spaghetti	1 lb.	9 c.
Kidney, lima and navy beans; split peas	1 c.	2¼ c.

How to Store Perishable Foods

Food is money—and it will pay you dividends in both dollars and food flavor to store it properly. Be sure to unpack groceries as soon as you get them home; put away the perishables as suggested here:

Meat, Poultry, Fish
Loosely wrap and store in the refrigerator. If fresh meat is packaged in moisture-vaporproof wrap, you can refrigerate as is for one or two days. After that, loosen wrapper at both ends. To store meat longer than the refrigerator time suggested below, freezer-wrap, label, date and freeze. Put two layers of waxed paper between individual servings packaged together. Refrigerate luncheon meat in original wrap until opened. Most canned hams need refrigeration, so check the label. Remove giblets from poultry and store separately in a loose wrap. Refrigerate fish in moisture-vaporproof bags or tightly covered containers.

	Time	
	In Refrigerator	*In Freezer* *0° or Lower*
Beef		
Roasts	5 to 6 days	6 to 12 months
Steaks	3 to 5 days	6 to 12 months
Ground beef, stew meat	1 to 2 days	3 to 4 months
Pork		
Roasts	5 to 6 days	3 to 6 months
Hams, picnics, whole	7 days	2 months
Bacon	5 to 7 days	Not recommended
Chops, spareribs . .	3 days	3 to 6 months
Veal		
Roasts	5 to 6 days	6 to 9 months
Chops	4 days	6 to 9 months
Lamb		
Roasts	5 days	6 to 9 months
Chops	3 days	6 to 9 months
Poultry		
Chicken, whole . .	2 to 3 days	12 months
Chicken, cut up . .	2 days	12 months
Turkeys, whole . .	4 to 5 days	12 months
Cooked Meats		
Leftover cooked meat .	4 to 5 days	2 to 3 months
Cooked poultry . .	2 days	6 months
Frankfurters . . .	4 to 5 days	Not recommended
Sliced luncheon meat .	3 to 7 days	Not recommended
Fresh Fish You Buy		
Cod, haddock, halibut, 　pollock, sea trout, 　king crab, shrimp, 　scallops	24 hours	4 to 6 months
Mullet, ocean perch, 　mackerel, salmon, 　butterfish, clams, 　oysters	24 hours	2 to 3 months

Frozen Fish You Buy	*Storage Time*
Cod, flounder, haddock, halibut, pollock	6 months
Sea trout, striped bass, ocean perch . .	3 months
King crabmeat	10 months
Shrimp	12 months

Vegetables

Wash and drain greens, celery, green onions, asparagus and cabbage. Refrigerate individually in moisture-vaporproof bags. Cut off tops of carrots, beets and radishes. Store in refrigerator in separate moisture-vaporproof bags. Keep white and sweet potatoes, onions, rutabagas and winter squash in a cool, dark, dry place with ventilation. A cool, dry place provides good storage for canned vegetables. Opened canned vegetables may be left in the can, covered and stored in the refrigerator.

Fresh	*Storage Time*
White and sweet potatoes, onions,	Up to 1 month in cool,
rutabagas, winter squash . .	dark place
Other fresh vegetables . . .	3 to 5 days in refrigerator
Frozen vegetables you buy . . .	8 months in freezer
Home frozen vegetables . . .	9 to 12 months in freezer

Fruits

Store fresh, ripened fruits in the refrigerator crisper, or uncovered. Keep dried fruit in covered containers and canned fruit in a dry, cool place.

Fresh	*Storage Time*
Apples, citrus	7 days
Most other fruits . . .	3 to 5 days
Frozen fruits you buy . . .	9 to 12 months in freezer
Home frozen fruits . . .	10 to 12 months in freezer
Frozen orange juice concentrate	12 months in freezer

Dairy Products, Eggs

Refrigerate butter, milk, cottage cheese and hard cheese tightly covered or wrapped. Butter and margarine will keep 1 to 2 weeks in the refrigerator, 3 months in the freezer. Use cottage cheese and milk within 3 to 5 days, hard cheese in 3 to 4 weeks after the original wrapper is removed. You can store eggs in their original carton in the refrigerator up to 3 weeks.

Thrifty Tips from Country Kitchens

Every homemaker has her pet economies. We present some favorite ways in which 500 members of FARM JOURNAL's Family Tests Group make every food dollar count. Sharing their economies may give you new time and money savers to add to your own:

I always try to feed my family as economically as possible without sacrificing good nutrition. I do not buy many mixes because my family prefers my own "from-scratch" dishes. Although we eat the same things when food prices are high, I serve smaller portions of the more expensive items.

*

I buy the food my family likes, but I cut down on luxury items that we can get along without.

*

Our eating habits change little when prices are high, but we do buy fewer snacks.

*

My cooking really does not change much because I always prepare "from-scratch" foods. My family thinks the prepared dishes you buy all taste the same. I am learning to bake yeast breads, which means we will have to use will power to avoid eating too much. The baking is time consuming, but breads freeze well.

*

We never throw away food. I keep a container for stews in my freezer and all compatible foods go into it. When filled, we have stew, soup or a meat pie with biscuits baked on top. I use bits of meat, combined with fresh vegetables, to make sweet-sour dishes and curries.

*

I save the broken bits of cookies and crumbs in a plastic bag stored in the refrigerator. Before long, there's enough to make a pie crust. Roll crumbs fine and follow directions for a graham cracker crust. I often combine different cookies, such as gingersnaps and vanilla wafers.

*

I make apple dumplings with scraps of leftover pastry. Peel and core an apple; place it on rolled-out pastry; fill apple with sugar, spice, raisins and a dot of butter. Seal pastry at top, wrap in foil and freeze. Bake when you have enough to serve the family.

*

I freeze leftover egg whites in foil-lined muffin-pan cups. When set, remove filled foil cups, fold tops to close, pack in a round carton and return to freezer.

*

I try to avoid waste by cooking no more than we need. Leftovers sometimes spoil in the refrigerator before I can use them. I now keep them in the freezer.

*

When I have leftovers, I freeze them for TV dinners. I package a complete meal in a disposable pie pan. They come in handy, especially when you need to serve one person.

*

I figure we are money ahead when I fix food my family likes so that they clean their plates! We encourage the children to take smaller portions and have seconds if they wish.

*

I continue to freeze and can as much food as possible when it's in season and therefore lower in cost.

*

I make cranberry sauce when the berries are in season and the most inexpensive. It freezes beautifully.

*

During the canning season, I put up fruit juices and pulp. When the weather is cooler and I have more time, I make these into butters and jellies.

*

If I have lemons and oranges that might spoil, I squeeze and freeze the juice in ice cube trays. Later I thaw as many cubes as I need.

*

When cooking meat for dinner, I prepare a little extra to use later in sandwiches. Costs less than buying lunch meats that may have less food value.

*

When I prepare stuffing, I double the recipe. Then I freeze the extra in 1-cup portions; use it to stuff chops, fish or rolled steak.

*

When I prepare Welsh rarebit, I make a double batch and store part in the refrigerator. It makes a tasty and nutritional sauce for vegetables. When you have garden surplus, serve a vegetable plain one day, with sauce the next.

*

Our splurges are fresh fruit and lettuce the year around. We love salads. Sometimes lettuce, due to crop conditions, is quite expensive. Then I substitute by adding more shredded carrots to salads for roughage. I also make good use of the least costly fruits, such as apples and bananas.

*

I don't think the high cost of living changes our eating very much, although I am really careful to save leftovers and use them. I'm fortunate, for I was trained from childhood not to waste food.

*

I divide expensive fruits into serving portions instead of letting everyone have as much as he likes. For snacks we use popcorn, cheese curls and fresh fruits rather than nutrition-empty candy and other sweets.

*

I sprout alfalfa seeds and beans and add the nutritious sprouts to salads.

*

Last summer a neighbor taught me how to fry squash blossoms. They taste delicious and came to me free from the garden. There are other interesting "free" foods—especially berries, nuts, some greens.

*

I save the leftover syrup from a jar of sweet or dill pickles. It's delicious poured over a ham before baking. Or I use it to thin mayonnaise or to marinate onion rings to add to a tossed salad.

*

I use the drained potato water plus dry milk as the liquid for mashing potatoes.

*

For a pretty and inexpensive garnish, I add pineapple tidbits or shredded coconut to the syrup that's left when all the maraschino cherries are used from a bottle.

*

When we have company or extra men to feed, I make homemade rolls. They go over real well and are filling—and stretch the meat.

*

I try to eliminate rich desserts and serve fresh fruits in season to cut costs. Also helps us with our weight problems.

*

I use nonfat dry milk in cooking. Also we have many oven meals in which I bake at least the main dish and dessert side by side, saving on electricity.

*

I make more main-dish soups now. I buy stewing hens when I can get them at a bargain; then dress, package and freeze them myself.

*

When we eat out we find that Mexican and Chinese dinners are relatively less expensive and my family likes them very much.

*

We entertain at picnics and suppers instead of large dinners.

*

During the hot summer months I keep an ice bucket full of ice on the sink counter. It saves frequent opening of the refrigerator and emptying of ice trays and thus saves electricity. Cubes keep up to 6 or 8 hours in a plastic foam container.

*

I serve more hot cereals, which are a better buy and more nutritious than ready-to-eat cereals.

*

We neighbors exchange plentiful foods. For example, I give one of them a box of cherries when our crop is ripe and she gives me a box of tomatoes she grows.

*

I try to keep my husband away from supermarkets. He's the champion impulse buyer.

*

Shopping early in the day helps me. I buy more if I shop late in the day when I'm hungry!

*

I plan menus around food specials advertised in newspapers.

*

It's wise, at least for me, to shop for food without the children. They want so many snacks. I do try to keep home-baked cookies on hand for them.

*

I do not buy nonfood items at the supermarket. We can get them elsewhere at a discount.

*

Cents-off coupons save money if you buy foods you need and those that will keep well. They might as well be on my shelf as on the supermarket's.

*

When I find a very good special on food that will keep well in my cool basement, I buy it in larger quantities than I otherwise would. I just returned home with 100 pounds of potatoes and spread them on the basement floor so the air can circulate around them.

*

It pays to shop less often, with a shopping list (and to stick to it).

*

Tuna is an excellent buy. I also save money on it by using the less expensive grated type for casseroles and reserving the chunk tuna for salads and dishes in which appearance is important.

*

I use the store's own brand of canned foods, which costs less and is good, at least those of my supermarket are.

*

I save money by making my own salad dressings.

*

I have a philosophy that helps me meet high food costs. The most economical thing to do is to plan more carefully and eat more selectively.

*

Variety in meals is important. My family enjoys a pot of hearty soup almost as much as a roast or steak, but I'm careful not to serve the same kind of soup too frequently.

*

I consider myself fortunate to have a good source of raw material (garden) and a skill (cooking) with which I can produce a highly desirable meal at a fairly low cost. We like to socialize at home around our dinner table and we entertain often. I love to cook and I have learned to combine cooking and entertaining easily. This helps. We save money by not eating out except on a very few occasions, such as during Fair week.

*

I entertain more with after-dinner desserts and I also have ice cream parties instead of inviting friends to a complete dinner.

*

Recently I had company for breakfast instead of for dinner. The food cost less and was delicious. Everyone had a wonderful time.

*

Careful planning of my menus helps me cope with high food costs.

*

We have two freezers. I buy broiler-fryers at a bargain and put a supply in the freezer. I just froze 60 chickens to use in the future.

*

When available, I buy day-old bread and store it in my freezer. This is quite a saving.

*

I make barbecue sauce using tomatoes, green peppers and onions from my garden when they are plentiful. The sauce freezes successfully and comes in handy. And, of course, it saves money.

*

I do not use many prepared foods and mixes from stores. I teach food preparation to 4-H girls and need to practice what I preach. Let's face it: You feel a sense of pride when you look at the food you have canned or open a freezer and see how you filled it with foods from your garden. You experience the same feeling when you get and serve a "from-scratch" meal that tastes good and stretched your food dollars.

CHAPTER 2

Homemade Mixes Save Time and Money

Food mixes originated in country kitchens where, with lots of cooking to do, time was at a premium. And money was "hard to come by." Supplies, other than those grown on the farm, often were miles and hours away. Creative women made their own combinations, especially of dry ingredients and shortening, to speed the preparation of menu staples such as biscuits, pancakes and pie crust.

Daughters of these pioneer mix-makers continued to use their family mixes to stretch time and money too—and to produce the wonderful-tasting baked foods their mothers made. Recipes passed as heirlooms from one generation to the next.

When commercially packaged mixes came to supermarkets and automobiles provided rapid transportation, fewer kitchens made their own. But, now, with higher food prices and the greater interest in thrifty meals the family *likes,* homemade mixes are coming back. New ones are being developed. In this chapter we include recipes for the best of the new and the longtime favorites. And we show how to use these "master mixes" with variety in tasty, economical dishes.

In our Test Kitchens we also tried different combinations of seasonings we had on the shelves, figured costs, and held them in economical dishes. Our taste panel, composed of different age groups, liked the results. We share recipe-size premeasured directions for seasoning mixes for you to store in handy aluminum foil packets.

Recipes for seasoning mixes that follow are good in meat loaves, spaghetti sauce, Spanish rice, hamburgers, chili. We have chicken, beef and curry flavors for rice. We also developed recipes for Seasoned Coating and Stuffing Mixes to enhance chicken and meats. Try Spanish Rice with Chicken or the Spanish Rice/Ham Dinner; both are seasoned just right with a mix. Make the Chicken/Stuffing Casserole and many other dishes expertly seasoned in a split second.

This chapter also contains recipes for mixes to use for baked foods. Among them are favorites country women shared with FARM JOURNAL food editors, such as gingerbread, corn bread, Oatmeal

Cookie and quick bread mixes. We developed new ones that include some of the nutritious and economical foods now available.

Nonfat dry milk, which contains the nutrients of fresh milk except the fat, is a good example. You will notice that some of the homemade mixes contain this milk which increases their protein content. White Sauce Mix with many uses is one of them. Potato Soup and Corn/Clam Chowder are two excellent dishes made with it. Super Mix for Baking is accompanied by recipes for eight different, distinctive specials you will enjoy serving—and eating.

Shortenings that require no refrigeration increase the time these mixes can be kept on hand. Look on the label of the container of shortening to be certain that *no refrigeration* is required before you use it in a mix to be stored on the shelf.

Home freezers revolutionized food storage and made it possible to keep partially prepared homemade foods on hand. Hamburger Mix is a splendid example. By packaging it in recipe-size amounts, serving a variety of appetizing and thrifty main dishes is only minutes away. The recipes for the meat mix and ways to use it, and for Frozen Hashed Brown Potatoes ready to brown are just some of the treats in this chapter. Make them up when they are most abundant for use when scarcity of supply causes prices to rise.

Pizza, unknown to most Americans a generation ago, now rates as a top choice across the country, especially with young people. The home economist who worked out the pizza recipes has three teen-age children, all of whom enthusiastically share the results with friends. The success secret is to prebake the crust 6 to 8 minutes, cool and freeze. To make pizza, all you do is fill the firm frozen crust and bake it directly on the oven rack (no pan). Pizzas so handled have a crisp crust that is unusual in other homemade pizzas.

We offer this collection of recipes for homemade convenience mixes as a practical and interesting way to get unusually good meals while holding down food costs.

Homemade Seasoning Mixes

With packets of homemade seasoning mixes in your cupboard, instant and expert seasoning is at your fingertips. While a taste panel approved our blends, you can tailor them to fit your family's taste. If you prefer less chili powder or instant minced garlic, for instance, you can alter the mix the next time you make it.

The easy way to package a mix is to spread the desired number of aluminum foil squares on the kitchen counter. Place the measurement of each ingredient on all the squares, then add others in turn.

These seasoning mixes will keep several months in the kitchen, but, as with spices and dried herbs, it is advisable to keep them in a dry place away from the heat of the range to reduce chances of flavor loss. They contain no preservatives as do commercial products. If you live in a warm, humid climate, put the little packets in a plastic bag and store them in the refrigerator.

You can buy packaged seasoning mixes at the supermarket and frequently they are enclosed with inexpensive meat extenders, such as rice and pasta. By comparing costs of commercial seasoning blends, you will discover you make a substantial saving by making your own. Also, you save money by seasoning your own macaroni, rice and spaghetti.

SPAGHETTI SAUCE MIX

Keep a few packages in a jar on the shelf ready to use.

1 tblsp. instant minced onion	1½ tsp. salt
1 tblsp. parsley flakes	½ tsp. instant minced garlic
1 tblsp. cornstarch	1 tsp. sugar
2 tsp. green pepper flakes	¾ tsp. Italian seasoning

Combine all ingredients. Place on 6″ square of aluminum foil and seal air tight. Repeat recipe to make as many packages as desired. Makes 1 package.

SPAGHETTI WITH MEAT SAUCE

The packaged mix is a real timesaver in this family favorite.

1 lb. ground beef	2 c. water
1 pkg. Spaghetti Sauce Mix	12 oz. spaghetti
1 (6 oz.) can tomato paste	Grated Parmesan cheese

Brown beef in skillet; drain off excess fat. Blend in Spaghetti Sauce Mix, tomato paste and water; bring to a boil. Cover and simmer 20 minutes, stirring once.

Meanwhile, cook spaghetti by package directions; drain. Serve topped with meat sauce. Sprinkle with cheese. Makes 6 servings.

Memo to Meal Planner: The perfect accompaniment for this main dish is Fresh Vegetable Relish Salad if you are serving it in the garden season. An excellent, inexpensive around-the-year choice is molded Country Vegetable Salad (see Index for recipes).

NOODLES WITH MEAT SAUCE

Share this noodle dish with friends when you want to serve something different, tasty and not too expensive.

1 lb. ground beef	12 oz. noodles
1 pkg. Spaghetti Sauce Mix	2 c. grated process sharp
1 (6 oz.) can tomato paste	American cheese (8 oz.)
2 c. water	

Cook ground beef in large skillet until browned; drain off excess fat. Stir in Spaghetti Sauce Mix, tomato paste and water. Bring to a boil. Reduce heat; cover and cook 20 minutes.

Meanwhile, cook noodles by package directions; drain well. Add cheese to meat mixture; stir until cheese is melted. Stir in noodles. Makes 6 servings.

Memo to Meal Planner: No salad tastes better with this main dish than one of lettuce or other greens. Also serve French bread. To make it a special-occasion treat, cut bread in ½″ slices, spread each slice with soft butter or margarine, reassemble loaf, wrap in aluminum foil and heat in 400° oven 15 to 20 minutes. Serve hot. Canned, fresh or frozen fruit makes a perfect dessert. Clusters of grapes, when in season, are a fine choice.

MEAT LOAF SEASONING MIX

Try this seasoning in meat balls, too. You'll like it.

2 c. dry bread crumbs	1 tsp. pepper
½ c. nonfat dry milk	¼ c. instant minced onion
2 tblsp. salt	¼ c. parsley flakes
4 tsp. poultry seasoning	

Combine all ingredients and mix thoroughly. Store in tightly covered container in a cool place. Stir to mix thoroughly before measuring to use. Makes 3 cups.

TASTY BEEF LOAF

Expertly seasoned—has tempting brown exterior, slices neatly.

½ c. water
1 egg, beaten.

¾ c. Meat Loaf Seasoning Mix
1½ lbs. ground beef

Blend water, egg and Meat Loaf Seasoning Mix. Let stand 2 minutes. Thoroughly mix in ground beef. Shape into an 8×4″ loaf in shallow baking pan.

Bake in 350° oven 1 hour and 15 minutes. Makes 6 servings.

Memo to Meal Planner: Loaf slices neatly and is a good hub around which to plan an oven meal. If appetites are hearty, consider also having Baked Butter Beans or Scalloped Corn Supreme. If you make the salad ahead, you will have almost no work to do in the hour before mealtime. Carrot/Cabbage Salad is a thrifty choice (see Index for recipes).

SLOPPY JOE SEASONING MIX

Save minutes by making several packages at a time—handy!

1 tblsp. instant minced onion
1 tsp. green pepper flakes
1 tsp. salt
1 tsp. cornstarch
½ tsp. sugar

½ tsp. instant minced garlic
¼ tsp. dry mustard
¼ tsp. celery seeds
¼ tsp. chili powder

Combine all ingredients. Place on 6″ square of aluminum foil and seal air tight. Repeat recipe to make as many packages as desired. Makes 1 package.

SLOPPY JOE BURGERS

Young people rate these hot sandwiches tops for lunch.

1 lb. ground beef
1 pkg. Sloppy Joe Seasoning
  Mix

1 (6 oz.) can tomato paste
1¼ c. water
6 hamburger buns

Brown beef in skillet; drain off excess fat. Blend in Sloppy Joe Seasoning Mix. Stir in tomato paste and water. Cover and simmer 10 minutes. Serve hot between split buns. Makes 6 sandwiches.

Memo to Meal Planner: Complete lunch with carrot sticks, glasses of milk, applesauce and peanut butter cookies.

NEW ORLEANS FRANKS

The peppy seasoning makes this a hard-to-resist main dish.

1 c. uncooked rice
1 lb. frankfurters
1 tblsp. salad oil
1 (6 oz.) can tomato paste
1¼ c. water

1 pkg. Sloppy Joe Seasoning Mix
1 (15 oz.) can kidney beans, drained and rinsed

Cook rice as directed on package.

Meanwhile, cut each frankfurter in fourths crosswise; brown in hot oil in skillet. Stir in tomato paste, water and Sloppy Joe Seasoning Mix. Add kidney beans. Bring to a boil; reduce heat, cover and simmer 10 minutes. Serve over cooked rice. Makes 6 servings.

CHILI SEASONING MIX

Children like to use this to make their own special chili.

3 tblsp. flour
2 tblsp. instant minced onion
1½ tsp. chili powder
1 tsp. salt
½ tsp. ground cumin

½ tsp. crushed dried red pepper (optional)
½ tsp. instant minced garlic
½ tsp. sugar

Combine all ingredients. Place on 6″ square of aluminum foil and seal air tight. Repeat recipe to make as many packages as desired. Makes 1 package.

RANCH-STYLE CHILI

It takes about 20 minutes to make this superior chili.

1 lb. ground beef
1 pkg. Chili Seasoning Mix
1 (1 lb.) can tomatoes, cut up

½ c. water
1 (15 oz.) can kidney beans, undrained

Brown beef in skillet; drain off excess fat. Blend in Chili Seasoning Mix. Stir in tomatoes, water and beans. Bring to a boil. Reduce heat; cover and simmer 10 minutes. Makes 4 to 6 servings.

Memo to Meal Planner: Include banana or pineapple (or a combination of both fruits) salad in menu. Or if you want to splurge to give your family pleasure, have a tossed salad and Pineapple Upside-down Cake for dessert (see Index).

TEXAS MEAT BALL STEW

A chili-seasoned, one-dish meal—just add a tossed salad.

1 lb. ground beef
1 egg, beaten
¼ c. fine bread crumbs
2 tblsp. milk
½ tsp. salt
1 tblsp. salad oil

1 (1 lb.) can tomatoes, cut up
1 (15 oz.) can kidney beans
1 c. elbow macaroni
1 pkg. Chili Seasoning Mix
2 c. water

Thoroughly mix together ground beef, egg, crumbs, milk and salt. Form into 1″ balls. Brown meat balls on all sides in hot oil in Dutch oven. Pour off excess fat.

Add tomatoes, kidney beans, macaroni, Chili Seasoning Mix and water; bring to a boil, stirring gently. Reduce heat and simmer 15 minutes, stirring occasionally. Makes 6 servings.

CHILI BEEF SHORT RIBS WITH ONION RICE

Blending of seasonings makes these ribs a special favorite.

4 lbs. short ribs
1 pkg. Chili Seasoning Mix
½ c. water
1 (1 lb.) can tomatoes, cut up
½ tsp. salt
1 c. chopped onion

2 tblsp. butter or regular
    margarine
1 c. uncooked rice
2 c. boiling water
1 tsp. salt

Brown short ribs on all sides in heavy Dutch oven; drain off excess fat. Cover and bake in 325° oven 1½ hours. Remove ribs from Dutch oven and drain off fat.

Blend Chili Seasoning Mix and ½ c. water in bottom of Dutch oven. Add tomatoes and ½ tsp. salt. Cook and stir until mixture is thick and bubbly. Add short ribs and stir to coat with sauce. Cover and return to oven 30 minutes, or until ribs are tender.

Meanwhile, cook onion in butter in saucepan until tender. Add rice, boiling water and 1 tsp. salt. Bring to a boil. Reduce heat; cover and cook about 25 minutes, until rice is tender. Serve short ribs over rice. Makes 6 servings.

TACO MIX

Use this mix in the two favorite Mexican recipes that follow.

2 tsp. instant minced onion	½ tsp. crushed dried red pepper
1 tsp. salt	½ tsp. instant minced garlic
1 tsp. chili powder	½ tsp. cornstarch
½ tsp. ground cumin	¼ tsp. dried orégano leaves

Combine all ingredients. Place on 6″ square of aluminum foil and seal air tight. Repeat recipe to make as many packages as desired. Makes 1 package.

TACOS

They carry the double role of sandwich and salad—try them!

1 lb. ground beef	Grated Cheddar cheese
1 pkg. Taco Mix	Chopped fresh tomatoes
¾ c. water	Finely shredded lettuce
Taco shells	

Cook ground beef in skillet until browned; drain off excess fat. Add Taco Mix and water; bring to a boil. Reduce heat and cook uncovered about 10 minutes, until liquid is reduced. Stir once or twice.

Serve 2 tblsp. beef mixture into each taco shell; top beef with cheese, tomatoes and lettuce. Makes 8 to 10 tacos.

Memo to Meal Planner: If your markets do not have taco shells (crisp tortilla pickets), serve beef mixture on corn chips.

TACO BAKE

A favorite Mexican dish with many north-of-the-border friends.

1 lb. ground beef
1 pkg. Taco Mix
2 tblsp. cornstarch
1 (12 oz.) can whole kernel
  corn

1 (8 oz.) can tomato sauce
1½ c. water
2 c. corn chips
½ c. grated Cheddar cheese
  (2 oz.)

Cook beef in skillet until browned; pour off excess fat. Remove from heat; stir in Taco Mix and cornstarch. Add undrained corn, tomato sauce and water. Cook, stirring until mixture reaches a boil. Reduce heat; simmer uncovered 15 minutes, stirring once or twice.

Add half the corn chips to beef mixture; pour into greased 2-qt. casserole. Top with remaining corn chips and cheese. Bake in 400° oven 10 minutes. Makes 5 or 6 servings.

Memo to Meal Planner: This is a good time to have a Mexican-type meal. Serve a big tossed salad and bake custards for dessert. Caramel and chocolate sauces will enhance chilled custards, an important milk and egg dessert. Remember that you can cut costs by using reconstituted nonfat dry milk in custards.

WHITE SAUCE MIX

Keep handy in the refrigerator to stretch time on busy days.

2 c. nonfat dry milk
1 c. sifted flour

3 tsp. salt
1 c. butter or regular margarine

Combine dry milk, flour and salt in large bowl. Cut in butter with pastry blender until mixture resembles tiny peas. Store tightly covered in refrigerator. Makes 5 to 5½ cups.

ENRICHED MEDIUM WHITE SAUCE

Use this recipe to introduce more milk into family meals.

½ c. White Sauce Mix
1 c. milk

Combine White Sauce Mix and milk in saucepan. Cook over medium heat, stirring until thick and bubbly. Makes 1 cup.

Variation
Regular Medium White Sauce: Substitute water for milk.

Memo to Meal Planner: To vary sauce, stir in 2 finely chopped hard-cooked eggs and serve with fish. Or stir in 1 c. shredded process American cheese.

POTATO SOUP

You can easily double this recipe for more servings.

2 c. cubed peeled potatoes	⅛ tsp. pepper
¼ c. chopped celery	1½ c. water
¼ c. chopped onion	¾ c. White Sauce Mix
1 tblsp. parsley flakes	3 c. milk
½ tsp. salt	

Combine potatoes, celery, onion, parsley, salt, pepper and water in saucepan; cook until vegetables are tender.

Meanwhile, combine White Sauce Mix and milk in large saucepan. Cook, stirring constantly, until mixture thickens and bubbles. Add undrained vegetables and heat. Makes about 5 cups.

Memo to Meal Planner: Good on a cold day with hot-from-the-oven California Corn Bread and Molded Tomato Salad (see Index).

CORN/CLAM CHOWDER

A rich-tasting, nutritious soup that's quick and easy to make.

¾ c. White Sauce Mix	1 (8 oz.) can minced clams
3 c. milk	1 tsp. parsley flakes
2 tsp. instant minced onion	½ tsp. seasoning salt
1 (1 lb. 1 oz.) can cream style corn	⅛ tsp. pepper

Combine White Sauce Mix, milk and onion in saucepan; cook, stirring constantly, until mixture thickens and bubbles. Add remaining ingredients and heat. Makes about 6 cups.

Memo to Meal Planner: Choose this for lunch with crisp crackers, carrot sticks and for dessert, applesauce with Oatmeal Chippers made from a mix (see Index).

SPANISH RICE SEASONING MIX

Keep packets of this handy to flavor many rice dishes.

1 tblsp. instant minced onion	1 tsp. sugar
1 tblsp. green pepper flakes	¼ tsp. instant minced garlic
2 tsp. parsley flakes	⅛ tsp. pepper
1½ tsp. salt	⅛ tsp. turmeric

Combine all ingredients. Place on 6″ square of aluminum foil and seal air tight. Repeat recipe to make as many packages as desired. Store in jar or plastic bag on cupboard shelf. Makes 1 package.

BASIC SPANISH RICE

Especially good teamed with chicken, ham or hamburgers.

1 c. uncooked rice	1 (1 lb.) can tomatoes, cut up
2 tblsp. melted butter, regular margarine or bacon drippings	1 pkg. Spanish Rice Seasoning Mix
1 c. boiling water	

Cook rice in butter in saucepan over medium heat, stirring constantly, until golden. Slowly add water, tomatoes and Spanish Rice Seasoning Mix; bring to a boil. Cover with tight-fitting lid and cook over low heat about 25 minutes, until rice is tender. Makes 4 cups.

SPANISH RICE WITH HAMBURGER

An easy, quick and good recipe—you'll make it often.

1 lb. ground beef	1 (1 lb.) can tomatoes, cut up
1 c. uncooked rice	1 pkg. Spanish Rice Seasoning Mix
1 tsp. salt	
1 c. boiling water	

Cook ground beef in skillet until browned; pour off excess fat. Stir in remaining ingredients; bring to a boil. Reduce heat; cover and simmer about 25 minutes, until rice is tender. Makes 6 servings.

SPANISH RICE/HAM DINNER

This nutritious dinner takes less than 30 minutes to prepare.

1 c. uncooked rice
2 tblsp. regular margarine or
  bacon drippings
1 (1 lb.) can tomatoes, cut up
1 c. boiling water

1 pkg. Spanish Rice Seasoning
  Mix
2 c. cubed cooked ham
1 (1 lb. 1 oz.) can peas

Cook rice in melted margarine in skillet until golden, stirring constantly. Add tomatoes, water, Spanish Rice Seasoning Mix and ham. Bring to a boil; reduce heat, cover and simmer 25 minutes. Stir in peas; simmer to heat. Makes 6 servings.

SPANISH RICE WITH CHICKEN

Different, distinctive way to team chicken with rice.

1 (2½ to 3 lb.) broiler-fryer,
  cut up
Salt
Pepper
1 c. uncooked rice
2 tblsp. regular margarine or
  bacon drippings

1 (1 lb.) can tomatoes, cut up
1 c. boiling water
1 pkg. Spanish Rice Seasoning
  Mix

Arrange chicken in bottom of greased 13×9×2″ baking pan. Sprinkle lightly with salt and pepper.

Cook rice in melted margarine over medium heat, stirring constantly, until rice is golden. Slowly add tomatoes, water and Spanish Rice Seasoning Mix. Bring to a boil. Pour over chicken. Cover pan with aluminum foil and bake in 375° oven 1 hour, or until chicken is tender. Makes 5 servings.

Memo to Meal Planner: Serve with buttered green beans and Waldorf salad. Make salad with 2 c. cubed peeled pears or unpeeled apples and 1 c. thinly sliced celery. Or for fruit, use 1 c. each apple and diced bananas. Have a chocolate dessert.

CHICKEN FLAVOR MIX FOR RICE

Gives plain rice a subtle, intriguing taste of chicken.

1 tblsp. instant chicken broth mix	1 tsp. celery flakes
1 tblsp. parsley flakes	1 tsp. sugar
1 tsp. instant minced onion	½ tsp. salt

Combine all ingredients. Place on 6″ square of aluminum foil and seal air tight. Repeat recipe to make as many packages as desired. Store in jar or plastic bag on cupboard shelf. Makes 1 package.

CHICKEN-FLAVORED RICE

You pay more for the chicken-flavored rice you buy in a box.

1 c. uncooked rice	2 c. water
2 tblsp. butter or regular margarine	1 pkg. Chicken Flavor Mix for Rice

Cook rice in butter over medium heat, stirring occasionally, until golden brown. Slowly add water. Stir in Chicken Flavor Mix for Rice. Reduce heat; cover and simmer 20 minutes, until rice is tender and liquid is absorbed. Makes 3 cups.

Memo to Meal Planner: Double the recipe if you need more servings. It's easy with flavor mix on hand. Good served with Baked Pork Steaks with Stuffing and Tender-crisp Carrots (see Index).

BEEF FLAVOR MIX FOR RICE

This mix gives plain rice the much favored taste of beef.

4 tsp. instant beef broth mix	½ tsp. salt
1 tblsp. instant minced onion	½ tsp. sugar
1 tblsp. parsley flakes	

Combine all ingredients. Place on 6″ square of aluminum foil and seal air tight. Repeat recipe to make as many packages as desired. Store in jar or plastic bag on cupboard shelf. Makes 1 package.

BEEF-FLAVORED RICE

An extra-good side dish to serve with grilled ground beef.

1 c. uncooked rice	1 pkg. Beef Flavor Mix for
2 tblsp. butter or regular	Rice
margarine	2 c. water

Cook rice in butter over medium heat, stirring frequently, until rice is golden brown. Stir in Beef Flavor Mix for Rice and water; heat to boiling. Reduce heat; cover and cook about 20 minutes, until rice is tender. Makes 6 servings.

Memo to Meal Planner: Rice is moist so you omit gravy from menu —a help to calorie watchers. Serve with meat loaf or beef pot roast. Either Homemade Stewed Tomatoes or Okra/Tomato Treat fit beautifully in this meal (see Index).

CURRY SEASONING MIX FOR RICE

Save money by making your own mix—it's really easy to do.

1 tblsp. instant minced onion	1 tsp. instant chicken broth mix
1½ tsp. curry powder	¼ tsp. instant minced garlic
1 tsp. sugar	⅛ tsp. ground turmeric
1 tsp. salt	

Combine all ingredients. Place on 6″ square of aluminum foil and seal air tight. Repeat recipe to make as many packages as desired. Store in jar or plastic bag on cupboard shelf. Makes 1 package.

CURRIED RICE

This makes a wonderful companion for chicken, turkey or lamb.

1 c. uncooked rice	2 c. water
2 tblsp. butter or regular	1 pkg. Curry Seasoning Mix for
margarine	Rice

Cook rice in butter over medium heat, stirring frequently, until golden brown. Slowly add water; stir in Curry Seasoning Mix for Rice. Bring to a boil. Reduce heat; cover and simmer 20 minutes, until rice is tender and liquid is absorbed. Makes 3 cups.

Memo to Meal Planner: Complete menu with Oven-fried Chicken, Lemon-buttered Broccoli and your favorite fruit salad (see Index).

SEASONED COATING MIX

Try this speedy, delicious seasoning for oven-fried chicken.

2 c. fine bread crumbs	2 tsp. poultry seasoning
½ c. flour	1 tsp. pepper
4 tsp. salt	½ c. shortening
4 tsp. paprika	

Combine bread crumbs, flour, salt, paprika, poultry seasoning and pepper in mixing bowl. Mix thoroughly. Cut in shortening until mixture resembles coarse crumbs. Place in covered container and store in a cool place. Makes 4 to 4½ cups.

SPECIAL OVEN-FRIED CHICKEN

Chicken takes on gorgeous rosy-brown color. Recipe can be doubled.

1 (3 lb.) broiler-fryer, cut up   1 c. Seasoned Coating Mix

Dip chicken pieces in water. Shake a few pieces at a time in plastic bag containing Seasoned Coating Mix until pieces are evenly coated. Place in a single layer in ungreased shallow baking pan; do not cover. Bake in 400° oven 40 to 50 minutes. Makes 4 servings.

STUFFING MIX

Save dry bread in the refrigerator to make this useful mix. Double recipe to make stuffing for a 10-lb. turkey.

4 c. bread cubes (6 slices)	½ tsp. rubbed sage
2 tblsp. salad oil	¼ tsp. salt
1 tblsp. parsley flakes	¼ tsp. pepper
½ tsp. poultry seasoning	

Spread bread cubes in shallow baking pan; toast in 300° oven 40 minutes. (Bread will shrink slightly.)

Sprinkle bread cubes with oil and toss to coat. Sprinkle with remaining ingredients and toss to coat evenly. Makes 3½ cups.

ROAST CHICKEN WITH STUFFING

The economical Stuffing Mix is a time-saver in this recipe.

¼ c. chopped onion	¼ c. hot water
¼ c. chopped celery	Salt
¼ c. butter or regular margarine	1 (3 to 5 lb.) roasting chicken
3½ c. Stuffing Mix	

Cook onion and celery in melted butter until soft, but not browned. Pour over Stuffing Mix; toss to coat. Add hot water and toss.

Lightly salt body cavity of chicken. Spoon in stuffing; do not pack. Roast in 375° oven 1½ to 2½ hours. Chicken is done when drumstick will move up and down and twist easily in socket. Serves 6.

CHICKEN/STUFFING CASSEROLE

You'll be proud to tote this casserole to potluck suppers.

1 (2½ to 3 lb.) broiler-fryer, cut up	½ c. chopped onion
4 c. water	¼ c. butter or regular margarine
1 small onion, sliced	7 c. Stuffing Mix
1 (6″) branch celery, cut up	3 c. chicken broth
1 tsp. salt	¼ c. flour
4 peppercorns	½ tsp. salt
½ c. chopped celery	Few drops bottled browning sauce

Place chicken with water, sliced onion, cut-up celery, 1 tsp. salt and peppercorns in kettle. Cover and bring to a boil. Reduce heat and simmer 50 minutes. Strain broth and reserve (you will need 3 c.). Cut meat from bones; discard skin.

Cook chopped celery and onion in butter until soft but not browned. Add to the Stuffing Mix and toss. Stir in 1 c. reserved chicken broth.

Place half of stuffing in bottom of greased 2½-qt. casserole. Top with cut-up chicken, then the remaining stuffing.

Blend ½ c. remaining chicken broth with flour and ½ tsp. salt in saucepan to make a smooth paste. Add remainder of chicken broth. Cook, stirring constantly, until mixture is bubbly and thickened. Add enough browning sauce to color sauce a light brown. Pour over mixture in casserole. Cover; bake in 350° oven 45 minutes. Serves 6.

Memo to Meal Planner: This is a fine casserole to serve guests, along with cranberries and sweet potatoes. For a memorable meal, end with homemade cake. Cranberry/Apple Salad and Plum Kuchen or Grandmother's Orange Cake fit beautifully in this menu (see Index).

CHEESE-SEASONED CROUTONS

Another economical use of bread—and a real time-saver.

6 c. bread cubes (9 slices)   3 tblsp. grated Parmesan cheese
½ c. melted butter or regular
  margarine

Toss bread cubes with butter; place in 13×9×2″ pan. Toast in 300° oven 1 hour. Toss with cheese. Cool and store in covered container in refrigerator. Makes 4 cups.

Memo to Meal Planner: Add to tossed salads or soup just before serving. Instead of seasoning bread cubes with cheese use ¾ tsp. garlic powder, dried marjoram or basil leaves, crushed.

ONION/CHEESE DIP MIX

Sour cream plus this flavorful mix add up to a marvelous dip.

1 tblsp. instant minced onion   1½ tsp. instant beef broth mix
2 tblsp. grated Parmesan cheese   ¼ tsp. garlic salt

Combine all ingredients. Place on 6″ square of aluminum foil and seal air tight. Repeat recipe to make as many packages as desired. Makes 1 package.

ONION/CHEESE SOUR CREAM DIP

For dippers have carrot and celery sticks, and small crackers.

1 pkg. Onion/Cheese Dip Mix   Parsley
1 c. dairy sour cream

Add Onion/Cheese Dip Mix to sour cream in bowl. Cover and chill at least 30 minutes before serving, or chill several hours. Garnish with parsley when serving. Makes 1 cup.

Memo to Meal Planner: Set glasses of tomato juice, a plate of crackers and a bowl of the luscious dip on a tray. Carry to living room.

CURRY DIP MIX

Add to sour cream and serve with raw vegetables and crackers.

1 tblsp. instant minced onion	¼ tsp. instant minced garlic
2 tsp. curry powder	¼ tsp. salt

Combine all ingredients; mix thoroughly. Place on 6″ square of aluminum foil and seal air tight. Repeat recipe to make as many packages as desired. Makes 1 package.

Curried Sour Cream Dip: Combine 1 c. dairy sour cream and 1 pkg. Curry Dip Mix. Chill at least 30 minutes. Makes 1 cup.

BACON FLAVOR DIP MIX

Another perfect accompaniment for raw vegetable appetizers.

2 tblsp. bacon flavor textured vegetable protein, crushed	1 tsp. instant beef broth mix
1 tblsp. instant minced onion	⅛ tsp. instant minced garlic

Combine all ingredients. Place on 6″ square of aluminum foil and seal air tight. Repeat recipe to make as many packages as desired. Makes 1 package.

Bacon/Sour Cream Dip: Combine 1 c. dairy sour cream and 1 pkg. Bacon Flavor Dip Mix. Chill at least 30 minutes. Makes 1 cup.

TACO DIP MIX

Making this mix prompts thoughts of happy times to come.

1 tblsp. instant minced onion	½ tsp. ground cumin
1½ tsp. instant beef broth mix	¼ tsp. salt
1 tsp. chili powder	⅛ tsp. instant minced garlic

Combine all ingredients. Place on 6″ square of aluminum foil and seal air tight. Repeat recipe to make as many packages as desired. Makes 1 package.

TACO SOUR CREAM DIP

Often the hit of the party and so easy to make. Serve it with corn chips or, if you prefer, with tortilla chips.

1 c. dairy sour cream	1 pkg. Taco Dip Mix
2 tsp. ketchup	

Thoroughly combine sour cream, ketchup and Taco Dip Mix. Place in bowl, cover and chill at least 30 minutes. Makes 1 cup.

INSTANT COCOA MIX

This mix makes it easy to fix hot cocoa for family meals, or for a pick-up snack between meals, if you have it on hand. For children's parties, you can give the beverage a festive appearance by providing red and white peppermint stick candy instead of spoons for stirring. Let young people make their own cocoa.

1 (1 lb.) pkg. nonfat dry milk	¼ tsp. salt
1 c. sugar	4 c. miniature marshmallows
¾ c. unsweetened cocoa	(optional)

Sift dry milk, sugar, cocoa and salt together twice. Add marshmallows. Place in tightly covered container and store in a cool, dry place. Shake or stir before using. Makes about 6⅓ cups without marshmallows.

Hot Cocoa: Measure ⅓ c. Instant Cocoa Mix into a serving cup. Almost fill with hot water; stir to blend thoroughly. (Some people prefer to use ¼ c. instead of ⅓ c. mix to 1 cup of hot water.) To make a larger amount, place 1⅓ c. cocoa mix in saucepan. Pour 4 c. hot water into pan and stir to mix.

BASIC COCOA SYRUP

You keep this syrup in the refrigerator. It's a real convenience—you can serve cocoa icy cold or steaming hot in no time.

2 c. sifted unsweetened cocoa	4 c. boiling water
4 c. sugar	4 tsp. vanilla
¼ tsp. salt	

Combine cocoa, sugar and salt in saucepan. Gradually add water, stirring until mixture is smooth. Cook over medium heat, stirring until mixture comes to a boil. Boil 1 minute without stirring. Remove from heat and cool; stir in vanilla. Pour into glass jar or other container; cover and refrigerate. Makes about 5 cups.

PARTY-STYLE HOT COCOA

Garnish each cup with a pink, green or white marshmallow.

6 c. milk   ¾ c. Basic Cocoa Syrup

Heat milk in 2-qt. saucepan until bubbles form around edge of pan. Add Basic Cocoa Syrup, stirring until well blended with milk. Pour into mugs. Makes 6 servings.

Iced Cocoa: Beat ¾ c. Basic Cocoa Syrup with 6 c. milk to blend. Use blender or electric mixer. Pour over ice cubes in glasses. (To make just 1 glass of beverage, use 2 tblsp. Basic Cocoa Syrup and 1 c. milk.) Makes 6 servings.

HAMBURGER MIX

Busy women vouch for the help this mix gives them—they find many pleasing ways to use it. We give you recipes for four favorites: Pizzaburgers, Italian Skillet Macaroni, Iowa Spanish Rice and Easy Chili con Carne. All of them produce quick, easy, tasty dishes.

2 c. finely chopped celery   4 tsp. salt
2 c. finely chopped onion   ½ tsp. pepper
¼ c. salad oil   2 tblsp. Worcestershire sauce
4 lbs. ground beef   2 (15 oz.) cans tomato sauce

Cook celery and onion in oil in large kettle 5 minutes, stirring occasionally. Add beef; cook until red color disappears. Drain off excess fat.

Add salt, pepper, Worcestershire sauce and tomato sauce to kettle. Cover and cook 10 minutes. Cool quickly. Pour into freezer containers the right size for your family, and freeze.

To thaw mix when using, place in refrigerator overnight, or set container in hot water until contents will pour. Makes 12 cups.

Memo to Meal Planner: When you are in a big hurry, instead of making one of the following dishes, just heat the Hamburger Mix.

Spoon it between split buns and you have appetizing hot sandwiches that you can fix in just 10 minutes if the mix is thawed. Tossed green salad is an excellent accompaniment. Fruit is an ideal dessert.

ITALIAN SKILLET MACARONI

While this Italian-type main dish tastes good the year around, it is especially appropriate for warm weather because it cooks on top the range and keeps unwelcome oven heat out of the kitchen. Cottage cheese is a surprise ingredient in it.

1 pt. Hamburger Mix	1 tsp. dried orégano leaves,
1 (1 lb.) can tomatoes, cut up	crushed
1 (8 oz.) can tomato sauce	1 (7 oz.) pkg. macaroni
2 c. water	1 c. creamed cottage cheese
1 tsp. salt	Parmesan cheese
2 medium cloves garlic, minced	

Combine Hamburger Mix, tomatoes, tomato sauce, water, salt, garlic and orégano in 12″ skillet. Bring to a boil. Add macaroni. Cover and simmer about 30 minutes, until macaroni is tender, stirring occasionally. Stir in cottage cheese; heat but do not let boil. Serve sprinkled with Parmesan cheese. Makes 6 servings.

Memo to Meal Planner: If you want a hot vegetable, broccoli fills the bill. Have a green salad and crusty rolls. For dessert, if the cantaloupe season is in full swing, cut chilled melon in thick slices, discard seeds and fill centers with scoops of vanilla ice cream.

EASY CHILI CON CARNE

One advantage of Hamburger Mix is the ease with which teen-agers can fill bowls with chili, their name for chili con carne. Using the mix, they can fix chili con carne for their friends and have fun doing it— it's an ideal after-the-football-game dish. Mother may need to set mix in the refrigerator several hours ahead to thaw it partially.

1 pt. Hamburger Mix	2 (15 oz.) cans kidney beans
1 (1 lb.) can tomatoes, cut up	2 to 3 tsp. chili powder
1 (1 lb.) can hominy	

Combine all ingredients in saucepan. Simmer 20 minutes, stirring occasionally. Makes 6 servings.

Memo to Meal Planner: Use 1 instead of 2 cans of beans for less than 6 servings. Crackers and dill pickles make good accompaniments. If a dessert is to be served, suggest banana sundaes and show how to make them. Here's how: Split a peeled banana in half lengthwise for 2 servings. Lay each half, cut side down, on dessert plate. Place a scoop of vanilla or chocolate ice cream in curve of banana and pour on a dessert sauce, such as butterscotch or chocolate sauce. Encourage youngsters to make their own sundaes.

PIZZABURGERS

These quick, easy and tasty sandwiches taste like pizza.

1 pt. Hamburger Mix	8 mozzarella cheese slices
¼ tsp. dried orégano leaves,	(about 6 oz.)
crushed	8 green pepper rings
4 hamburger buns, split	

Combine Hamburger Mix and orégano in saucepan; heat.

Toast buns. Spoon hamburger mixture on bun halves; top each with a cheese slice and green pepper ring. Place under broiler just long enough to melt cheese. Makes 8 sandwiches.

Memo to Meal Planner: The green pepper rings are optional, but they add color and flavor. Use them when plentiful. You can substitute process American cheese for the mozzarella, but it's the Italian-type cheese that provides the pizza taste. To complete supper on a summer evening, have sliced tomatoes, potato salad and ice cream or ice milk. For supper on a wintry evening have hot tomato soup or chilled tomato juice, buttered grean beans, a relish plate and chilled Skillet Custards (see Index for recipe).

IOWA SPANISH RICE

Rice cooks in the skillet with the other ingredients.

1 pt. Hamburger Mix	1 tsp. salt
1 (1 lb.) can tomatoes, cut up	1 c. uncooked rice
½ c. chopped green pepper	1 c. shredded process American
1½ c. water	cheese (4 oz.)

Combine Hamburger Mix, tomatoes, green pepper, water and salt in saucepan; bring to a boil. Stir in rice. Reduce heat, cover and simmer 25 minutes, or until rice is tender. Sprinkle with cheese and continue cooking about 5 minutes, just until cheese is melted. Makes 6 servings.

Memo to Meal Planner: Succotash tastes good with this main dish. Include a crisp salad, such as coleslaw, in the meal. Use your imagination in making the slaw. Add a new touch. It might be a chopped unpeeled red apple, a bit of minced onion, a few raisins, ¾ tsp. celery seeds, or shredded carrots. You can convert a plain-Jane salad into something special. A milk pudding makes an appealing dessert. Why not try Vanilla Pudding made with our Pudding Mix (see Index)? To dress it up, alternate layers of pudding and fresh or thawed frozen strawberries in dessert glasses. Or top with strawberry preserves.

PIZZA CRUSTS

These partially baked crusts freeze well—they're really handy.

2 pkgs. active dry yeast	2½ c. warm water (110 to
7 to 8 c. flour	115°)
1 tsp. salt	

Combine yeast, 2½ c. flour, salt and warm water in large bowl. Beat at low speed of mixer 30 seconds, scraping sides of bowl constantly. Beat 3 minutes at high speed. By hand, stir in enough remaining flour to make a moderately stiff dough. Knead on lightly floured surface until smooth and elastic, 8 to 10 minutes. Shape into a ball; place in greased bowl and turn dough over to grease top. Cover and let rise in warm place until doubled, about 45 minutes.

Punch down dough; divide in fourths. Roll each part to make an 11" circle. Stretch each circle to fit a greased 12" pizza pan. (Or roll each portion of dough into a 12×10" rectangle; place on baking sheet and build up edges slightly.)

Bake in 500° oven 6 to 8 minutes, until crust starts to brown. (Crust will be somewhat uneven due to baked-in air bubbles, but they will not affect finished pizza.) Cool. Freeze in pans or on flat surface, then wrap each crust separately in foil or freezer paper and return to freezer. Or make pizza when crust is cool and bake. You can leave crust at room temperature 24 hours before making pizza. Makes 4 partially baked crusts.

Directions for Baking Pizza in Partially Baked Crusts:

Place pizza directly on rack (not in pan) at lowest position in 500° oven. Time as follows: unfrozen pizza about 5 minutes; frozen crust with unfrozen topping, about 7 minutes; frozen pizza about 10 minutes. Check bottom of pizza. When baked, the crust will be golden brown.

Use a baking sheet for a giant spatula to remove pizza from oven. Follow these directions and the crust will not be soggy, but delightfully crisp.

PIZZA SAUCE

You can freeze ¾ cup portions of sauce in cup containers.

2 (6 oz.) cans tomato paste
2 c. water
3 tblsp. parsley flakes
4 tsp. instant minced onion
1 tsp. dried orégano leaves, crushed

1 tsp. dried basil leaves, crushed
2 cloves garlic, minced

Combine all ingredients. Bring to a boil; reduce heat, cover and simmer 10 minutes. Makes 3 cups.

SAUSAGE PIZZA

Especially popular with teen-agers who like the pizza sausage.

½ lb. pizza sausage
¾ c. Pizza Sauce
1 Pizza Crust, partially baked

1 c. shredded mozzarella cheese (4 oz.)

Cook sausage in skillet until browned; drain on paper toweling.
Spread Pizza Sauce over Pizza Crust. Top with pizza sausage, then sprinkle with cheese. Bake in 500° oven according to Directions for Baking Pizza. Makes 1 (12″) pizza.

PEPPERONI PIZZA

Almost everyone rates this the top pizza favorite—try it.

¾ c. Pizza Sauce
1 Pizza Crust, partially baked
1 (1½ oz.) stick pepperoni
1 c. shredded mozzarella cheese (4 oz.)

2 onion slices, separated into rings (optional)

Spread Pizza Sauce over Pizza Crust.

Slice and remove skin from pepperoni. Top Pizza Sauce with pepperoni, cheese and onion rings. Bake in 500° oven according to Directions for Baking Pizza. Makes 1 (12″) pizza.

Memo to Meal Planner: If pizza is the main dish, there is no better salad to serve than one of lettuce or a combination of greens tossed with Homemade Italian Salad Dressing. Vanilla ice cream or ice milk makes an excellent dessert, or if you prefer, have a fruit cup and Oatmeal Drop Cookies (see Index for recipes).

HAMBURGER PIZZA

Another interesting way to use ground beef to please youngsters.

½ lb. ground beef
¾ c. Pizza Sauce
1 Pizza Crust, partially baked
½ tsp. salt

½ green pepper, cut in strips
1 c. shredded mozzarella
  cheese (4 oz.)

Cook ground beef until lightly browned; drain off excess fat.

Spread Pizza Sauce over Pizza Crust. Top with ground beef; sprinkle with salt. Top with green pepper and cheese. Bake in 500° oven; see Directions for Baking Pizza. Makes 1 (12″) pizza.

FROZEN HASHED BROWN POTATOES

The ingredients used in this recipe are for 4 generous servings. You will need enough potatoes to make 4 cups grated, after cooking. Cook 2 skilletfuls if you need more than 4 servings. Men always praise these golden, crisp-coated potatoes.

Unpeeled baking-type potatoes
1½ tsp. salt

½ c. shortening

Boil potatoes in their jackets until just tender but still firm. Drain, cool and peel. Grate on coarse grater (you will need 4 c.).

Line a 10″ skillet with aluminum foil, bringing foil up to cover sides. Mix potatoes and salt; pack into skillet, pressing down firmly. Hold onto foil and remove potatoes from skillet, keeping the shape intact. Seal package, label, date and freeze. Repeat recipe until you stock your freezer.

To cook, heat shortening over medium heat in same skillet in

which potatoes were shaped for freezing. Remove foil and add disk
of frozen potatoes to skillet. The shortening will spatter so quickly
cover skillet. Cook over medium heat 5 minutes. Uncover and continue cooking 10 to 12 minutes, or until potatoes are browned on bottom. Cut in 4 wedges; turn each piece with a spatula or pancake
turner. Continue cooking 5 minutes, or until attractively browned.
Makes 4 servings.

MAKE-AHEAD BATTER FOR BRAN MUFFINS

Bake any amount of muffins you want with this mix on hand.

5 c. sifted flour	2 c. sugar
5 tsp. baking soda	1 c. shortening
2 tsp. salt	4 eggs, well beaten
2 c. boiling water	1 qt. buttermilk
2 c. whole bran cereal	4 c. whole bran cereal buds

Sift together flour, baking soda and salt.

Pour boiling water over whole bran cereal; set aside.

Cream together sugar and shortening in 6-qt. bowl until light. Add
eggs and beat well. Blend in buttermilk, bran buds and the soaked
whole bran cereal. Add sifted dry ingredients; mix well. Store in
tightly covered container in refrigerator. Batter will keep up to 6
weeks. Makes enough for 5 dozen muffins.

To make muffins, fill greased muffin-pan cups two thirds full of
batter. Bake in 400° oven about 20 minutes.

Memo to Meal Planner: Enhance meals featuring baked beans with
this hot bread. Also good served with Baked Lentils Supreme, Hot
Bologna Salad and Green Pea/Salmon Salad (see Index).

Convenient Baking Mixes

Many women feature thrifty home-baked foods in their meals to
add the special touch to economy menus and step up enthusiasm for
the entire meal. Using premeasured mixes on busy days cuts the time
in getting the food in the oven and you'll have something "fresh
baked."

Take Super Mix for Baking as a versatile example. From it you can
make such a variety of foods as California Corn Bread, Peanut But-

ter Cookies, Onion/Cheese Bread, Plum Kuchen and Spicy Breakfast Rolls! And when you taste Old-fashioned Buttermilk Hot Cakes, made from a mix, you will think pancakes never were better.

Try all the recipes for baked foods that follow—they provide a practical way to save money and time while treating your family and friends to mighty good eating—the kind for which country kitchens are famous.

SUPER MIX FOR BAKING

You'll find this mix versatile and a real convenience.

9 c. sifted flour
⅓ c. baking powder
1 tblsp. salt
½ c. nonfat dry milk
2 c. shortening

Combine flour, baking powder, salt and dry milk; sift together. Cut in shortening until mixture resembles coarse cornmeal. Store in covered container in cool place. Makes 12 cups.

CALIFORNIA CORN BREAD

Wonderful with tossed salad and ham or chicken dishes.

¾ c. cornmeal
½ tsp. salt
3 tblsp. sugar
¾ tsp. chili powder
1½ c. Super Mix for Baking
¾ c. milk
1 egg
1 (8 oz.) can cream style corn

Stir together cornmeal, salt, sugar, chili powder and Super Mix for Baking.

Beat milk and egg together; add to dry ingredients. Stir until slightly blended, but not smooth (there will be some lumps). Fold in corn. Bake in greased 9″ square pan in 400° oven 20 to 25 minutes, until golden brown. Makes 9 servings.

PEANUT BUTTER COOKIES

Perfect with glasses of cold milk and fruit for dessert.

1 c. sugar
2 eggs, beaten
1 c. smooth peanut butter
3 c. Super Mix for Baking
1 to 2 tblsp. milk
Chocolate candy kisses
  (optional)

Stir sugar, eggs and peanut butter into Super Mix for Baking; blend thoroughly. If dough seems dry, add milk. Shape into 1″ balls; place about 3″ apart on ungreased baking sheet. Press a candy kiss in each ball, if desired. Or, for everyday cookies, omit candy and flatten balls with a fork. Bake in 375° oven 15 to 20 minutes. Makes 6 dozen.

RANCH-STYLE BISCUITS

Serve these golden biscuits piping hot in a basket.

3 c. Super Mix for Baking   ⅔ c. milk

Put mix in bowl; blend in milk with 20 strokes. Turn onto lightly floured surface. Gently knead 10 to 12 times. Pat or roll dough ½ to ¾″ thick; cut with floured biscuit cutter. Bake on ungreased baking sheet in 425° oven 12 to 15 minutes. Makes 15 or 16 biscuits.

ONION/CHEESE BREAD

Serve this on special occasions and enjoy the compliments.

2 c. Super Mix for Baking   1 tblsp. butter or regular
½ c. cold water   margarine
1 tblsp. instant minced onion   1 tsp. poppy seeds
¾ c. shredded sharp Cheddar
  cheese (3 oz.)

Combine Super Mix for Baking, water and onion. Blend in cheese. Spread dough in well-greased 9″ pie pan. Spread with soft butter and sprinkle with poppy seeds. Bake in 400° oven 18 to 20 minutes, until lightly browned. Serve cut in wedges. Makes 6 servings.

PLUM KUCHEN

Serve this coffee cake for breakfast or dessert—it's good!

1½ c. Super Mix for Baking   1 (1 lb. 13 oz.) can plums,
¼ c. sugar   drained, cut in halves and
1 egg, beaten   pitted
1 tsp. vanilla   ¼ c. sugar

Combine Super Mix for Baking and ¼ c. sugar.
Combine egg and vanilla; add to mix and blend. Pat dough evenly in greased 9″ round layer cake pan. Arrange plum halves over

dough; sprinkle with ¼ c. sugar. Bake in 350° oven 1 hour. Makes 6 servings.

WHEAT GERM MUFFINS

Share these tasty, nutritious muffins with guests.

2 c. Super Mix for Baking	⅔ c. milk
2 tblsp. brown sugar	¼ c. chopped dates
2 tblsp. wheat germ	¼ c. chopped nuts
1 egg, beaten	

Combine Super Mix for Baking, brown sugar and wheat germ.

Combine egg and milk; stir into mix until flour is slightly moistened. Batter will not be smooth. Add dates and nuts; stir 2 or 3 times to distribute them. Do not overmix. Pour into well-greased large muffin-pan cups, filling two thirds full. Bake in 425° oven 20 minutes. Makes 12 large muffins.

COUNTRY SUPPER MUFFINS

You can depend on this hot bread to perk up the meal.

2 c. Super Mix for Baking	1 egg, beaten
3 tblsp. sugar	⅔ c. milk

Combine Super Mix for Baking and sugar. Stir egg and milk together and add to mix, stirring 12 to 15 strokes, until flour is moistened but still lumpy. Do not overmix. Pour into greased muffin-pan cups, filling two thirds full. Bake in 425° oven 20 minutes. Makes 12 muffins.

SPICY BREAKFAST ROLLS

Take these hot rolls to the table in a napkin-lined basket for breakfast on Sunday or any other day of the week. And serve them hot from the oven to friends. The tender, rich, golden-crusted rolls literally melt in the mouth and win many compliments whenever they appear. The busy woman finds them quick to bake, and kind to her budget. The rolls contain no expensive ingredients.

2 c. Super Mix for Baking	1 c. brown sugar, lightly
½ c. milk	packed
¼ c. butter or regular margarine	1 tsp. ground cinnamon

Toss together Super Mix for Baking and milk, and stir until dough leaves the sides of bowl and forms a ball. Turn onto lightly floured waxed paper; knead gently about 10 times. Flatten to 1" thickness.

Melt butter in small skillet. In a bowl combine brown sugar and cinnamon. Break off pieces of dough the size of large walnuts; dip or roll in butter in skillet and drop in brown sugar-cinnamon mixture. Roll until dough is well coated with sugar mixture, pressing a little extra on outside of ball.

Place balls of dough at least 1" apart on lightly greased baking sheet. Bake in 425° oven 12 to 15 minutes. Serve at once. Makes 12 to 16 rolls.

QUICK BREAD MIX

A thrifty, easy way to provide milk in family meals.

8 c. sifted flour	1 c. sugar
1⅓ c. nonfat dry milk	¼ c. baking powder
3 tsp. salt	1 c. shortening

Sift together dry ingredients 3 times. Cut or rub in shortening until thoroughly mixed. Store in tightly covered container in cool place. Will keep up to 1 month. Makes about 12 cups.

SPEEDY MUFFINS

A good recipe for busy days when you want homemade muffins.

3 c. Quick Bread Mix	1 egg, beaten
1 c. water	

Combine Quick Bread Mix, water and egg, stirring about 15 strokes around bowl. Batter should be lumpy. Fill greased medium muffin-pan cups two thirds full. Bake in 425° oven 18 to 20 minutes, until golden brown. Makes 12 medium muffins.

Speedy Waffles: To 3 c. Quick Bread Mix add 1½ c. water and 1 egg yolk. Stir just to mix. Fold in 1 egg white, stiffly beaten. Bake on preheated waffle iron.

Memo to Meal Planner: Serve for supper with creamed chicken for the main dish and with syrup and butter or margarine for dessert. A salad will add appetite appeal, especially if it's Peach Salad with French Celery Seed Salad Dressing (see Index for recipes).

BISCUIT MIX

You'll like the three outstanding recipes made from this mix.

8 c. sifted flour
1 c. nonfat dry milk
¼ c. baking powder

4 tsp. salt
1⅓ c. shortening

Sift together dry ingredients 3 times. Rub or cut in shortening until well mixed. Store in tightly closed jar. Makes about 12 cups.

HOT BISCUITS

For the best results measure the Biscuit Mix lightly.

⅔ to ¾ c. water   3 c. Biscuit Mix

Stir water into Biscuit Mix with about 25 strokes. (Use enough water to make a soft dough you can handle.) Turn onto lightly floured surface, round up dough and knead lightly 10 times. Pat or roll to ½″ thickness. Cut close together with floured 2″ cutter. Place 1″ apart on greased baking sheet for crusty sides, close together for soft sides. Bake in 425° oven 12 to 15 minutes, until browned. Serve at once. Makes 15 biscuits.

ORANGE PINWHEELS

You can use 1 tsp. ground cinnamon instead of orange peel. Serve warm.

3 c. Biscuit Mix
⅔ to ¾ c. water
½ c. sugar
⅓ c. melted butter or regular
   margarine

2 tsp. grated orange peel
1 tblsp. melted butter or regular
   margarine

Combine Biscuit Mix and enough water to make a soft dough. Stir with fork or spoon 25 times. Turn onto lightly floured surface and knead lightly 10 times. Roll into an 18×8″ rectangle.

Blend together sugar, ⅓ c. butter and orange peel; spread over dough. Starting at long side, roll as for jelly roll. Pinch edges to seal. Cut in 1″ slices; place in greased muffin-pan cups. Brush tops with 1 tblsp. butter. Bake in 400° oven 15 to 20 minutes. Makes 18.

SHORTCAKES

Serve these with sugared berries or fruit for dessert.

3 tblsp. sugar
3 c. Biscuit Mix
3 tblsp. shortening

⅔ to ¾ c. water
Melted butter or regular
  margarine

Combine sugar and Biscuit Mix; stir to mix thoroughly. Cut in shortening and add water to make a soft dough. Pat or roll to ½″ thickness; brush with melted butter. With floured cutters, cut an equal number of 2½″ and 2″ rounds. Stack smaller rounds on top of larger ones. Bake in 425° oven 12 to 15 minutes, until golden. Makes 6 shortcakes.

HOT CAKES MIX

An old-time country kitchen favorite—always in style.

6 c. sifted flour
1 tblsp. baking soda
1 tblsp. baking powder

1 tblsp. salt
6 tblsp. sugar

Sift together all ingredients. Store in air-tight container. Makes about 6 cups.

OLD-FASHIONED BUTTERMILK HOT CAKES

Help pancakes live up to their name—serve them hot.

1¼ c. Hot Cakes Mix
1 egg, beaten
1 c. buttermilk

2 tblsp. milk
2 tblsp. salad oil

Measure Hot Cakes Mix into medium bowl.

In another bowl combine egg, buttermilk, milk and oil; stir to blend. Add liquid to mix and stir until dry ingredients are just moistened. Batter will look lumpy.

Pour batter from spoon or pitcher onto preheated hot griddle and bake until pancakes are golden brown on both sides, turning once. Serve immediately. Makes 16 medium cakes.

Old-fashioned Cakes from Basic Homemade Mix

Long before commercial mixes became available, farm women were making their own. Cakes made from our homemade mix will be light and tender with wonderful flavor.

If you prefer to bake these cakes in a 13×9×2″ pan, increase the baking time 5 minutes (from 30 to 35 minutes). Be sure to use shortening that requires no refrigeration when making this and other mixes for baking.

We give you four recipes to make from the basic mix for cakes popular in country kitchens—and even one cookie!

HOMEMADE CAKE MIX

Make right-side-up and upside-down cakes and cookies with this mix.

9 c. sifted flour	1 tblsp. salt
⅓ c. baking powder	1 tsp. cream of tartar
¼ c. sugar	2 c. shortening

Stir together flour, baking powder, sugar, salt and cream of tartar. Sift three times. Cut in shortening until mixture resembles cornmeal. Store in covered container at room temperature. To measure mix when using, spoon lightly into measuring cup and level off with spatula. Makes about 15 cups.

JIFFY TWO-EGG CAKE

When you are in a big hurry, this is the cake to bake.

3 c. Homemade Cake Mix	2 eggs, slightly beaten
1¼ c. sugar	1 tsp. vanilla
1 c. milk	

Stir together Homemade Cake Mix and sugar in large bowl.

Combine milk, eggs and vanilla. Add half of liquid to mix; beat 1 minute at medium speed, scraping bowl with spatula. Add remaining liquid and continue beating 2 minutes.

Grease and line bottom of two 8″ round layer cake pans with paper. Spread batter evenly in pans; bake in 375° oven 25 to 30 minutes. Let cake cool in pans 10 minutes. Turn out on racks and continue cooling. Frost cooled cake as desired.

SPEEDY CHOCOLATE CAKE

Doubly good when spread with Fast-fix Chocolate Frosting.

1½ c. sugar	2 eggs, slightly beaten
½ c. cocoa	1 tsp. vanilla
3 c. Homemade Cake Mix	Fast-fix Chocolate Frosting
1¼ c. milk	

Stir together sugar and cocoa; stir into Homemade Cake Mix in large bowl of mixer.

Combine milk, eggs and vanilla. Stir half of liquid into mix; beat 1 minute at medium speed, scraping bowl with spatula. Add remaining liquid and continue beating 2 minutes.

Grease and line bottom of two 8″ round layer cake pans with paper. Spread batter evenly in pans; bake in 375° oven 25 to 30 minutes. Cool in pans 10 minutes. Turn out on racks and continue cooling. When completely cool, spread Fast-fix Chocolate Frosting between layers and on sides and top of cake.

Fast-fix Chocolate Frosting: Mix together ⅓ c. soft butter or regular margarine and 3 c. sifted confectioners sugar. Add 1 tsp. vanilla and enough milk to make mixture of spreading consistency (about 3 tblsp.). Melt and cool 3 squares unsweetened chocolate; stir into frosting.

GRANDMOTHER'S ORANGE CAKE

It has the wonderful flavor of freshly squeezed orange juice.

3 c. Homemade Cake Mix	Juice of 1 orange
1½ c. sugar	2 eggs, slightly beaten
2 tsp. grated orange peel	Easy Orange Frosting

Stir together Homemade Cake Mix, sugar and orange peel in large bowl of mixer.

Add enough water to orange juice to make 1 c. Combine with eggs. Add half of liquid to the mix; beat 1 minute at medium speed, scraping bowl with spatula. Add rest of liquid; beat 2 minutes.

Grease and line bottom of two 8″ round layer cake pans with paper. Spread batter evenly in pans; bake in 375° oven 25 to 30 minutes. Cool in pans 10 minutes. Turn out on racks and continue cooling. When completely cooled, spread Easy Orange Frosting between layers and on sides and top of cake.

Easy Orange Frosting: Mix together ⅓ c. soft butter or regular margarine and 3 c. sifted confectioners sugar. Add 2 tsp. grated orange peel and enough orange juice to make a mixture of spreading consistency (about 3 tblsp.).

PINEAPPLE UPSIDE-DOWN CAKE

Company dessert that retains its popularity year after year.

¼ c. butter or regular margarine
½ c. brown sugar, firmly
  packed
1 (8¼ oz.) can sliced
  pineapple, drained
8 maraschino cherries
1½ c. Homemade Cake Mix

⅔ c. sugar
1 egg, slightly beaten
½ c. milk
½ tsp. vanilla
Vanilla ice cream or whipped
  dessert topping

Melt butter in 9″ round layer cake pan set over high heat. Sprinkle brown sugar evenly over butter. Place 1 pineapple slice in center of pan. Cut remaining pineapple slices in halves. Arrange halves, cut side out, around center pineapple slice. Place cherries in centers of pineapple slices.

Mix Homemade Cake Mix and sugar in small bowl of mixer.

Combine egg, milk and vanilla. Add half of liquid to mix; beat 1 minute at medium speed, scraping bowl with spatula. Add remaining liquid and continue beating 2 minutes. Spread batter over pineapple in pan. Bake in 375° oven 25 to 30 minutes, or until wooden pick inserted in center comes out clean. Invert on plate; let stand a few minutes. Lift off pan. Serve warm with vanilla ice cream. Makes 8 servings.

Topping: You can make an inexpensive topping by combining ½ c. ice water and ½ c. nonfat dry milk in chilled small mixer bowl. Beat with chilled beaters until soft peaks form. Beat in 3 tblsp. sugar and 3 tblsp. lemon juice; continue beating until stiff peaks form. Makes about 2½ cups.

CHOCOLATE DROP COOKIES

To dress up cookies, spread tops with an easy white frosting.

3 c. Homemade Cake Mix	1 egg, beaten
1 c. sugar	1 tsp. vanilla
⅓ c. cocoa	½ c. chopped nuts (optional)
½ c. milk	

Stir together Homemade Cake Mix, sugar and cocoa.

Combine milk, egg and vanilla. Stir into mix until well blended. Stir in nuts. Drop by teaspoonfuls 2″ apart onto greased baking sheet. Bake in 350° oven 12 to 15 minutes. Makes 4 dozen.

GINGERBREAD MIX

Use this mix to make the following five recipes—they taste just as wonderful as gingerbreads Grandmother used to make.

8 c. sifted flour	3 tblsp. ground cinnamon
2¼ c. sugar	1 tsp. ground cloves
2½ tsp. baking soda	1 tblsp. salt
2 tblsp. baking powder	2¼ c. shortening
3 tblsp. ground ginger	

Sift together twice all ingredients except shortening. Cut in shortening with two knives or pastry blender until mixture resembles cornmeal. Store tightly covered in refrigerator. Mix will keep up to 3 months. Makes enough mix for six 8″ square pans gingerbread.

COUNTRY GINGERBREAD

You can double recipe and bake batter in a 13×9×2″ pan.

2 c. Gingerbread Mix	½ c. dark molasses
1 egg, beaten	½ c. boiling water

Put Gingerbread Mix in bowl. Combine remaining ingredients; stir half of mixture into Gingerbread Mix, blending just until smooth. Add remaining mixture; blend until smooth. Pour into greased 8″ square pan. Bake in 350° oven 35 minutes. Makes 4 to 6 servings.

Country Gingerbread Variations

Mincemeat Gingerbread: Add 1 c. prepared mincemeat to Gingerbread Mix, then add liquid mixture. Bake in 350° oven 50 minutes.

Gingerbread/Orange Squares: Spread Country Gingerbread batter in pan and sprinkle top with mixture of 2 tblsp. melted butter, 3 tblsp. grated orange peel, ¼ c. sugar and ⅓ c. chopped nuts. Bake in 350° oven 35 minutes.

Gingerbread/Pear Upside-down Cake: Make Country Gingerbread batter, reducing molasses to ⅓ c. and boiling water to ¼ c. Cut 8 canned pear halves in lengthwise halves; drain well. Melt 2 tblsp. butter in greased 9″ round cake pan; add ¼ c. brown sugar, firmly packed, and spread over bottom of pan. Arrange pears in pan; pour on gingerbread batter. Bake in 350° oven 45 minutes.

GINGERBREAD PANCAKES

Sprinkle with confectioners sugar and serve with melted butter.

1 egg, beaten	⅔ c. milk
⅓ c. molasses	2 c. Gingerbread Mix

Combine egg, molasses and milk. Add to Gingerbread Mix; stir to just moisten dry ingredients. Batter will be lumpy. Bake on greased griddle. Makes 2 dozen.

OATMEAL COOKIE MIX

The all-time top favorite FARM JOURNAL *cookie mix.*

8 c. sifted flour	6 c. brown sugar, firmly packed
4 tsp. salt	3 c. shortening
2 tsp. baking powder	8 c. quick-cooking rolled oats
2 tsp. baking soda	

Sift together 3 times flour, salt, baking powder and soda into big dishpan. Stir in brown sugar. Cut in shortening until mixture is crumbly. Stir in oats; mix well. Place in gallon glass jars or other covered containers. Store in a cool place. Makes 6½ quarts.

OATMEAL CHIPPERS

Oatmeal cookies with chocolate—children especially like them.

2 eggs, beaten	1 (6 oz.) pkg. semisweet
½ c. milk	chocolate pieces
2 tsp. vanilla	½ c. chopped nuts
6 c. Oatmeal Cookie Mix	

Stir eggs, milk and vanilla into Oatmeal Cookie Mix; add chocolate pieces and nuts. Drop by teaspoonfuls about 2″ apart onto greased baking sheets. Bake in 350° oven 12 to 15 minutes. Makes 4 dozen.

Variation
Peanut Cookies: Omit vanilla, chocolate and nuts from recipe for Oatmeal Chippers. Add 1 c. peanut butter. Shape dough in 1″ balls, place on greased baking sheets; flatten with fork. Bake as directed.

MINCEMEAT BARS

Bake some of these fruity cookies for the holidays.

4 c. Oatmeal Cookie Mix	1½ c. prepared mincemeat
¼ c. milk	

Blend Oatmeal Cookie Mix with milk; spread half of mixture in bottom of greased 9″ square pan. Spread with mincemeat. Cover with remaining cookie mixture; pack lightly. Bake in 350° oven 30 minutes. Cool; cut in bars. Makes about 2 dozen.

Variation
Prune Bars: Omit the mincemeat from Mincemeat Bars; use a mixture of ½ tsp. ground nutmeg and 1½ c. chopped cooked prunes.

RAISIN/SPICE COOKIES

These are always a welcome addition to the cookie tray.

2 eggs, beaten	½ tsp. ground cloves
½ c. milk	6 c. Oatmeal Cookie Mix
1 tsp. ground cinnamon	1 c. raisins
½ tsp. ground nutmeg	½ c. chopped nuts

Stir eggs, milk and spices into Oatmeal Cookie Mix. Add raisins and nuts. Drop by teaspoonfuls about 2" apart onto greased baking sheet. Bake in 350° oven 12 to 15 minutes. Makes 4 dozen.

BROWNIE MIX

Mix makes bar cookies that really taste like fudge.

4 c. sifted flour	8 c. sugar
4 tsp. baking powder	2½ c. sifted unsweetened cocoa
4 tsp. salt	2 c. shortening

Sift together flour, baking powder and salt.

Combine sugar and cocoa; add to flour mixture and mix thoroughly. (A good way to mix ingredients is to pour them into a large paper bag. Fold open end over, grasp both ends of bag and shake back and forth. Pour into a large bowl or dishpan.) Cut in shortening with pastry blender. Store in covered container in a cool dry place, or in refrigerator. Makes 16 cups.

SHORT-CUT BROWNIES

Brownies are crisp outside, soft and fudgy inside.

2 eggs, beaten	2 c. Brownie Mix
1 tsp. vanilla	½ c. chopped nuts

Combine eggs and vanilla; blend into Brownie Mix. Mixture will not be smooth. Stir in nuts. Spread in greased 8" square pan.

Bake in 350° oven 20 to 25 minutes, until slight imprint remains when lightly touched with finger. Cool in pan set on rack 10 minutes, or cool completely in pan. Cut in 2" squares. Makes 16.

QUICK BROWNIE CAKE

So easy to make and so wonderful served à la mode.

3 eggs, separated	2 c. Brownie Mix
3 tblsp. milk	Ice cream
1 tsp. vanilla	

Beat egg yolks; stir in milk, vanilla and Brownie Mix.

Beat egg whites until stiff and fold into batter. Spread in greased and waxed-paper lined 8" square pan. Bake in 350° oven about 35 minutes, or until done. Cool on rack. Cut in squares and serve with vanilla or peppermint stick ice cream on top. Or spoon Fudge Sauce (recipe follows) over cake. Makes 6 servings.

FUDGE SAUCE

For fudge sundaes spoon hot over vanilla ice cream, or cool and use as cake topping or as filling for a 9″ layer cake.

1 c. Brownie Mix	½ c. water

Blend Brownie Mix and water in saucepan. Cook over medium heat, stirring constantly, until mixture reaches a boil. Reduce heat, cover and simmer until sauce is thick and smooth.

PIE CRUST MIX

Keep this in the refrigerator—it's so handy during the busy holiday season when pies are especially popular.

6 c. sifted flour	1 tblsp. sugar
1½ tsp. salt	1 (1 lb.) can shortening

Sift together flour, salt and sugar. Cut in half the shortening with two knives or pastry blender until mixture resembles cornmeal. Cut in remaining half of shortening until mixture resembles small peas. Store in air-tight container in refrigerator, or a cool dry place. Makes about 8 cups.

How to Use Pie Crust Mix:

For Pie Shell: For 8″ single crust, use 1¼ c. Pie Crust Mix; for 9″ single crust, use 1½ c. mix. Add 2 to 4 tblsp. cold water.

For 2-Crust Pie: For 8″ pie, use 2 to 2¼ c. Pie Crust Mix; for 9″ pie, use 2¼ to 2½ c. mix. Add 4 to 6 tblsp. cold water.

Directions for Combining Ingredients: Measure Pie Crust Mix into bowl. Sprinkle on cold water, a little at a time (about 1 tblsp.). Stir quickly and evenly with fork after each addition of water, adding just enough water that dough holds together in a ball.

Country-style Granola

Many cereal mixes appear on supermarket shelves and in food health stores, but none of them surpasses the taste and delightful crispness of homemade country granola—nor the economy. If you make your own mix from the recipe that follows, you can be sure it is nutrition-packed. It bakes slowly for an hour and requires some stirring to insure even toasting without scorching. So make it when you are going to be busy in the kitchen and can watch it.

While the cereal mix tastes great served as a cereal, it also appeals to snackers. Mothers appreciate its contribution to good nutrition— often lacking in commercially prepared snacks that cost more. Try Granola Cookies and Granola/Apple Crisp for special treats.

Peanuts, an excellent source of vegetable protein, are considerably less expensive than most other nuts included in some granolas. Their flavor and texture accounts for a large share of the popularity of Country-style Granola.

COUNTRY-STYLE GRANOLA

This homemade mix is a gold mine of good nutrition and country kitchen flavors. You'll find many uses for it.

5 c. old-fashioned rolled oats	½ c. brown sugar, firmly packed
1½ c. wheat germ	½ c. salad oil
1 c. shredded coconut	⅓ c. water
1 c. chopped peanuts	2 tsp. vanilla
½ c. whole wheat bran	

Stir together oats, wheat germ, coconut, peanuts, bran and brown sugar in a large bowl.

Combine oil, water and vanilla; pour over cereal mixture and mix thoroughly. Turn into 15½ ×10½ ×1″ pan, or other large, shallow pan. Bake in 350° oven 1 hour, stirring every 15 minutes. Cool and store in covered container. Makes about 10 cups.

Memo to Meal Planner: Use as a cereal to lure members of the family who are not hungry early in the day to eat breakfast and enjoy it. Serve it in bowls like any ready-to-eat cereal. When friends stop by in the evening, set a bowl of Country-style Granola on the coffee table and watch nibblers gravitate to it. Almost everyone likes this snack that you can keep on hand to serve on short notice. Sprinkle some of it on vanilla or chocolate ice cream or chilled pudding just before serving. It is a quick dress-up for many other desserts.

GRANOLA COOKIES

Bake a batch of these new country drop cookies soon.

½ c. butter or regular margarine	½ tsp. baking soda
½ c. brown sugar, firmly packed	½ tsp. salt
½ c. sugar	2 c. Country-style Granola
1 egg	1 (6 oz.) pkg. semisweet
1 tsp. vanilla	chocolate pieces
¾ c. sifted flour	

Cream butter; gradually add sugars, beating until light and fluffy. Beat in egg and vanilla.

Sift together flour, soda and salt; add to creamed mixture. Stir in Country-style Granola and chocolate pieces. Drop by teaspoonfuls about 2″ apart onto greased baking sheet. Bake in 350° oven 10 to 12 minutes, until lightly browned. Makes about 4 dozen.

GRANOLA/APPLE CRISP

Peanuts and coconut in mix add good flavor to apple crisp.

4 c. sliced peeled apples	⅓ c. flour
¼ tsp. ground cinnamon	⅓ c. melted butter or regular
1½ c. Country-style Granola	margarine
⅔ c. brown sugar, firmly packed	

Place apples in greased 8″ square pan. Sprinkle with cinnamon.

Combine Country-style Granola, brown sugar and flour. Thoroughly mix in butter. Sprinkle mixture over apples. Bake in 350° oven 35 minutes. Makes 6 servings.

Economical Pudding Mixes

Mothers who are always looking for desserts that contribute milk to family meals will welcome the recipes that follow for pudding mixes. Nonfat dry milk is an important ingredient in them.

When you keep homemade mixes on hand, it takes only a few minutes to make delicious Vanilla, Caramel and Chocolate Puddings. Use simple garnishes on the individual servings to add variety and appeal. Bits of leftover fresh or canned fruits dress up the thrifty dessert quickly as do scraps of other leftover foods, such as a few nuts, miniature marshmallows, cookie or cake crumbs and jelly or jam.

PUDDING MIX

Keep mix on hand to help get a good dessert fast.

1½ c. sugar	¾ c. cornstarch
2¾ c. nonfat dry milk	1 tsp. salt

Combine all ingredients; stir until well blended. Store in tightly covered container. Makes about 24 servings of pudding.

VANILLA PUDDING

You can dress up this delicious pudding with chocolate sauce.

1¼ c. Pudding Mix	1 egg, slightly beaten
2½ c. milk or water	1½ tsp. vanilla
1 tblsp. butter	

Combine Pudding Mix and milk in heavy 2-qt. saucepan. Cook over medium heat, stirring constantly, until thickened. Add butter and remove from heat.

Stir some of hot mixture into egg. Blend egg into pudding; cook 1 minute. Remove from heat, and add vanilla. Pour into dessert glasses. Serve warm or chilled. Makes 6 servings.

CHOCOLATE PUDDING MIX

Blame the chocolate taste for the way mix disappears.

1½ c. sugar
5 c. nonfat dry milk
1¼ c. flour

1 tsp. salt
¾ c. unsweetened cocoa

Stir together all ingredients until thoroughly blended. Store in covered container in a cool place. Makes about 24 servings of pudding.

CHOCOLATE PUDDING

You can depend on this budget dessert to win friends.

1¼ c. Chocolate Pudding Mix
1 egg, beaten
2½ c. water

1 tblsp. butter or regular
margarine
¾ tsp. vanilla

Place Chocolate Pudding Mix in saucepan.

Combine egg and water, and stir into mix. Cook, stirring constantly, until mixture thickens and is smooth. Remove from heat and add butter and vanilla. Serve warm or chilled. Makes 6 servings.

Memo to Meal Planner: Sprinkle flaked coconut on puddings just before serving. Or top with scoops of vanilla ice cream or whipped dessert topping. Chopped salted peanuts make a delightful garnish.

CARAMEL PUDDING MIX

Keep mix on hand to make thrifty, quick desserts.

1½ c. brown sugar, firmly
packed
5 c. nonfat dry milk

1¼ c. flour
1 tsp. salt

Stir all ingredients together to blend thoroughly. Store in covered container in a cool place. Makes about 24 servings of pudding.

CARAMEL PUDDING

An easy, economical way to include milk in meals.

1¼ c. Caramel Pudding Mix	1 tblsp. butter or regular
1 egg, beaten	margarine
2½ c. water	¾ tsp. vanilla

Place Caramel Pudding Mix in saucepan.

Combine egg and water; add to mix. Cook, stirring constantly, until mixture thickens and is smooth. Remove from heat; add butter and vanilla. Serve warm or chilled. Makes 6 servings.

Memo to Meal Planner: To dress up dessert, alternate pudding and sliced bananas in dessert dishes just before serving. Or top with sliced bananas. For a change, garnish with pineapple chunks.

Frozen Sauce Cubes for Vegetables

Many women lament that they "can't get the kids to eat vegetables." To help make these healthful foods acceptable, home economists in our Test Kitchens developed recipes for Tomato and Cheese Sauce Cubes, along with two other mixtures, to freeze and quickly add to cooked vegetables. The recipes have been so popular that we repeat them in this cookbook, just in case you've missed seeing them in another FARM JOURNAL cookbook. They will help you enhance many of the economical vegetables which you may have in your freezer or garden.

TOMATO SAUCE CUBES

Sauce Cubes are instant—no need to thaw before using.

¼ c. butter or regular margarine	2 tsp. salt
½ c. flour	½ tsp. dried basil leaves
1 (6 oz.) can tomato paste	¼ tsp. pepper
1 tsp. prepared mustard	¼ tsp. garlic powder
2 tsp. sugar	1 tblsp. salad oil
2 tsp. onion powder	¾ c. water

Melt butter in saucepan; remove from heat. Add flour; stir until moistened. Add remaining ingredients, except water. Stir until smooth. Gradually stir in water. Pour into 8½ × 4½ × 2½" loaf pan. Freeze to consistency of ice cream. Cut in 32 cubes. Carefully transfer cubes to baking sheet; freeze solid. Package in plastic freezer bags. Label and freeze. Makes 32.

TOMATO-SAUCED GREEN BEANS

You will discover many other good ways to use Sauce Cubes.

1 (1 pt.) pkg. frozen green beans	½ c. water, lightly salted
	4 Tomato Sauce Cubes

Cook beans in water until tender. Add Tomato Sauce Cubes. Stir and continue cooking until sauce is smooth and thick.

Variations

Tomato-sauced Zucchini: Use 1 pt. sliced zucchini, cooked, and ¼ c. cooking liquid, for the green beans.
Tomato-sauced Celery: Use 1 pt. sliced celery, cooked, with ¼ c. cooking liquid, for the green beans.
Tomato-sauced Onions: Use 1 pt. small onions, cooked, with ¼ c. cooking liquid, for the green beans.

Memo to Meal Planner: If you are alone for lunch and do not want to spend much time getting a meal, fix yourself a cup of tomato soup. Use 5 frozen Tomato Sauce Cubes. Add them to ¾ c. milk and cook, stirring, until soup is smooth and thickened. Team with toast and salad for an enjoyable lunch.

LEMON/BUTTER SAUCE CUBES

Spoon sauce made with cubes over hot cooked vegetables.

½ c. butter or regular margarine	½ tsp. grated lemon peel
¼ c. flour	3 tblsp. lemon juice
1 tblsp. sugar	¾ c. water
2 tsp. salt	Yellow food color
1 tsp. ground nutmeg	

Melt butter; add flour and stir until moistened. Stir in remaining ingredients, using a few drops of yellow food color. Cook, stirring constantly, until mixture begins to bubble and thicken. Pour into 8½ × 4½ ×2½″ loaf pan. Freeze to the consistency of ice cream. Cut in 32 cubes. Transfer to baking sheet and freeze solid. Package in plastic freezer bags. Label and freeze. Makes 32.

LEMON/BUTTER SAUCE

Sauce is good with most vegetables, but serve it on fish too.

8 Lemon/Butter Sauce Cubes ¼ c. water

At serving time combine cubes and water in saucepan. Heat and stir until smooth. Keep warm over low heat, but do not let boil. Serve with the following vegetables.

Lemon-sauced Asparagus: Cook 1 (10 oz.) pkg. frozen asparagus by package directions. Spoon Lemon/Butter Sauce over asparagus just before serving.

Lemon-sauced Carrots: Spoon Lemon/Butter Sauce over hot cooked diced or sliced carrots just before serving.

Lemon-sauced Beets: Just before serving, spoon Lemon/Butter Sauce over hot cooked diced beets.

CHEESE SAUCE CUBES

Sauce made from cubes is as smooth as velvet and tasty.

8 oz. process sharp American cheese	1½ tsp. salt
¾ c. water	1 tsp. dry mustard
⅓ c. butter or regular margarine	2 tsp. Worcestershire sauce
½ c. flour	½ c. nonfat dry milk
	2 tblsp. water

Grate chilled cheese; add to ¾ c. water in saucepan. Cook over low heat, stirring occasionally until cheese is melted and smooth.

Melt butter in another saucepan; remove from heat. Add flour; stir until smooth. Stir in salt, dry mustard and Worcestershire sauce. Add melted cheese and stir until smooth. Add dry milk and 2 tblsp. water; stir until smooth.

Pour sauce into 8½ ×4½ ×2½″ loaf pan. Freeze to the consistency of ice cream. Cut in 32 cubes. Carefully transfer cubes to baking sheet; freeze solid. Package in plastic freezer bags. Label and freeze. Makes 32.

CHEESE SAUCE

Serve over cooked green beans, cauliflower, broccoli, small onions and boiled potatoes. You'll find many ways to use it.

6 Cheese Sauce Cubes   ¾ c. milk

Add frozen Cheese Sauce Cubes to milk; cook over medium heat until sauce is smooth and thick. Makes ¾ cup.

Cheese-sauced Lima Beans: Cook 1 (1 pt.) pkg. frozen lima beans in ¾ c. lightly salted water until tender. Add 8 Cheese Sauce Cubes; stir and cook until sauce is smooth and thick.

CURRY SAUCE CUBES

Tasty sauce enhances the delicate flavor of peas.

½ c. butter or regular   ⅔ c. flour
  margarine   ¼ c. nonfat dry milk
2 tsp. salt   ¾ c. warm water
¾ tsp. curry powder   2 tblsp. grated Parmesan
½ tsp. onion powder   cheese

Melt butter in saucepan; remove from heat. Add salt, curry powder and onion powder. Stir to dissolve. Gradually add flour; stir until moistened. Slowly add milk and water; stir in cheese. Pour into 8½ × 4½ × 2½″ loaf pan. Freeze to the consistency of ice cream. Cut in 32 cubes. Transfer to baking sheet and freeze solid. Package in plastic freezer bags. Label and freeze. Makes 32.

CURRY-SAUCED PEAS

Serve these curry-flavored peas when you have pork for dinner.

1 (1 pt.) pkg. frozen peas   8 Curry Sauce Cubes
⅔ c. water, lightly salted

Cook peas in water until tender. Add Curry Sauce Cubes and continue to cook and stir until sauce is smooth and thick. Do not overcook peas. (For less sauce, use ⅓ c. water and 4 sauce cubes.)

Homemade Salad Dressings

Bottled salad dressings from the supermarket cost more than those you can make at home. Get out your pencil and compare the costs of a French dressing you buy with an equal measurement of Basic French Dressing made from the recipe that follows. You will see that it pays you to shake up your own. Another advantage of making it is that you can season the dressing the way your family likes it best.

BASIC FRENCH DRESSING

Thrifty women save pennies by making salad dressings.

2 tsp. salt	½ c. wine or cider vinegar
2 tsp. sugar	1½ c. salad oil
½ tsp. dry mustard	Dash of ground red pepper
¼ tsp. pepper	

Combine all ingredients in glass jar or bottle. Cover, shake well and store in refrigerator. Shake again before using or making additions. Makes 2 cups.

DISTINCTIVE SALAD DRESSINGS

Add the following ingredients to 1 c. Basic French Dressing at least 1 hour before serving with tossed or other vegetable salads. Shake before using.

Curry: Add 1 tsp. curry powder, ¼ tsp. dry mustard and 2 finely chopped or sieved hard-cooked eggs.

Florentine: Add 2 tblsp. minced raw spinach leaves.

Garlic: Add 2 crushed cloves garlic.

Parmesan: Add ¼ c. grated Parmesan cheese. Good with both fruit and vegetable salads.

Vinaigrette: Add 2 tsp. chopped chives and 2 finely chopped hard-cooked eggs.

IMAGINATIVE SALAD DRESSINGS

Start with 1 c. Basic French Dressing to make these.

For Tossed and Vegetable Salads
Chiffonade: Add 4 tsp. minced pimiento, 4 tsp. minced fresh parsley and 1 finely chopped hard-cooked egg.
Herb: Add 4 tsp. snipped fresh parsley and 1 tsp. minced fresh basil or tarragon.
Indian Rose: Add 1 small cooked beet, finely chopped or sieved, 1 tsp. minced onion and ½ tsp. celery seeds.
Parisian: Add 2 tblsp. chopped green pepper, 2 tblsp. chopped celery, 2 tsp. chopped onion, ½ tsp. Worcestershire sauce and ½ tsp. salt.
Spicy Red: Add ⅓ c. ketchup, 1 tsp. chopped onion, 1 tsp. Worcestershire sauce and 2 tblsp. chopped sweet pickle.

For Fruit Salads
Honey/Celery Seed: Add ½ c. honey and 1 tsp. celery seeds.
Honey/Lemon: Add 2 tblsp. honey, 4 tsp. lemon juice and ½ to 1 tsp. grated lemon peel.
Celery Seed: Add ½ tsp. celery seeds. Chill at least 3 hours.
Mint: Add ¼ c. chopped fresh mint leaves and 4 tsp. sugar.
Sweet French: Add ¼ c. confectioners sugar.
Cheese: Add 2 to 4 tblsp. crumbled blue or Roquefort cheese (more expensive but good on both fruit and vegetables).

SPECIAL HERB FRENCH DRESSING

This herb blend lifts salads above the commonplace.

1 c. bottled French dressing	1 tsp. dried basil leaves,
1 tblsp. lemon juice	crumbled
1 tsp. dried orégano leaves,	½ tsp. dried dill weed
crumbled	¼ tsp. celery salt
1 tsp. parsley flakes, crumbled	

Pour French dressing into a jar. Add remaining ingredients. Cover and shake vigorously. Refrigerate 1 week to give herbs time to flavor dressing. Makes 1 cup.

MAYONNAISE WHIP

Creamy and mild, a combination of old-fashioned cooked salad dressing and mayonnaise—excellent for sandwiches.

3 c. water	⅓ c. sugar
1 c. white vinegar	2 tsp. dry mustard
½ c. cornstarch	2 tsp. salt
⅔ c. cold water	½ tblsp. white vinegar
⅓ c. sugar	1 c. salad oil
3 egg yolks	1½ tblsp. water

Heat 3 c. water and 1 c. vinegar to boiling.

Make a paste of cornstarch and ⅔ c. cold water; add to boiling mixture. Cook, stirring constantly, until thick and smooth. Remove from heat; blend in ⅓ c. sugar. Set in pan of cold water to cool.

Combine egg yolks, ⅓ c. sugar, dry mustard, salt and ½ tblsp. vinegar. Beat with electric mixer until light and lemon-colored. Alternately add salad oil and 1½ tblsp. water, a little at a time, starting with ½ tsp. oil and doubling the amount after each addition, and a few drops of water; end with oil. Beat thoroughly after each addition until smooth and thick.

Add the cooked vinegar mixture, beating just enough to blend. Store in covered glass jar in refrigerator. Whip will keep up to 2 weeks. Makes about 6 cups.

Memo to Meal Planner: Use Mayonnaise Whip as a base for salad dressings and a help in sandwich making.

SALAD DRESSINGS AND SANDWICHES

Use Mayonnaise Whip to make these tasty country favorites.

Farmhouse Salad Dressings
For Fruit Salad: Thin Mayonnaise Whip with juice from canned fruit, as for peach/cottage cheese salad.
For Coleslaw: Mix equal portions Mayonnaise Whip and dairy sour cream. Add seasonings as desired.
For Tossed and Other Lettuce Salads: Combine equal parts Mayonnaise Whip and chili sauce (a good reason for canning chili sauce when tomatoes are plentiful).

Fillings for Four Hostess Sandwiches

Chicken or Ham Salad: To 1 c. chopped cooked chicken or ham add ½ c. drained crushed pineapple, 2 tblsp. Mayonnaise Whip and, if you like, ¼ c. chopped nuts and a dash of ground nutmeg. Makes filling for 4 sandwiches.

Egg/Onion: Chop 3 hard-cooked eggs; blend with 1 tblsp. prepared mustard, 1 tblsp. minced onion, 1 tblsp. minced green pepper and 2 tblsp. Mayonnaise Whip. Makes filling for 4 sandwiches.

Prune/Cheese: Pit and chop ½ c. soft prunes; mix with ½ c. grated Cheddar cheese, 1 tblsp. grated orange peel, 1 tsp. lemon juice and 2 tblsp. Mayonnaise Whip. Makes filling for 4 sandwiches.

Tuna/Celery: Flake 1 (7 oz.) can tuna; add ¼ c. each chopped celery, ¼ c. chopped green pepper, 1 tsp. lemon juice and 3 tblsp. Mayonnaise Whip. Makes filling for 4 sandwiches.

CHAPTER 3

Economical Meat Dishes

Recipes for meat dishes so good you would want to make them even if they were not thrifty—that's what you will find in this chapter's carefully selected and tested collection. The fact that they take some of the pressure off grocery bills increases their appeal.

Their variety proves that the more costly meat cuts are not necessarily more versatile—or more appetizing. We have paid special attention to good nutrition; certain dishes containing less meat are fortified with other protein ingredients with no sacrifice of appetite appeal.

Here are a few examples of economical dishes from this chapter: Beef/Corn Pie to put in the oven on a chilly day, for instance. It is the winter version of grilled hamburgers and corn on the cob in July. Baked Pork Steaks with Stuffing really please the men. Tasty Beef/Bean Loaf cuts like a charm, every slice falling off the carving knife without breaking.

These budget recipes provide specialties for company occasions. Set Beef/Macaroni Hostess Special on the buffet table and you can be proud to invite guests to help themselves. Treat your family and friends to inexpensive Buttermilk Stroganoff. Serve Beef-stuffed Buns to the young crowd and watch their enthusiasm.

Some of these thrifty dishes are time-savers, too. If you need to be away from home in the afternoon, put Four-hour Beef Stew in the oven to cook while you are away. You can serve a wonderful evening meal on time.

Every one of our recipes calls for a thrifty meat. Meat usually costs more per serving than other foods, but when you consider what it does for the family's nutrition, you are wise to plan your meal around it. We Americans like meat and we expect to find it on the table.

Women everywhere register concern when meat prices are high. Sometimes people in cities blame the farmers, supermarkets, government and whomever they suspect of unnecessarily boosting the prices. Women living on the land, whose husbands may produce beef, hogs and lamb, also feel the increases in cost. They know that the steer or hog slaughtered to provide their meat would have added to their income if it had been sold instead. They also know firsthand about the high cost of feeds for livestock and the work involved. Meat is money to the grower. That is why farm women always have made thrifty use of it in their kitchens and why we turned to their favorite recipes in making this collection.

This chapter contains the best meat recipes from country kitchens, all tried and perfected in the FARM JOURNAL Test Kitchens. For more recipes that include economical meat as an ingredient, turn to the chapters on Hearty Main-dish Soups and Homemade Mixes.

Tasty Beef Specials

One way to please the family with economical meat dishes is to substitute less expensive for the more costly traditional cuts. Rarely does the family recognize the change. A classic example is Economy Swiss Steak made with round-bone chuck instead of the usual round steak. The gourmet casserole recipe for Continental Beef Shanks uses meat commonly cooked in the soup kettle. In Second-choice Roast Beef, a chuck cut cooks in dry rather than in the customary moist heat.

The names of beef cuts, as well as those of veal, pork and lamb have been standardized so they can be the same in all parts of the country. (See inside back cover of this cookbook for charts showing the standard terms for beef and pork cuts and from what part of the carcass they come.) From more than 1,000 names for meat cuts the number has been reduced to about 300. This helps the shopper by advising her what she is buying and it avoids the confusion of strictly regional names.

Stews in which vegetables extend beef rate high in country kitchens. You will find some different vegetables in some of the recipes that follow. Short ribs (instead of stew meat) team with onion, green pepper, canned tomatoes, kidney and pinto beans in Lone Star Beef Stew. Autumn Beef/Vegetable Stew contains the harvest season's fresh vegetables, such as tomatoes, zucchini or yellow crookneck squash, green beans, carrots, cabbage and green pepper. It salvages the last of the garden before frost arrives.

ECONOMY SWISS STEAK

This beef tastes so good family and guests will never know you made it with chuck instead of more expensive round steak.

2½ to 3 lbs. round-bone chuck
    steak, cut 1" thick
¼ c. flour
2 tsp. salt
¼ tsp. pepper

3 tblsp. salad oil
1 (1 lb.) can tomatoes, cut up
½ c. chopped onion
½ c. chopped celery
½ tsp. Worcestershire sauce

Cut meat in 5 or 6 portions.

Combine flour, salt and pepper; pound into meat on both sides using edge of heavy saucer. Set aside flour mixture that is left. Brown meat in skillet containing hot oil. Remove from skillet.

Blend remaining flour mixture with drippings in skillet. Add tomatoes, onion, celery and Worcestershire sauce; cook, stirring, until mixture comes to a boil. Return meat to skillet, spooning gravy over each piece. Cover and bake in 350° oven about 2 hours, until meat is tender. Makes 5 or 6 servings.

Memo to Meal Planner: Serve this simply delicious Swiss steak with Tender-crisp Carrots or Corn with Crisp Topping, Green Bean Salad Bowl or Apple Coleslaw (see Index for recipes).

CONTINENTAL BEEF SHANKS

Thrifty beef shanks leave soup kettle and go glamorous.

6 cross-cut slices beef shank,
    1½" thick
¼ c. flour
3 tblsp. salad oil
1½ c. chopped onion
1 carrot, peeled and chopped
½ c. chopped celery

1½ tsp. salt
½ tsp. dried thyme leaves,
    crushed
¼ tsp. pepper
1 (8 oz.) can tomato sauce
½ c. dry red wine

Coat both sides of beef shank slices with flour. Brown on both sides in hot salad oil in large skillet. Place meat in 3-qt. casserole. Top with onion, carrot, celery and seasonings. Pour tomato sauce and wine over top. Cover and bake in 350° oven about 2 hours, until meat is tender. Makes 6 servings.

Memo to Meal Planner: Serve this special main dish with fluffy, hot rice, a green salad and for dessert, Cherry Crisp (see Index for recipe). For a pleasing touch, top dessert servings with small scoops of ice cream or ice milk.

SECOND-CHOICE ROAST BEEF

Everyone who tastes this cut of beef, prepared by these USDA directions, likes it better than the same cut cooked as pot roast, or with water added. Chuck is coarser than a rib roast, but the taste is similar—consider it when cost is a factor.

> 1 (4 lb.) round-bone chuck roast, cut 2" thick   Meat tenderizer

Treat meat with tenderizer as directed on jar label. Place on rack in shallow roasting pan or skillet. Bake in 325° oven 1½ to 2½ hours, depending on doneness desired. Test doneness by cutting meat in thickest part with a sharp knife and checking color. Carve across grain in *thin* slices. Makes 8 servings.

CONTINENTAL POT ROAST

When the prime rib roast of beef you'd like to serve for a special occasion is too expensive, try this distinctive pot roast. Beef, vegetables and gourmet seasonings bake in foil wrap.

> 1 (3 to 4 lb.) round-bone chuck roast
> 1 onion, thinly sliced
> 1 branch celery, thinly sliced
> 1 carrot, peeled and thinly sliced
> 1 tblsp. parsley flakes
> 2 tsp. salt
>
> 1 tsp. dried thyme leaves, crushed
> ¼ tsp. pepper
> 2 bay leaves
> 1 clove garlic, minced
> 1 c. dry red wine
> 2 tblsp. cornstarch
> 2 tblsp. water

Tear off a piece of foil large enough to completely wrap meat and vegetables. Place foil in shallow roasting pan, arrange meat in center and turn back edges of foil. Place pan under broiler, 3 to 5" from source of heat, and brown meat on both sides. Remove pan.

Top meat with vegetables, seasonings and wine. Pull edges of foil around meat and seal tightly. Bake in 300° oven 3 hours. Strain off juices. Remove bay leaves. Keep meat and vegetables warm.

Blend together cornstarch and water in saucepan. Add enough additional water to pan juices to make 2 c. Stir into cornstarch mixture. Cook, stirring constantly, until gravy bubbles and is thickened. Serve meat with vegetables; pass the gravy. Makes 6 servings.

Memo to Meal Planner: Serve this pot roast with a bowl of fluffy hot rice so everyone can ladle some of the lovely gravy over it. Buttered peas, a mixed green salad and hard rolls will complete the main course in fine fashion. Serve a simple dessert. Consider having pretty, light Fruited Pink Whip (see Index for recipe).

LONE STAR BEEF STEW

Texans like hot biscuits with this. End meal with lemon sherbet.

4 lbs. short ribs
1 c. chopped onion
1 c. chopped green pepper
2 cloves garlic, minced
2 tblsp. chili powder
2 tsp. salt
1 (1 lb.) can tomatoes, cut up
1 beef bouillon cube

1 c. boiling water
1 (15 oz.) can kidney beans, drained
1 (15 oz.) can pinto beans, drained
1 (17 oz.) can whole kernel corn, drained

Rub fat side of a short rib over bottom of heated heavy Dutch oven to coat with fat. Add short ribs; brown on all sides. Remove ribs. Add onion, green pepper and garlic to drippings. Cook until soft; drain off fat.

Return beef to Dutch oven; add chili powder, salt, tomatoes, bouillon cube and water. Cover and simmer about 2 hours, until meat is tender and falls away from bones. Stir occasionally.

Remove meat from broth; remove bones and discard. Skim fat from broth. (If time permits, chill meat and broth separately; remove hardened fat from broth). Return beef to Dutch oven, add beans and corn; simmer 20 to 25 minutes. Makes 8 servings.

AUTUMN BEEF/VEGETABLE STEW

Big recipe for a main dish to serve a crowd. A cross between a stew and soup, it uses dry kidney beans and the harvest season's vegetables when they are lowest in cost.

1 lb. dry red kidney beans	2 c. chopped fresh tomatoes
2½ qts. water	2 small zucchini or yellow
1 lb. stewing beef, cut in 1″	crookneck squash, sliced
cubes	1 c. cut green beans (1″
2 cloves garlic, minced	pieces)
2 c. chopped onion	1 c. sliced peeled carrots
2 tsp. salt	1 c. shredded cabbage
¼ tsp. pepper	½ c. chopped green pepper
4 beef bouillon cubes	

Wash and pick over kidney beans; put in large kettle and add water. Cover and bring to a boil; boil 2 minutes. Remove from heat and let stand 1 hour.

Add beef, garlic, onion, salt, pepper and bouillon cubes. Cover and simmer 2 hours, or until beans are tender. Add remaining ingredients and simmer 35 to 45 minutes, until vegetables are tender. Makes 3¾ quarts.

Memo to Meal Planner: You can dress up servings of this stew by sprinkling it with Parmesan cheese. Serve with hot garlic bread, pickles and apple pie.

DANISH BEEF STEW

Beer takes role more expensive wine often has in European meat dishes. This is an economy recipe for gourmet eating.

2½ lbs. lean stewing beef	1 (12 oz.) can beer
¼ c. salad oil	2 tsp. salt
4 large onions, sliced and	1 tsp. sugar
separated into rings	½ tsp. dried thyme leaves,
3 cloves garlic, minced	crushed
3 tblsp. flour	¼ tsp. pepper
1 c. water	2 tblsp. prepared mustard
1 tblsp. prepared mustard	8 (1″) slices French bread
2 beef bouillon cubes	

Brown meat on all sides in 3 tblsp. oil in large skillet. Remove with slotted spoon to 13×9×2″ baking pan. Add remaining 1 tblsp. oil to skillet. Add onion rings and garlic; cover and cook until onions are limp, stirring frequently.

Blend flour with ½ c. water. Stir in remaining ½ c. water and 1 tblsp. mustard. Add to skillet along with bouillon cubes, beer, salt, sugar, thyme and pepper. Cook, stirring, until mixture comes to a boil and is slightly thickened. Add to baking pan, stirring to distribute beef. Cover with foil and bake in 350° oven about 2 hours, until beef is tender.

Spread 2 tblsp. mustard on one side of bread slices. Place bread, mustard side down, on top of beef, pushing halfway down into the sauce. Return to oven and cook uncovered 15 minutes, then broil 3 to 5″ from heat 2 to 3 minutes until bread browns. Serves 8.

Memo to Meal Planner: You can build an interesting oven meal for guests around the stew. You may wish to try Dijon-type mustard instead of the prepared mustard you use regularly. It costs a little more, but adds a telling flavor touch. Choose a vegetable that you reheat or cook in the oven alongside the stew. This might be stuffed baked potatoes made ahead and frozen, or baked sweet potatoes. You can use the same recipe as for Sweet Potatoes for Freezing, but do not freeze them. Include a green salad or relish plate and apple pie, or Apple Cobbler in the menu. The cobbler bakes in the oven with the stew. If you want to splurge and the budget will permit, top the warm cobbler with vanilla ice cream (see Index for recipes).

BEEF/POTATO BAKE

Meat makes gravy as it bakes under layer of sliced potatoes.

1½ lbs. lean stewing beef, cut in 1½″ cubes	¼ tsp. pepper
2 tblsp. salad oil	⅛ tsp. dried thyme leaves, crushed
1 large onion, sliced and separated into rings	1¾ c. water
¼ c. flour	5 c. sliced peeled potatoes
1½ tsp. salt	½ tsp. salt
	Dash of pepper

Brown beef cubes in hot oil. Combine with onion rings in 2½-qt. casserole. Sprinkle with flour, 1½ tsp. salt, ¼ tsp. pepper and thyme.

Pour water into casserole. Cover and bake in 350° oven 1½ hours. Remove from oven.

Top meat with potatoes; sprinkle with ½ tsp. salt and dash of pepper. Cover and bake about 45 minutes, until potatoes are tender.

Remove cover and place casserole under broiler about 3 minutes, until potatoes are lightly browned. Makes 6 servings.

Memo to Meal Planner: The woman who shares this recipe used to make this dish with round steak. She learned by experimenting that less costly stew meat is equally good. Once the casserole is in the oven, it looks out for itself during the 1½ hours of baking before time to add the potatoes. After the potatoes are added, there is time to get the remainder of the dinner. One reason for the popularity of the dish is that most men and boys like meat, potato and gravy meals.

SHORT RIBS WITH NOODLES

Precooking short ribs in very hot oven removes excess fat. Men especially praise this substantial beef main dish.

⅓ c. flour	4 c. hot water
1 tsp. salt	1 envelope onion soup mix
¼ tsp. pepper	1 (8 oz.) pkg. noodles
3 lbs. short ribs	

Combine flour, salt and pepper in paper or plastic bag.

Cut off excess fat from meat. Shake short ribs, a few at a time, in flour mixture to coat thoroughly. Place in 13×9×2″ pan, keeping pieces slightly apart. Bake in 475° oven 30 minutes.

Remove from oven and drain off excess fat. Add water and onion soup mix; cover pan tightly with foil. Bake in 325° oven 1½ to 2 hours, until meat is tender.

Stir noodles into liquid in pan. Cover and cook 15 minutes. Stir, adding more hot water if needed. Continue cooking, covered, about 15 minutes, until noodles are tender. Makes 6 servings.

Memo to Meal Planner: Serve with a green vegetable, pickled beets, lettuce salad and cherry pie. Or if you prefer, or do not have time to bake a pie, have canned pears, chilled, with chocolate syrup poured over for dessert. If you have crisp cookies, serve them with pears.

BEEF/NOODLE STEW

Colorful, tasty beef stew features homemade noodles.

1 lb. stewing beef
2 tblsp. salad oil
1 tsp. salt
⅛ tsp. pepper
3 beef bouillon cubes
3½ c. water
1 c. chopped onion

1 c. chopped celery
1 c. sliced peeled carrots
Homemade Noodles or 6 oz.
  packaged noodles
½ c. frozen loose-pack green
  beans

In Dutch oven brown beef in hot oil. Add salt, pepper, bouillon cubes and water. Bring to a boil; reduce heat, cover and simmer about 1½ hours, until beef is tender.

Add onion, celery, carrots and Homemade Noodles; cover and simmer 20 minutes. Add green beans; simmer 10 minutes longer. Makes 8 servings.

Homemade Noodles: Combine 1 egg, beaten, 2 tblsp. milk, ½ tsp. salt and 1 c. sifted flour to make a stiff dough. Knead 5 or 6 times; roll as thin as possible, and place between towels until partially dry (looks like chamois skin). Roll up like jelly roll; cut in slender strips, shake out and let dry. (These can be made a day ahead.)

Memo to Meal Planner: Serve with your favorite cottage cheese salad to boost protein and to please the family.

FOUR-HOUR BEEF STEW

You put stew in oven and forget about it for 4 hours. It captures that wonderful, old-fashioned taste our grandmothers achieved with their wood-and-coal-burning ranges. Choose it for a day when you need to be out of the kitchen most of the time.

1½ lbs. lean stewing beef
3 potatoes, peeled and
  quartered
6 carrots, peeled and cut in 1″
  pieces
2 onions, quartered
1 c. sliced celery

2 tsp. seasoned salt
⅛ tsp. pepper
1 (15 oz.) can tomato sauce
1 c. water
¼ c. flour
½ c. water

Combine beef and vegetables in heavy Dutch oven. Sprinkle with seasoned salt and pepper. Pour on tomato sauce and 1 c. water; stir to mix. Cover and bake in 275° oven 4 hours. Remove to range top.

Combine flour and ½ c. water; blend until smooth. Add to stew; cook until liquid thickens and bubbles, stirring often. Serves 6.

Memo to Meal Planner: You do not brown the beef, but the tomato sauce imparts appealing color. The vegetables are more tender than they are in many stews, but they hold their shape and have beautifully blended flavors. Serve stew with hot rolls.

BEEF STEW WITH DUMPLINGS

Fluffy Paprika Dumplings give stew an appealing look.

1 lb. stewing beef, cut in 1½″ cubes	1 tsp. paprika
¼ c. flour	¼ tsp. pepper
2 tblsp. salad oil	3 potatoes, peeled and quartered
1 c. chopped onion	2 c. sliced peeled carrots
1 (1 lb.) can stewed tomatoes	½ c. chopped celery
½ c. water	Paprika Dumplings
2 tsp. salt	1 tsp. paprika

Shake beef cubes a few pieces at a time in paper or plastic bag with flour. Brown in hot oil. Add onion, tomatoes, water, salt, 1 tsp. paprika and pepper. Cover and simmer about 1½ hours, or until meat is tender.

Add potatoes, carrots and celery. Simmer about 30 minutes, until almost tender.

Meanwhile, make Paprika Dumplings. Drop from tablespoon onto vegetables and meat in stew. Sprinkle on 1 tsp. paprika. Simmer uncovered 10 minutes; cover and simmer 10 minutes more. Serves 6.

Paprika Dumplings: Sift together 1½ c. sifted flour, 3 tsp. baking powder and ¾ tsp. salt. Combine with ¾ c. milk and 3 tblsp. salad oil. Stir just to moisten the flour mixture. Use as directed.

BEEF/RICE SCRAMBLE

Eggs and cheese team with cured beef to contribute body-building protein. Cook rice ahead and you have a 15-minute main dish.

1 c. uncooked rice	½ tsp. hot pepper sauce
3 tblsp. regular margarine	½ tsp. salt
½ c. chopped onion	½ c. shredded process
⅓ c. chopped green pepper	American cheese (2 oz.)
(optional)	4 eggs, slightly beaten
1 (3 oz.) pkg. smoked sliced	
beef	

Cook rice by package directions.

Melt margarine in skillet; add onion and green pepper and cook until soft, but not browned.

Shred smoked beef; add to skillet and heat. Add rice and cook, stirring, until thoroughly heated. Add remaining ingredients and cook, stirring, just until cheese is melted and eggs are set. Makes 6 servings.

Memo to Meal Planner: Chilled tomato juice, toast and cooked frozen mixed vegetables are good accompaniments for this easy, quick and flavorful supper dish. Serve a simple dessert, such as sliced bananas in pineapple juice. Or if you prefer, have instant or regular vanilla pudding with well-drained mandarin orange sections.

Oriental-style Beef

Take a tip from Chinese kitchens in preparing thrifty dishes with less tender beef steaks. Cut the meat in slender strips for cooking. Recipes for two excellent examples follow; both are adapted to American taste and are worthy of serving friends when you want something different and distinctive. Their special merits are economy and intriguing color and flavor—contrasts introduced by vegetables.

BEEF STEAK, ORIENTAL STYLE

Color bright, flavorful main dish to make in summer when vegetables are most plentiful. Serve with ice cream and coconut cookies.

1½ lbs. arm steak, cut 1½″ thick
2 tblsp. salad oil
1 c. water
¼ c. soy sauce
½ tsp. sugar
⅛ tsp. pepper
3 fresh tomatoes, peeled and cut in wedges

2 green peppers, cut in strips
6 green onions, cut in 1″ lengths
2 tsp. cornstarch
2 tblsp. water
1 c. uncooked rice

Cut meat in 3×½″ strips; brown in hot oil in skillet. Add 1 c. water, soy sauce, sugar and pepper. Cover and simmer about 1½ hours, until meat is tender. Add tomato wedges, green pepper and onions; simmer 10 minutes, or until vegetables are tender-crisp.

Blend together cornstarch and 2 tblsp. water. Stir into beef mixture and heat to bubbling.

Meanwhile, cook rice by package directions. Serve meat mixture over hot rice. Makes 6 servings.

BEEF CHOW MEIN

Country hostess version of a famous Chinese dish.

1½ lbs. chuck steak
2 tblsp. salad oil
2 beef bouillon cubes
1½ c. water
¼ c. soy sauce
½ tsp. ground ginger
1 (1 lb.) can bean sprouts
1 green pepper

1 onion
1 c. bias sliced celery
3 tblsp. cornstarch
¼ c. water
1½ c. uncooked rice
1 (3 oz.) can chow mein noodles

Cut beef in 1×½″ pieces. Brown beef in hot oil in large skillet. Add bouillon cubes, 1½ c. water, soy sauce and ginger. Cover and simmer 30 to 45 minutes, until beef is tender. Add bean sprouts.

Meanwhile, cut green pepper in strips; slice onion and separate into rings. Add with celery to skillet. Continue simmering 10 minutes, until vegetables are tender-crisp.

Blend cornstarch with ¼ c. water; add to skillet. Cook, stirring, until mixture is thickened and comes to a boil.

Cook rice as directed on package; drain. Serve meat mixture over rice; sprinkle with noodles. Makes 6 servings.

Memo to Meal Planner: Serve with peas and spiced peaches, and ice milk and crisp cookies for dessert.

Popular Ground Beef

Thrifty ground beef is at the top in meat popularity even when price is not a consideration. It is so adaptable! And children are so fond of it. That is why this cookbook contains more recipes using ground beef than any other meat.

Ground beef is a good mixer. Farm women combine it with many cost-cutting ingredients, such as rice, bread, cornmeal, hominy, macaroni, noodles, rolled oats, textured soybean products, spaghetti and just about every vegetable that grows in their gardens. None of these foods contain the amount or quality of protein as meat, but they help bring to the table thrifty, delicious dishes that retain the beef taste.

Some of the recipes make extra-quick main dishes. Smothered Burgers, Beef/Hominy and Beef/Sauerkraut Skillets are good examples. In Oven Beef Cakes in Gravy, ground beef tastes like country-fried steak and costs less.

Cheese teams with ground beef in many dishes contributing additional protein to a small amount of meat and providing flavor change. Try Cheeseburger Bake and Beef Lasagne—both are delicious.

ECONOMY POT ROAST

Ground beef is the meat you cook and serve like a pot roast.

1½ lbs. lean ground beef
1½ c. soft bread cubes
¾ c. milk
2 eggs, beaten
1½ tsp. salt
⅛ tsp. pepper
2 tsp. Worcestershire sauce
6 medium potatoes, peeled and
    cut in halves

6 medium carrots, peeled and
    cut in halves crosswise, then
    lengthwise
1 onion, cut in 6 wedges
2 tblsp. melted butter or
    regular margarine
½ tsp. salt
Dash of pepper
Topping

Thoroughly mix together beef, bread cubes, milk, eggs, 1½ tsp. salt, ⅛ tsp. pepper and Worcestershire sauce. Form into an 8×4″ loaf in center of 12″ skillet with a tight fitting lid. Arrange potatoes, carrots and onion around loaf; drizzle them with melted butter and sprinkle with ½ tsp. salt and dash of pepper. Cover and bake in 350° oven about 1 hour and 10 minutes, until vegetables are tender.

Spread Topping over meat loaf; return to oven and bake uncovered 3 to 5 minutes, until Topping is heated. Spoon pan drippings over vegetables when serving. Makes 6 servings.

Topping: Combine ⅓ c. ketchup, 1 tblsp. brown sugar and 1 tblsp. prepared mustard.

Memo to Meal Planner: If you are looking for a single-dish meal, try this specialty of a Missouri country woman, who serves a wreath of the vegetables around the meat on the platter. There is space in the oven to bake a dessert alongside the meat and vegetables. Baked apples, crowned with scoops of vanilla ice cream at serving time, end the meal pleasantly.

VEGETABLE/MEAT LOAF

No one complains of having to eat vegetables when they are baked with ground beef in a loaf. Serve this with ketchup or homemade chili sauce if you have it on hand.

2 eggs, slightly beaten	2 lbs. ground beef
2 c. shredded peeled potatoes	2 tsp. salt
1 c. shredded peeled carrots	¼ tsp. pepper
⅓ c. shredded onion	¼ c. nonfat dry milk
1 tblsp. parsley flakes	

Combine all ingredients and shape into a 10×5″ loaf in shallow baking pan. Bake in 350° oven 1 hour 30 minutes. Makes 8 servings.

Memo to Meal Planner: Complete the menu with Cabbage Skillet and Apple/Pineapple Salad (see Index for recipes).

BEEF/BEAN LOAF

If you are looking for a recipe for an unusually good meat loaf, call off the search. This is it, and it slices beautifully, hot or cold. Canned kidney beans, mashed to a paste, economically stretch the beef. They contribute valuable protein and pleasing flavor. And they also help keep the tender loaf moist.

2 eggs, beaten	¼ tsp. pepper
½ c. ketchup	1½ lbs. ground beef
¼ c. milk	1 (15 oz.) can kidney beans,
1 c. soft bread cubes	drained and mashed
1½ tsp. salt	¼ c. finely chopped onion

Thoroughly blend together eggs, ketchup, milk, bread cubes, salt and pepper in mixing bowl. Mix in ground beef, mashed beans and onion. Shape into 10×4″ loaf in a shallow baking pan. Bake in 350° oven 1 hour and 15 minutes. Makes 8 to 10 servings.

Memo to Meal Planner: Serve the neat, shapely slices on a warm platter. Use the cold slices for sandwiches or add them to a plate of cold cuts. Scalloped potatoes or carrots, baked in the oven with the meat loaf, are a fine accompaniment. For a second vegetable, choose peas or green beans.

INDIVIDUAL MEAT LOAVES

You cook meat loaves on top of the range in a sauce.

1 egg
1 c. soft bread cubes
¼ c. milk
1½ tsp. garlic salt
1 tsp. parsley flakes
⅛ tsp. pepper
1½ lbs. ground beef
6 Cheddar cheese sticks (2½ ×
⅓ × ½")
3 tblsp. salad oil

2 (15 oz.) cans tomato sauce
½ c. chopped onion
3 tsp. parsley flakes, crumbled
½ tsp. dried orégano leaves,
crumbled
¼ tsp. dried basil leaves,
crumbled
¼ tsp. garlic salt
12 oz. elbow spaghetti, or 1"
pieces

Beat egg in large bowl; stir in bread cubes, milk, 1½ tsp. garlic salt, 1 tsp. parsley and pepper. Mix into ground beef. Divide mixture in 6 equal parts and shape each into a loaf around a cheese stick. Brown on top and bottom in hot oil in skillet; remove from skillet and drain off fat.

Add tomato sauce, onion, 3 tsp. parsley, orégano, basil and ¼ tsp. garlic salt to skillet. Heat and stir, loosening brown particles from bottom of skillet. Add meat loaves; spoon sauce over the top. Cover and simmer 25 minutes.

Meanwhile, cook spaghetti by package directions. Drain. Serve meat loaves and sauce over hot spaghetti. Makes 6 servings.

Memo to Meal Planner: Include broccoli in menu.

Barbecued Meat Balls and Twin Meat Loaves

When you shop at the meat counter these days, you may find fresh ground beef "plus textured vegetable protein," which is made from soybeans. TVP, as it is sometimes called, is nutritious, containing approximately the same protein per pound as red meat.

Textured vegetable proteins were introduced in national school lunch programs when the USDA approved their use in 1971. Now they are in supermarkets, both in meat as an extender and separately for the homemaker's use. An excellent protein value at low cost.

Though soybeans are nutritious they have a strong pungent flavor that most Americans find distasteful. However, researchers have developed ways to eliminate the objection. The granulated form is used as an extender.

In addition, there are simulated meat products that are also 100 per cent soy protein. They resemble meat or poultry as closely as possible in texture, flavor, odor and color. There are many varieties of these "meatless meats"—simulated fried chicken, beef, ham and Salisbury steak are just a few.

Vegetable proteins are a budget helper and will doubtless become more prominent. Here are two recipes which we have developed that use textured soybean protein as an ingredient. Look in the Index for recipes for Exceptional Tuna Patties, Oatmeal Drop Cookies and Bacon Flavor Dip Mix. All three also contain the protein supplement—try them!

BARBECUED MEAT BALLS

This recipe combines textured vegetable protein and ground beef.

¾ c. textured vegetable protein	1 tsp. salt
½ c. water	⅛ tsp. pepper
1 egg, beaten	1 lb. ground beef
¼ c. milk	Special Barbecue Sauce
2 tblsp. finely chopped onion	Hot cooked rice (optional)

Combine textured vegetable protein and water.

Stir together egg, milk, onion, salt and pepper. Mix in textured vegetable protein and ground beef. Shape in small balls about 1″ in diameter, using 1 tblsp. meat mixture for each ball (you'll have about 35). Place in 15½ ×10½ ×1″ baking pan. Bake in 375° oven 25 to 30 minutes, until lightly browned.

Meanwhile, make Special Barbecue Sauce.

Add meat balls to sauce and simmer several minutes. Serve over hot cooked rice, if desired. Makes 6 servings.

Special Barbecue Sauce: Combine 1 c. ketchup, ¼ c. chopped onion, ¼ c. brown sugar, firmly packed, ¼ c. water, 2 tblsp. vinegar, 2 tblsp. butter or regular margarine and ½ tsp. chili powder in skillet. Cover and simmer 5 minutes.

TWIN MEAT LOAVES

It's as easy and quick to mix and bake two loaves as one.

1 (4 oz.) pkg. textured
    vegetable protein (1½ c.)
1 c. water
2 eggs, beaten
1 (8 oz.) can tomato sauce
2 tsp. salt

½ tsp. dry mustard
¼ tsp. pepper
2 tsp. Worcestershire sauce
½ c. finely chopped onion
2 lbs. ground beef
Ketchup or chili sauce

Mix vegetable protein and water; stir until water is absorbed.

Blend together eggs, tomato sauce, salt, dry mustard, pepper and Worcestershire in large bowl. Stir in onion and vegetable protein mixture. Thoroughly mix in ground beef.

Form mixture into two 8×4″ loaves in 13×9×2″ baking pan. Bake in 350° oven 1 hour. Serve with heated tomato ketchup or chili sauce. Each loaf makes 6 servings.

Memo to Meal Planner: Cool and refrigerate to slice the next day for exceptionally good sandwiches. Or freeze one loaf; reheat when serving. Slice and spread barbecue sauce on both sides. Place in 13×9×2″ pan in 325° oven until warm.

YORKSHIRE MEAT BALLS

Topping on meat balls tastes like Yorkshire pudding—an ideal main dish for company.

1½ lbs. ground beef
¼ c. ketchup
1 envelope onion soup mix
1 tblsp. parsley flakes
¼ tsp. pepper
1 egg, beaten
1 tblsp. water
1½ c. sifted flour

1½ tsp. baking powder
1 tsp. salt
4 eggs
1½ c. milk
3 tblsp. melted regular
    margarine
Fast-fix Cheese Sauce

Thoroughly combine ground beef, ketchup, onion soup mix, parsley, pepper, 1 egg and water. Form mixture into 24 balls and place in 6 rows of 4 meat balls each in *well-greased* 13×9×2″ baking pan.

Sift together flour, baking powder and salt.

Beat 4 eggs until foamy; blend in milk and margarine. Add dry ingredients all at once; beat with rotary beater just until smooth. Pour over meat balls. Bake in 350° oven 45 to 50 minutes. Serve with Fast-fix Cheese Sauce. Makes 8 servings.

Fast-fix Cheese Sauce: Combine ¾ lb. process cheese spread (Velveeta), cubed, ⅓ c. milk and ¼ tsp. Worcestershire sauce in saucepan. Cook over medium heat, stirring, until cheese is melted. Makes 1½ cups.

OVEN BEEF CAKES IN GRAVY

Quick, easy main dish inspired by meat balls but patties are easier to shape. They cook in oven and require no pot-watching. Brown gravy adds flavor and eye appeal.

2 eggs, slightly beaten	2 tblsp. butter or regular
½ c. milk	margarine
⅔ c. coarse cracker crumbs	¼ c. flour
¼ c. finely chopped onion	2 c. milk
1 tsp. salt	3 beef bouillon cubes
⅛ tsp. pepper	¼ tsp. salt
½ tsp. Worcestershire sauce	Dash of pepper
1½ lbs. lean ground beef	Mashed potatoes for 6 servings

To eggs, add ½ c. milk, cracker crumbs, onion, 1 tsp. salt, ⅛ tsp. pepper and Worcestershire sauce. Mix in ground beef.

Melt butter in large skillet. Form beef mixture into 18 patties. Arrange in skillet so patties do not touch each other. Bake in 375° oven 35 minutes. Remove patties from skillet.

Stir flour into drippings in skillet, scraping to remove brown particles that adhere to skillet. Add 2 c. milk, bouillon cubes, ¼ tsp. salt and dash of pepper. Cook, stirring constantly, until mixture comes to a boil and bouillon cubes are dissolved. Return meat cakes to skillet. Spoon gravy over them. Cover and simmer 5 minutes. Serve over mashed potatoes. Makes 6 servings.

Memo to Meal Planner: Serve with Homemade Stewed Tomatoes, Cornhusker Bean/Corn Salad and for dessert, applesauce with Scotia Oat Squares (see Index for recipes).

CHEESEBURGER BAKE

Cheeseburger taste assures success for this casserole.

8 slices white bread	⅛ tsp. pepper
Regular margarine	1 c. shredded sharp process
1 lb. ground beef	American cheese (4 oz.)
½ c. chopped onion	1 egg, beaten
¼ c. chopped celery	¾ c. milk
1 tblsp. prepared mustard	½ tsp. salt
½ tsp. salt	

Toast bread. Spread both sides lightly with margarine and cut each slice in 3 lengthwise pieces.

Cook ground beef in skillet with onion and celery until meat is browned. Stir in mustard, ½ tsp. salt and pepper. Place half the toast slices in greased 9″ square pan. Top with half the ground beef mixture and ½ c. cheese. Repeat layers.

Combine egg, milk and ½ tsp. salt. Pour over layers in pan. Bake in 350° oven 30 to 35 minutes. Makes 6 servings.

Memo to Meal Planner: Start dinner with chilled tomato juice or cups of tomato soup. Succotash or broccoli answers for the hot vegetable. The dessert may be small, but see that it is big in taste. One of the best ways to win praise from your family is to serve luscious desserts. This time it might be peanut butter brownies topped with vanilla or chocolate ice cream.

BEEF/CORN PIE

Seasoned beef makes the "pie crust," corn the filling.

2 eggs	⅛ tsp. pepper
¼ c. fine bread crumbs	1 (12 oz.) can Mexicorn,
¼ c. ketchup	drained
2 tblsp. finely chopped onion	2 tblsp. fine bread crumbs
1 lb. ground beef	½ c. shredded Cheddar cheese
1 tsp. chili powder	(2 oz.)
1 tsp. salt	

Beat 1 egg. Mix thoroughly with ¼ c. bread crumbs, ketchup, onion, ground beef, chili powder, salt and pepper. Pat mixture evenly over sides and bottom of 9″ pie pan.

Beat remaining egg; combine with Mexicorn and 2 tblsp. bread crumbs. Pour into center of beef-lined pie pan. Bake in 350° oven about 40 minutes, until corn filling is set. Sprinkle cheese over corn and return to oven about 5 minutes to melt cheese. Cut in wedges to serve. Makes 6 servings.

Memo to Meal Planner: Serve this beef and corn pie with a green vegetable, such as asparagus in spring, broccoli in other seasons. Include lettuce salad or a relish plate in the meal. Bake a dessert alongside the pie. It might be a delicious rhubarb, cherry or apple crisp.

DOWN-EAST GOULASH

Serve this hearty beef-bean dish on a cold winter night.

¼ c. chopped bacon or bacon ends and pieces	1 tblsp. Worcestershire sauce
½ c. chopped onion	2 (15 oz.) cans kidney beans, drained
1 lb. ground beef	1 tsp. salt
1 c. chopped celery	¼ tsp. pepper
½ c. ketchup	

In skillet partially cook bacon. Add onion and continue cooking until soft. Stir in ground beef, breaking it into about ½″ pieces; brown. Add remaining ingredients. Cover and cook over low heat 15 minutes. Stir well. Continue cooking, covered, 15 minutes. Makes 6 servings.

Memo to Meal Planner: You can dress up this main dish special at serving time by sprinkling on shredded cheese or sliced green onion. Serve with crusty bread or rolls, tossed salad and a hot vegetable like buttered corn. Pineapple sherbet makes a good dessert.

BEEF/SPAGHETTI BAKE

Excellent main dish to tote to the potluck supper.

1 lb. ground beef
1 c. chopped onion
1 c. chopped celery
½ c. chopped green pepper
　(optional)
1 clove garlic, minced
2 (8 oz.) cans tomato sauce
¼ tsp. dried thyme leaves,
　crushed

1½ tsp. salt
1 tsp. chili powder
⅛ tsp. pepper
1 (12 oz.) can whole kernel
　corn, drained
1 (7 oz.) pkg. elbow spaghetti,
　or 1″ pieces
1 c. shredded Colby cheese
　(4 oz.)

In large skillet cook beef, onion, celery, green pepper and garlic until meat is browned. Add tomato sauce, thyme, salt, chili powder and pepper. Cover and simmer 25 minutes. Stir in corn.

Meanwhile, cook spaghetti by package directions; drain. In 2½-qt. casserole layer half the spaghetti, half the meat sauce and half the cheese. Top with remaining spaghetti, then meat sauce. Bake in 350° oven 30 minutes. Remove from oven and sprinkle remaining cheese over top; bake 5 minutes longer. Makes 8 servings.

Memo to Meal Planner: For a family supper serve this main dish with a mixed green salad and brownies à la mode. Bread sticks also are a fine addition to the menu.

BEEF/ONION HASH

Southwesterners call this hearty rice casserole Texas hash.

3 large onions, sliced and
　separated into rings
3 tblsp. salad oil
1 lb. ground beef
1 c. chopped green pepper
1 c. uncooked rice
2 tsp. chili powder

2 tsp. salt
⅛ tsp. pepper
1 (1 lb. 12 oz.) can tomatoes,
　cut up
½ c. water
3 (1 oz.) rectangular slices
　process Swiss cheese

Cook onion rings in hot oil in large skillet until soft; remove from skillet. Brown beef in same skillet; drain off excess fat. Add onion rings, green pepper, rice, chili powder, salt, pepper, tomatoes and water. Heat thoroughly. Pour into a greased 2½-qt. casserole. Cover and bake in 350° oven about 1 hour, until rice and vegetables are tender. Stir once or twice during baking.

Cut cheese slices in diagonal halves. Place around edge of casserole petal fashion. Return to oven about 3 minutes, to melt cheese. Makes 6 servings.

Memo to Meal Planner: Serve this casserole with crusty rolls and green beans, French style. Have a tossed or other green salad and for dessert, peach pie.

BEEF/HOMINY SKILLET

Ideal quick, easy main dish for dinner on a busy day.

1 lb. ground beef	⅛ tsp. pepper
½ c. chopped onion	1 (10¾ oz.) can condensed
¼ c. chopped green pepper	cream of chicken soup
2 (14½ oz.) cans hominy	⅓ c. milk
1 tsp. salt	Shredded process cheese
¼ tsp. garlic salt	

Cook ground beef, onion and green pepper in skillet until beef is browned. Stir in remaining ingredients, except cheese. Cover and simmer 20 minutes, stirring several times. Sprinkle with cheese and serve. Makes 6 servings.

Memo to Meal Planner: You can omit the cheese garnish, but it boosts the protein and adds color contrast and flavor. If you use it, complete the menu with green beans, carrot-cabbage slaw, applesauce and peanut butter cookies. If you omit the cheese garnish, substitute fruit-cottage cheese salad for the slaw, have carrot sticks on the side and omit applesauce. You can use 2 (16 oz.) cans hominy, but larger cans throw recipe off balance.

ITALIAN BEEF CASSEROLE

It's like lasagne, with rice substituting for noodles.

1 c. uncooked rice
1 lb. ground beef
½ c. chopped onion
¼ c. chopped green pepper
1 clove garlic, minced
1 (1 lb.) can tomatoes, cut up
1 (8 oz.) can tomato sauce
2 tblsp. parsley flakes
1 tsp. salt
½ tsp. dried basil leaves,
  crushed

½ c. dried orégano leaves,
  crushed
¼ tsp. pepper
1½ c. creamed cottage cheese
  (12 oz.)
½ c. grated Parmesan cheese
  (2 oz.)
½ c. grated mozzarella cheese
  (2 oz.)

Cook rice by package directions.

Meanwhile, cook beef, onion, green pepper and garlic in skillet until beef is browned. Add tomatoes, tomato sauce, parsley, salt, basil, orégano and pepper. Simmer uncovered 10 minutes.

Pour half the meat sauce into 2½-qt. casserole. Top with rice, then cottage cheese and Parmesan cheese. Pour over remaining meat sauce. Bake in 350° oven 35 to 40 minutes. Sprinkle top with mozzarella cheese; return to oven about 3 minutes, until cheese melts. Makes 8 servings.

Memo to Meal Planner: Serve this company special with garlic bread, tossed green salad and a fruit dessert.

GREEN PEPPER CASSEROLE

Tastes like stuffed peppers but it is easier to make.

1 c. uncooked rice
2 tblsp. melted regular
  margarine
3 green peppers, cut in strips
3 chicken bouillon cubes
2 c. boiling water
1 lb. ground beef
1 c. chopped onion
1 c. chopped celery

1 clove garlic, minced
1 (15 oz.) can tomato sauce
1 tsp. dried orégano leaves,
  crushed
1 tsp. salt
¼ tsp. pepper
1½ c. shredded Cheddar cheese
  (6 oz.)

Cook rice in margarine in skillet until lightly toasted, stirring frequently. Spread in greased 13×9×2″ baking pan. Arrange green pepper on top.

Dissolve bouillon cubes in boiling water; pour over rice mixture. Cover with foil and bake in 375° oven 20 minutes.

Meanwhile, cook ground beef, onion, celery and garlic in same skillet until meat is browned. Stir in tomato sauce, orégano, salt and pepper. Cover and simmer 5 minutes. Pour over peppers and rice. Cover and continue baking 15 minutes. Remove cover, sprinkle with cheese and bake uncovered 5 minutes. Makes 6 servings.

Memo to Meal Planner: Serve with corn on the cob, raw vegetable relish marinated in Italian dressing and fresh pears.

MEAT-AND-POTATO DINNER

You can fix this main dish in 30 minutes. The flavor combination especially pleases meat and potato fans.

1 lb. ground beef	1 (8 oz.) can tomato sauce
2 tblsp. flour	Instant mashed potato flakes
½ tsp. salt	for 8 servings
½ tsp. garlic salt	2 c. cubed process cheese
⅛ tsp. pepper	spread (Velveeta, 8 oz.)
⅛ tsp. dried thyme leaves	⅓ c. milk

Thoroughly mix together ground beef, flour, salt, garlic salt, pepper and thyme. Add tomato sauce and mix well. Drop from tablespoon into 15½ ×10½ ×1″ pan to make 12 mounds. Bake in 425° oven 20 minutes.

Meanwhile, prepare mashed potatoes as directed on package.

In small saucepan heat together cheese and milk, stirring constantly until cheese is melted.

Make a nest of potatoes on each individual dinner plate; place 2 beef mounds in each. Top with cheese sauce. Makes 6 servings.

Memo to Meal Planner: Serve quick-to-fix dinner with a hot green vegetable and relishes. For dessert have vanilla ice cream with maple syrup on top.

BEEF/SAUERKRAUT SKILLET

This is a fine way to include sauerkraut in a dinner menu, a different appetizing way to fix ground beef.

1 lb. ground beef	1 c. uncooked rice
1 c. chopped onion	1 (1 lb.) can sauerkraut
1½ tsp. salt	2 (8 oz.) cans tomato sauce
¼ tsp. pepper	¼ c. water

Cook ground beef and onion in skillet until beef is browned. Stir in remaining ingredients. Cover and simmer about 35 minutes, or until rice is tender. Makes 6 servings.

Memo to Meal Planner: Complete dinner with cooked carrots, apple-celery salad and hot cheese biscuits. If you have a flower pot of chives in your window-sill garden, chop a little of them and heat in margarine, toss with the hot carrots. Or use dried chives.

To make cheese biscuits, use your standard recipe calling for 2 c. sifted flour. Stir ½ c. shredded cheese of your choice into the milk and add to the dry ingredients blended with the shortening. Skip the dessert or, if you want to end the meal with a touch of sweetness, try small servings of a make-ahead, chilled pudding, like butterscotch.

TAMALE PIE

Cornmeal and cheese extend beef in this casserole.

1 lb. ground beef	1 tsp. salt
1 c. chopped onion	Dash of pepper
½ c. chopped green pepper	1½ c. shredded process
1 (15 oz.) can tomato sauce	American cheese (6 oz.)
1 (12 oz.) can whole kernel	¾ c. yellow cornmeal
corn, drained	½ tsp. salt
1 clove garlic, minced	2 c. cold water
1 tblsp. chili powder	1 tblsp. regular margarine

Cook beef, onion and green pepper in large skillet until meat is browned. Add tomato sauce, corn, garlic, chili powder, 1 tsp. salt and pepper; stir to mix thoroughly. Cover and simmer 20 to 25 minutes. Add cheese and stir until melted.

Meanwhile, stir cornmeal and ½ tsp. salt into cold water. Cook, stirring, until thick. Stir in margarine.

Pour meat mixture into greased 2-qt. casserole. Spoon cornmeal mixture over top. Bake in 375° oven 40 minutes. Makes 6 servings.

Memo to Meal Planner: The perfect companions to this main dish are a big tossed salad and lemon meringue pie.

HAMBURGER/VEGETABLE STEW

Fluffy mashed potatoes atop give stew eye appeal. Kidney beans stretch the beef by adding protein. Both help cut food bills.

1 lb. ground beef	1½ tsp. salt
2 medium onions, sliced	½ tsp. chili powder
1 c. sliced peeled carrots	¼ tsp. pepper
1 c. shredded cabbage	1 (15 oz.) can kidney beans,
½ c. diced celery	drained
1 (1 lb.) can tomatoes, cut up	Instant mashed potato flakes
1½ c. water	for 8 servings

In 12″ skillet cook beef until browned; drain off excess fat. Add onions, carrots, cabbage, celery, tomatoes, water, salt, chili powder and pepper. Cover and simmer 15 minutes.

Add beans. Cover and simmer 15 to 20 minutes longer.

Meanwhile, prepare mashed potatoes as directed on package. Serve stew in bowls; top with potatoes. Makes 6 servings.

Memo to Meal Planner: Biscuits hot from the oven are a great escort for this stew. They will answer for dessert too, if there's strawberry jam on the table. Be on the safe side and bake plenty of biscuits.

MEXICALI CASSEROLE

This main dish has Mexican overtones with a hint of chili powder, but not highly seasoned. Ripe olives are a California touch (available in small cans, 4½ oz.). The ready-to-use chopped olives are economical of time and money.

4 oz. fine noodles
1 lb. ground beef
1 medium onion, chopped
1 (1 lb.) can tomatoes, cut up
1 tsp. garlic salt
1 (8 oz.) can whole kernel
    corn

¼ c. chopped ripe olives
½ tsp. chili powder
½ c. grated Cheddar cheese
    (2 oz.)
½ c. crushed corn chips

Cook noodles by package directions; drain.

Cook meat and onion in large skillet until meat is lightly browned; drain off excess fat. Add tomatoes and garlic salt; simmer 10 minutes. Combine noodles, meat mixture, corn, olives, chili powder and cheese. Pour into greased 2-qt. casserole. Sprinkle with corn chips. Bake in 350° oven 1 hour. Makes 6 servings.

BUTTERMILK STROGANOFF

Tasty buttermilk costs less than half as much as sour cream commonly used in stroganoff and has fewer calories. The cheese, like all process cheese, shreds easiest if first chilled.

1 lb. ground beef
1 c. chopped onion
6 oz. noodles
1¾ c. buttermilk
¼ c. flour
¾ tsp. salt
⅛ tsp. pepper

¼ c. ketchup
2 tsp. Worcestershire sauce
1 (4 oz.) can chopped
    mushrooms
1 c. shredded process cheese
    spread (Velveeta, 4 oz.)

Cook ground beef and onion in skillet until beef is browned.

Meanwhile, cook noodles as package directs; drain.

Blend part of buttermilk into flour to make a smooth paste, then stir in remaining buttermilk. Add salt, pepper, ketchup, Worcestershire sauce and mushrooms.

Combine beef mixture, noodles and sauce. Spoon into 2-qt. casserole. Bake in 350° oven 30 minutes. Remove from oven and sprinkle with cheese. Return to oven about 3 minutes, long enough to melt cheese. Makes 6 servings.

Memo to Meal Planner: Complete menu with broccoli, fruit salad and brownies or chocolate cake or cupcakes.

BEEF/NOODLE CASSEROLE

This main dish tastes like pizza but you bake it in a casserole. It's easy to fix and serve, and totes well to potluck suppers.

1 lb. ground beef	1 tsp. garlic salt
1 c. chopped onion	1 tsp. salt
1 (1 lb.) can tomatoes, cut up	⅛ tsp. pepper
1 (10¾ oz.) can condensed	12 oz. noodles
tomato soup	1 c. shredded mozzarella
1 tsp. dried orégano leaves,	cheese (4 oz.)
crushed	

In skillet cook beef and onion until beef is browned. Add tomatoes, tomato soup, orégano, garlic salt, salt and pepper. Simmer 10 minutes.

Meanwhile, cook noodles by package directions; drain. Combine with beef mixture; spoon into a greased 2½-qt. casserole. Bake in 350° oven 30 minutes. Remove from oven, and sprinkle cheese over top. Return to oven about 3 minutes, just until cheese is melted. Makes 8 servings.

Memo to Meal Planner: When the Illinois country woman who shares this recipe fixes it for home meals she likes to serve quick-cooked cabbage and a molded fruit salad with it. If you want to have a dessert, try chocolate tapicoa pudding.

BEEF LASAGNE

Make 2 pans of this main dish if company is coming.

1 (8 oz.) pkg. lasagne noodles
¾ lb. ground beef
2 cloves garlic, minced
½ c. chopped onion
1½ tsp. salt
⅛ tsp. pepper
1 tsp. dried orégano leaves,
  crushed
1 tblsp. parsley flakes

1 (8 oz.) can tomato sauce
1 (6 oz.) can tomato paste
¾ c. water
1 egg, beaten
1 (12 oz.) carton creamed
  cottage cheese
1 c. shredded mozzarella.
  cheese (4 oz.)

Cook noodles as package directs. Add cold water until noodles can be handled. Lift out; do not drain them.

Meanwhile, lightly brown beef in large skillet. Add garlic, onion, salt, pepper, orégano, parsley, tomato sauce, tomato paste and ¾ c. water. Simmer 5 minutes.

Mix together egg and cottage cheese.

In greased 9″ square pan spread layers of one fourth meat sauce, half the noodles, one fourth meat sauce, half the cottage cheese mixture and half the mozzarella. Add another fourth meat sauce, remaining cottage cheese and mozzarella, remaining noodles and remaining meat sauce. Bake in 350° oven 30 minutes. Remove from oven and let stand 10 minutes before cutting. Makes 6 servings.

BEEF/MACARONI HOSTESS SPECIAL

More work to fix than some main dishes, but worth it.

1 (8 oz.) pkg. elbow macaroni
1 lb. ground beef
1 c. chopped onion
1 (15 oz.) can tomato sauce
1½ tsp. salt
¼ tsp. pepper

⅓ c. fine dry bread crumbs
1 egg
Velvety Sauce
1 c. grated Parmesan cheese
  (4 oz.)

Cook macaroni by package directions; drain. Cool to lukewarm.

Meanwhile, cook beef and onion in skillet to brown meat. Add tomato sauce, salt and pepper; cover and simmer 30 minutes. Stir in bread crumbs.

Beat egg in large bowl, add macaroni and toss together.

In greased 13×9×2" pan layer half the macaroni, meat mixture, Velvety Sauce and cheese. Repeat.

Bake in 375° oven 30 minutes (40 minutes if you make ahead and chill), or until lightly browned. Remove from oven and let stand 10 minutes, then cut into squares. Makes 8 servings.

Velvety Sauce: Melt ⅓ c. regular margarine in large saucepan. Blend in ⅓ c. flour, 1 tsp. salt and ¼ tsp. pepper. Add 2½ c. reconstituted nonfat dry milk and cook, stirring, until mixture boils; remove from heat. Beat 2 eggs and ½ c. reconstituted nonfat dry milk; add to sauce. Cook, stirring, until sauce thickens slightly.

STUFFED MANICOTTI

Beef-stuffed macaroni shells make fine company fare.

1 (8 oz.) pkg. manicotti	¾ c. milk
(about 14)	1½ tsp. salt
1½ lbs. ground beef	¼ tsp. pepper
1 egg, beaten	Tangy Tomato Sauce
½ lb. mozzarella cheese, diced	Parmesan cheese
3 slices bread, cubed	

Cook manicotti by package directions. Do not drain. Run cold water over it until water in pan is cold; leave manicotti in water until needed.

Meanwhile, combine ground beef, egg, cheese, bread, milk, salt and pepper. Divide mixture in half; form each half in 7 equal parts. Stuff 1 part into each manicotti shell. Place in greased 13×9×2" baking pan. Pour Tangy Tomato Sauce over top, cover with foil and bake in 350° oven 50 minutes (1 hour if made ahead and chilled). Pass grated Parmesan cheese when serving. Makes 7 servings.

Tangy Tomato Sauce: Combine 2 (15 oz.) cans tomato sauce, 1½ tblsp. parsley flakes, 1½ tblsp. instant minced onion, 1 tsp. dried orégano leaves, crumbled, ½ tsp. dried basil leaves, crumbled, ¼ tsp. salt and 2 cloves garlic, minced. Simmer 15 minutes.

Memo to Meal Planner: Serve with tossed salad and peas.

BEEF FLORENTINE CASSEROLE

Always a success at buffets and so easy to make.

1½ lbs. ground beef	½ tsp. salt
1 medium onion, chopped	¼ tsp. ground red pepper
1 clove garlic, minced	1 (7 oz.) pkg. shell macaroni,
1 (10 oz.) pkg. frozen chopped	cooked
spinach	1 c. shredded sharp Cheddar
Water	cheese (4 oz.)
1 (1 lb.) can spaghetti sauce	½ c. soft bread crumbs
1 (6 oz.) can tomato paste	2 eggs, well beaten
1 (8 oz.) can tomato sauce	2 tblsp. salad oil

Cook ground beef, onion and garlic in large skillet until meat is lightly browned; drain off excess fat.

Cook spinach by package directions; drain, saving liquid. Add water to spinach liquid to make 1 c. Combine spinach liquid, spaghetti sauce, tomato paste, tomato sauce, salt and red pepper; stir into meat mixture. Simmer 10 minutes.

Combine spinach with macaroni, cheese, crumbs, eggs and oil. Spread in 13×9×2″ baking pan. Top with meat mixture. Bake in 350° oven 30 minutes. Let stand 10 minutes before serving. Makes about 10 servings.

Memo to Meal Planner: Serve this delightful dish of Italian inspiration with hard rolls, tossed salad, chocolate cake and lemon sherbet.

ITALIAN SPAGHETTI

Ideal for supper when boys gather around the table.

1 lb. ground beef	1 tsp. dried orégano leaves,
1 c. chopped onion	crushed
½ c. chopped green pepper	½ tsp. dried basil leaves,
(optional)	crushed
1 clove garlic, minced	⅛ tsp. pepper
1 (1 lb.) can tomatoes, cut up	1 bay leaf
1 (15 oz.) can tomato sauce	1 (1 lb.) pkg. spaghetti
1 tblsp. sugar	Grated Parmesan cheese
1½ tsp. salt	

In Dutch oven cook ground beef, onion, green pepper and garlic until meat is browned. Drain off excess fat. Add tomatoes, tomato sauce, sugar, salt, orégano, basil, pepper and bay leaf; cover and simmer 30 minutes. Uncover and continue cooking 15 to 20 minutes more, or until sauce is slightly thickened. Remove bay leaf.

Cook spaghetti by package directions, drain and place on warm platter. Pour hot sauce over and sprinkle with Parmesan cheese, or pass cheese at the table. Makes 6 servings.

Memo to Meal Planner: Many women like to double the recipe for the sauce. They cool and freeze half of it to use later.

SPAGHETTI SUPPER

Heap on platter for a wonderful springtime supper.

½ lb. ground beef
3 green onions, sliced
1 clove garlic, minced
1 (1 lb. 12 oz.) can tomatoes
    cut up
1¼ tsp. salt

½ tsp. celery seeds
¼ tsp. pepper
¼ tsp. Worcestershire sauce
1 (8 oz.) pkg. thin spaghetti
1 c. shredded sharp Cheddar
    cheese (4 oz.)

In 2-qt. saucepan cook and stir beef, onions and garlic until meat is lightly browned; add tomatoes, salt, celery seeds, pepper and Worcestershire sauce. Cover and simmer 1 hour.

Meanwhile, cook spaghetti by package directions; drain. Add to tomato mixture. Simmer uncovered about 30 minutes, stirring occasionally. Just before serving stir in cheese. Makes 6 servings.

Memo to Meal Planner: If you like a pronounced garlic taste, use 2 instead of 1 garlic clove. With this main dish serve garden lettuce or sliced radish salad. Bake your favorite chocolate sheet cake for dessert. Cut unfrosted cake in squares and serve topped with scoops of chocolate or vanilla ice cream.

SMOTHERED BURGERS

Use this recipe to make ground beef go further.

1 egg	1 lb. ground beef
⅓ c. water	2 tblsp. salad oil
3 slices bread, cubed	1 (10¾ oz.) can condensed
¼ c. finely chopped onion	cream of mushroom soup
1 tsp. salt	2 tblsp. water
¼ tsp. pepper	3 hamburger buns
1 tsp. Worcestershire sauce	

Beat egg. Thoroughly mix in ⅓ c. water, bread cubes, onion, salt, pepper, Worcestershire sauce and ground beef. Form into 6 patties. Brown on both sides in large skillet in hot oil. Remove meat. Drain off excess fat.

Combine soup and 2 tblsp. water in same skillet. Heat, stirring and scraping brown particles from bottom of skillet. Return patties to skillet; spoon some of the sauce over them. Cover and simmer 20 minutes. Serve on hamburger buns, split and toasted. Makes 6 open-face sandwiches.

OPEN-FACE BURGERS

You will find that these main dish knife-and-fork sandwiches appeal alike to youngsters and adults. The beans stretch the beef, complement its flavor and increase protein content of the sandwich filling.

1 tblsp. instant minced onion	¼ tsp. pepper
½ c. milk	1 (15½ oz.) can
1½ lbs. ground beef	chili-flavored beans
1 egg, slightly beaten	¼ c. ketchup
½ c. quick-cooking rolled oats	8 slices French bread
1½ tsp. salt	

Soak onion in milk several minutes. Combine with ground beef, egg, rolled oats, salt and pepper. Spread evenly in 10″ skillet.

Combine beans and ketchup. Pour over meat mixture in even layer. Simmer uncovered 20 to 25 minutes. Cut in 8 wedges.

Cut French bread in diagonal slices. Top with wedges of the meat mixture. Makes 8 sandwiches.

Memo to Meal Planner: Serve the sandwiches for supper or lunch with hot tomato soup, carrot salad and butterscotch cookies. Shred carrots, combine them with crushed pineapple and flavor with a little salad dressing. Serve on lettuce leaves.

BEEF-STUFFED BUNS

One pound ground beef makes 12 new-style hamburgers. Cheese and eggs step up protein in sandwiches.

12 hamburger buns	½ c. ketchup
1 lb. ground beef	2 hard-cooked eggs, chopped
1 c. diced process American	¼ c. salad dressing
cheese (4 oz.)	2 tblsp. prepared mustard
½ c. chopped sweet pickle	1 tsp. salt
2 tblsp. minced onion	⅛ tsp. pepper

Slice tops off buns; scoop out soft centers. Reserve 1 c. crumbs. Set aside bun tops and shells.

Brown ground beef; drain off excess fat. Combine with reserved crumbs and remaining ingredients. Pile filling into bun shells. Cover with tops.

Place in 13×9×2" pan, stacking as necessary. Cover with foil. Heat in 350° oven 20 minutes, or until cheese is melted. Serve hot. Makes 12 sandwiches.

Memo to Meal Planner: You can use ground cooked beef if you have it. Refrigerate leftover crumbs to use later. You can stuff buns several hours ahead and chill in covered pan. Heat them 10 minutes longer than when unchilled. Good with tomato soup, potato chips, carrot sticks, canned pears and peanut butter cookies.

BEANBURGERS

Spring a surprise with these kidney bean-beef sandwiches.

2 tblsp. chopped onion	1½ tsp. salt
1 clove garlic	1 tsp. chili powder
1 tblsp. salad oil	2 tblsp. ketchup
1 (15 oz.) can kidney beans,	½ tsp. Worcestershire sauce
drained and rinsed	6 slices process American
¾ lb. ground beef	cheese
1 egg, beaten	6 hamburger buns, split

Cook onion and garlic in salad oil until soft; remove garlic. Combine onion, beans, beef, egg, salt, chili powder, ketchup and Worcestershire sauce and mix well. Divide mixture into 6 patties and place in 13×9×2″ baking pan. Bake in 350° oven 30 minutes.

Place a patty and a cheese slice between each split bun. Place on baking sheet; return to oven 3 to 5 minutes, until cheese melts. Makes 6 sandwiches.

Memo to Meal Planner: Serve these favorites of youngsters as the main dish for supper or dinner, and have buttered carrots or a raisin/carrot salad. Canned fruit and cookies answer deliciously for dessert.

Nutritious Liver

Beef liver is an economical and health promoting meat. One way to win favor with it is to make new, interesting dishes instead of pan-frying it every time. Best-ever Liver Loaf provides remarkably good eating at low cost. If your family "dislikes" liver, disguise it—that is exactly what Polynesian Liver does—successfully.

BEST-EVER LIVER LOAF

Liver in biscuit coat with tomato sauce on top. Chopped bacon ends and pieces cooked crisp make a tasty garnish.

1 lb. beef liver	2 c. sifted flour
1½ c. water	3 tsp. baking powder
1 small onion	½ tsp. salt
½ tsp. salt	¼ c. shortening
½ tsp. seasoning salt	¾ c. milk
⅛ tsp. pepper	Hasty Tomato Sauce
¼ c. ketchup	

Combine liver and water in saucepan; cover and simmer 15 minutes. Put through food chopper with onion. Add ½ tsp. salt, seasoning salt, pepper and ketchup.

Sift together flour, baking powder and ½ tsp. salt. Cut in shortening to make coarse crumbs. Mix in milk just to moisten all particles. Knead 20 light strokes on floured surface, then roll into 12×10″ rectangle. Shape liver mixture in loaf down center of 12″ length, leaving ½″ dough uncovered at each end. Roll dough around liver;

seal edges. Bake in 425° oven 20 to 25 minutes. Serve hot, sliced and drizzled with Hasty Tomato Sauce. Makes 6 servings.

Hasty Tomato Sauce: Blend and heat 1 (10¾ oz.) can condensed tomato soup, ¼ tsp. dried basil leaves, crumbled, and 2 tblsp. water.

POLYNESIAN LIVER

Liver is so disguised in this dish that even people who don't ordinarily like it are converts. It's a thrifty food with lots of good nutrition.

1 (8 oz.) can pineapple chunks	3 tblsp. cornstarch
2 c. tomato juice	¼ c. water
2 tblsp. vinegar	1 green pepper, cut in strips
1 tblsp. soy sauce	1 onion, sliced and separated
2 tblsp. brown sugar	into rings
1 tsp. instant beef bouillon, or	Hot cooked rice
1 beef bouillon cube	
1½ lbs. beef or pork liver, cut	
in 1″ strips	

Drain pineapple, reserving juice. Add water to juice to make ½ cup; combine with tomato juice, vinegar, soy sauce, brown sugar and bouillon in skillet. Bring to a boil. Add liver; reduce heat, cover and simmer 15 minutes.

Blend together cornstarch and water. Add to liver mixture and cook, stirring, until thickened. Stir in green pepper, onion and pineapple. Cover and simmer about 7 minutes, until vegetables are tender-crisp. Serve over hot cooked rice. Makes 8 servings.

Memo to Meal Planner: If you wish to serve a vegetable with this oriental-type dish on rice, it might be broccoli or a cabbage salad. For dessert, have Peanut Cookie Balls or Lemon Crisp Supreme (see Index for recipes) and tea. A good menu for entertaining!

Fresh, Smoked and Ground Pork

Pork steaks cost less than pork chops and they taste exceptionally good in many thrifty, substantial dishes. But there are times when you want to serve pork chops. In the recipe for Pork Chops with Dressing, seasoned bread stuffing bakes on the chops—a truly delicious main dish. You will notice the chops are ½″ thick rather than ¾″ or double chops, and that one of them makes a serving. The other recipes featuring this favorite pork cut extend the meat successfully.

Baked Pork Steaks with Stuffing also taste wonderful. And for a dish with a great country flavor, try Pork/Cabbage Casserole. It, too, is economical.

Smoked pork shoulder roll (butt) is more economical than ham. You can save money by using it in any of the recipes in this cookbook that call for cubed cooked ham, but if you are lucky enough to have leftover ham, you will be money ahead to salvage it. Buying cooked ham to make the dishes is a different story.

Ham/Sweet Potato Bake is a sepcial treat; cider or apple juice—whichever you have—enhances the flavor. Baked Ham/Cheese Sandwiches are one of the best hot sandwiches ever invented.

Fresh pork, ground and seasoned with sage, enjoys fame as "country sausage." This chapter contains several thrifty recipes for main dishes using it. They fit beautifully into lunch, supper and dinner menus.

Country women take pains to handle pork sausage to prevent dishes including it from becoming "greasy." They drain off excess fat after precooking the meat and before combining it with other ingredients. In two of our recipes, Sausage with Split Peas and Sausage/Potato Bake, the directions go a step further and suggest that you drain the meat thoroughly on paper toweling.

Pork sausage has more fat per pound than most meats—and less protein. That is why in the recipes that follow we supplement the excellent sausage protein with such foods as eggs, cheese and split peas. In the menus including sausage main dishes, we suggest the enrichment of the protein with other dishes such as baked beans and tossed salad with cottage cheese dressing.

PORK CHOPS WITH DRESSING

Pork chops baked this way are company fare. They're delicious.

6 pork chops, ½″ thick	6 c. soft bread cubes
2 tblsp. butter or regular margarine	¼ c. water
	¼ tsp. poultry seasoning
½ tsp. salt	¼ tsp. salt
Dash of pepper	⅛ tsp. pepper
¼ c. chopped onion	1 (10¾ oz.) can condensed
¼ c. chopped celery	cream of mushroom soup
¼ c. butter or regular margarine	⅓ c. water

Brown pork chops on both sides in 2 tblsp. melted butter in large skillet. Arrange in 13×9×2″ baking pan. Sprinkle with ½ tsp. salt and dash of pepper.

In same skillet cook onion and celery in ¼ c. butter until soft. Combine with bread cubes, ¼ c. water, poultry seasoning, ¼ tsp. salt and ⅛ tsp. pepper. Press mixture in mounds on top of chops.

Combine soup with ⅓ c. water; heat in skillet, scraping to remove browned bits from bottom. Pour over chops and dressing, cover with foil and bake in 350° oven 30 minutes. Remove foil and bake uncovered 30 minutes longer. Makes 6 servings.

Memo to Meal Planner: Serve pork chops with succotash, green salad or coleslaw and have cherry or apple pie for dessert.

PORK DINNER BAKE

Meat and vegetables bake together without attention.

1 (20 oz.) pkg. loose-pack frozen green beans	¼ tsp. pepper
	6 pork chops, ½″ thick
4 c. sliced peeled potatoes	2 tblsp. salad oil
1 (10¾ oz.) can condensed cream of mushroom soup	Salt
	Pepper
1 (10¾ oz.) can cream of celery soup	1 (3 oz.) can French fried onions
½ tsp. salt	

Spread beans in greased 13×9×2″ pan to partially thaw.

Cook potatoes in boiling water 5 minutes; drain.

Combine mushroom and celery soup, ½ tsp. salt and ¼ tsp. pepper. Spread half of soup mixture over beans. Top with potatoes, then rest of soup.

Meanwhile, brown pork chops in hot oil in skillet. Arrange on top of potatoes. Sprinkle lightly with salt and pepper. Cover with foil. Bake in 350° oven about 45 minutes, until potatoes are tender. Remove foil cover. Sprinkle onions over top. Return pan to oven about 5 minutes, just to heat onions. Makes 6 servings.

Memo to Meal Planner: You can omit onions but they add a special touch. Serve with relish tray; have canned peaches and sugar cookies for dessert.

PORK/RICE BAKE

This main dish is pretty and delicious enough for a company dinner —it has great flavor combination.

1 c. uncooked rice	Salt
2 tblsp. parsley flakes	Pepper
1 tsp. salt	6 onion slices, ½" thick
6 lean pork chops, ½" thick	18 unpeeled apple wedges
2 tblsp. salad oil	(1½ apples)
2 c. chicken broth	

Spread rice in bottom of 13×9×2" baking pan. Sprinkle parsley and 1 tsp. salt over top.

Brown pork chops in hot oil in skillet. Remove chops. Pour chicken broth into skillet. Bring to a boil, stirring to loosen brown particles from skillet. Pour over rice. Arrange pork chops on top; sprinkle lightly with salt and pepper. Top each chop with an onion slice, then with 3 apple wedges. (Cut apples in 6 crosswise slices and divide each slice in thirds.) Cover with foil and bake in 350° oven 1 hour. Makes 6 servings.

Memo to Meal Planner: If you do not have chicken broth, you can use 1 (13¾ oz.) can chicken broth plus ¾ c. water. Serve with broccoli or Harvard beets, a relish tray and gingerbread, baked alongside main dish. Top gingerbread with whipped dessert topping.

PORK CHOP/BEAN DINNER

Fast-to-fix, good-to-eat country skillet special.

6 pork chops, ½" thick	½ tsp. salt
2 tblsp. salad oil	1 tblsp. vinegar
½ c. chopped onion	1 (15 oz.) can kidney beans,
½ c. chopped green pepper	drained
1 (15 oz.) can tomato sauce	1 (1 lb.) can lima beans, drained
2 tblsp. brown sugar	

Brown pork chops in hot oil in skillet; remove. Cook onion and green pepper in drippings until soft. Add tomato sauce, brown sugar, salt and vinegar; cover and simmer 30 minutes. Return pork chops to skillet and add kidney and lima beans. Cover and continue cooking 20 minutes. Makes 6 servings.

Memo to Meal Planner: Cooked carrots and a tray of celery sticks and other relishes complete the main course. You may wish to bake a quick bread to rush hot from the oven to the table. Corn bread and corn sticks complement the main dish. If you want to serve a simple dessert that looks fancy, chilled canned peach halves, each holding a raspberry or lime sherbet ball, will fill the bill.

BAKED PORK STEAKS WITH STUFFING

This wonderful main dish is a good example of carefree cooking. Once the pork steaks are in the oven, they bake without attention.

4 c. bread cubes	¼ tsp. salt
½ c. chopped celery	⅛ tsp. pepper
½ c. chopped onion	1 beef bouillon cube
¼ c. melted butter or regular margarine	½ c. boiling water
2 c. chopped unpeeled apples	6 pork steaks, ½" thick
½ c. seedless raisins (optional)	2 tblsp. salad oil
½ tsp. poultry seasoning	½ tsp. salt
½ tsp. rubbed sage	Dash of pepper

Toast bread cubes in 300° oven 45 minutes.

Cook celery and onion in butter until soft, but not brown. Combine bread cubes, celery and onion mixture, apples, raisins, poultry seasoning, sage, ¼ tsp. salt and ⅛ tsp. pepper.

Dissolve bouillon cube in boiling water. Add to stuffing and toss.

Trim and discard excess fat from pork steaks. Brown steaks on both sides in hot oil. Place steaks in a 13×9×2" baking pan, overlapping slightly if necessary. Sprinkle with ½ tsp. salt and dash of pepper. Cover each steak with a layer of the bread stuffing. Cover pan tightly with foil. Bake in 350° oven 1 hour. Makes 6 servings.

Memo to Meal Planner: Bake sweet potatoes alongside the pork. A molded vegetable salad and a chilled dessert complete the meal in an admirable fashion. Consider Molded Tomato Salad and Frosty Lemon Squares (see Index for recipes) for this menu. Both the salad and dessert are exceptionally good—attractive, too.

PORK/CABBAGE CASSEROLE

Colorful, delicious favorite of a Nebraska family.

1½ lbs. pork shoulder steaks, cut in 1×½" strips	2 tsp. salt
2 tblsp. salad oil	½ tsp. chili powder
1 c. chopped onion	¼ tsp. pepper
1 c. uncooked rice	4 c. tomato juice
8 c. shredded cabbage	2 c. shredded process American cheese

Brown pork in hot oil in skillet. Remove from skillet. Add onion and rice to drippings. Cook and stir until rice is lightly browned.

Spread half the cabbage in 13×9×2" pan. Top with onion-rice mixture, pork strips, then remaining cabbage. Sprinkle with salt, chili powder and pepper. Pour tomato juice over; cover with foil. Bake in 350° oven about 1 hour and 15 minutes, until rice is tender.

Remove from oven and sprinkle cheese over top. Return to oven 3 to 5 minutes to melt cheese. Makes 8 servings.

Memo to Meal Planner: Serve with peas, carrot-raisin salad and rye bread. Bake peach upside-down cake in oven with casserole. Serve it faintly warm for dessert.

PORK/POTATO PIE

Meat, potatoes and gravy unite in this dinner pie.

1½ lbs. pork steak, cut in 1×½" strips	1 (10¾ oz.) can condensed cream of chicken soup
1 tblsp. salad oil	2 tsp. salt
2 c. thinly sliced peeled carrots	¼ tsp. pepper
1 c. sliced celery	Potato Topping
⅔ c. chopped onion	¼ c. shredded process American cheese (1 oz.)
⅔ c. boiling water	

Brown pork in hot oil in skillet; drain. Place pork in greased 2½-qt. casserole.

Meanwhile, cook carrots, celery and onion in boiling water 5 minutes; drain, reserving liquid. Add vegetables to pork.

Remove skillet from range, spoon soup into it; blend in reserved liquid, a little at a time. Heat and stir to loosen brown particles. Stir into casserole; sprinkle with salt and pepper. Cover and bake in 350° oven 1 hour.

Meanwhile, prepare Potato Topping. Drop by big spoonfuls over hot mixture in casserole. Sprinkle cheese over potatoes. Return casserole to oven and bake uncovered 15 minutes. Serves 8.

Potato Topping: Prepare instant mashed potato flakes for 8 servings by package directions, but set aside the milk. Stir ¾ c. shredded process American cheese into the potatoes. Add enough of the milk so that potatoes hold their shape when dropped from a spoon.

SWEET-SOUR PORK

Tasty, budget adaptation of a great Oriental special.

1½ lbs. lean smoked pork shoulder roll (butt), cut in 2×½″ strips

2 tblsp. salad oil

1 (13¼ oz.) can pineapple chunks

⅓ c. vinegar

2 tblsp. soy sauce

¼ c. brown sugar, firmly packed

1 carrot, peeled and cut in ¼″ bias slices

1 (1 lb.) can bean sprouts, drained

1 onion, sliced and separated into rings

1 green pepper, cut in thin strips

3 tblsp. cornstarch

¼ c. water

1½ c. uncooked rice

Brown pork in hot oil in skillet; drain off excess fat.

Meanwhile, drain pineapple, reserving syrup. Add enough water to pineapple syrup to make 1¼ c. Add to pork in skillet along with vinegar, soy sauce and brown sugar. Cover and simmer 1 hour. Add carrot; cook 2 minutes. Add pineapple chunks, bean sprouts, onion and green pepper. Cover and cook 8 to 10 minutes, until vegetables are tender-crisp.

Blend together cornstarch and water; add to skillet and cook, stirring, until mixture is thickened and bubbly.

Meanwhile, cook rice by package directions. Serve pork mixture over hot rice. Makes 6 servings.

Memo to Meal Planner: Serve with buttered green beans. Lemon-coconut cake or cookies are fine for dessert.

SMOKED PORK WITH SAUERKRAUT

Flavorful meal in a dish that's easy to get and eat.

2 (1 lb.) cans sauerkraut	6 medium potatoes, peeled
2 c. apple juice	2 onions, quartered
½ tsp. caraway seeds	6 carrots, peeled and halved
1½ to 2 lbs. smoked pork	lengthwise, then crosswise
shoulder roll (butt)	

Combine sauerkraut, apple juice and caraway seeds in Dutch oven. Bring to a boil. Add smoked pork shoulder; cover, reduce heat and simmer 1 hour.

Add potatoes, onions and carrots. Cover and simmer about 45 minutes, until vegetables are tender. Makes 6 servings.

Memo to Meal Planner: Serve with fresh rye bread and fruit salad. You may want to introduce your family to one of Grandmother's favorite salads, an old-fashioned children's special. To make it, cut bananas in chunks, roll in finely chopped salted peanuts and serve on lettuce with salad dressing alongside. For dessert consider warm gingerbread with whatever topping you prefer. Whipped dessert topping, warm applesauce and lemon sauce are good on squares of the spicy gingerbread and so is a frosting made with confectioners sugar, flavored with a bit of grated lemon peel.

MIDWESTERN BAKED BEANS

Put the surplus in the freezer to use on busy days.

2 lbs. dry pea beans	2 (1 lb.) cans tomatoes, cut up
3 tblsp. brown sugar	1 medium onion, sliced
2 tsp. dry mustard	1½ to 2 lbs. smoked pork
2 tsp. salt	shoulder roll (butt), cut in
⅓ c. molasses	cubes

Wash beans. Cover beans with cold water in kettle. Bring to a boil; cook 2 minutes. Remove from heat and let stand 1 hour. Add enough cold water to cover beans; cover kettle, bring to a boil, reduce heat. Cover and simmer until skins burst 1 to 1½ hours.

Meanwhile, blend together brown sugar, dry mustard and salt. Stir in molasses, tomatoes and onion. Add to beans. Turn into 5½-qt.

Dutch oven or bean pot. If liquid does not cover beans, add hot water. Cover and bake in 300° oven 3 hours.

Stir in smoked pork. Continue baking until beans are tender, 3 to 5 hours, adding more hot water as needed to keep beans covered. Remove cover the last 30 minutes of baking. Makes about 5 quarts.

Memo to Meal Planner: Serve with hot rolls, coleslaw, mixed pickles and an apple dessert. It might be raisin-stuffed baked apples.

PIONEER LIMA BEAN/PORK SPECIAL

No one will be hungry after eating this nutritious main dish.

1 lb. small dry lima beans	⅓ c. brown sugar, firmly
6 c. water	packed
⅓ c. chopped bacon ends and	1 tblsp. salt
pieces	⅛ tsp. pepper
3 lbs. pork neck bones	1½ c. chopped onion
2 c. water	

Wash and sort lima beans. Combine in large saucepan with 6 c. water. Bring to a boil; boil 2 minutes. Remove from heat; cover and let soak 1 hour. (Or soak beans overnight.)

Meanwhile, cook bacon pieces in Dutch oven until crisp; remove to large bowl with slotted spoon. Cook pork neck bones in hot bacon drippings, a few pieces at a time, until brown on all sides. Place in bowl with bacon.

Stir 2 c. water, brown sugar, salt and pepper into drippings in Dutch oven; stir until browned bits are loosened and mixture is blended. Return meat to pan. Cover and simmer 1 hour.

Drain beans. Add beans and onion to mixture in Dutch oven; simmer 1½ hours, until beans and meat are tender. Makes 3 quarts.

Memo to Meal Planner: With this thrifty dish include hot corn bread or muffins and make-ahead Country Vegetable Salad (see Index). You will have a money-saving meal that wins praises.

HAM/SWEET POTATO BAKE

Cider points up the best ham-sweet potato flavors.

5 c. mashed cooked sweet
   potatoes (about 3½ lbs.)
½ c. milk
¼ c. regular margarine
1 tsp. salt
Dash of pepper
¼ c. brown sugar, firmly
   packed

2 tblsp. cornstarch
1 tsp. dry mustard
½ tsp. salt
1½ c. apple cider or juice
2 tblsp. vinegar
3 c. cubed cooked ham
¼ c. raisins

Beat together mashed sweet potatoes, milk, margarine, 1 tsp. salt and pepper.

Blend together brown sugar, cornstarch, dry mustard and ½ tsp. salt in saucepan. Stir in cider and vinegar. Cook, stirring constantly, until mixture thickens and boils. Stir in ham and raisins.

Place half of sweet potatoes in bottom of greased 2½-qt. casserole. Top with ham mixture and then with remaining sweet potatoes, swirling them. Bake in 350° oven 30 to 35 minutes. Serves 6.

Memo to Meal Planner: Serve this delicious casserole with frozen mixed vegetables, cooked and seasoned, a relish tray and sherbet.

BAKED HAM/CHEESE SANDWICHES

Quick, tasty, hot main dish for summer lunch or supper.

1½ c. cubed cooked ham
1 c. diced process American
   cheese (4 oz.)
2 hard-cooked eggs, chopped
2 tblsp. chopped green pepper

2 tblsp. chopped onion
2 tblsp. chopped dill pickle
½ c. salad dressing
2 tsp. prepared mustard
8 hamburger buns, split

Combine all ingredients, except buns. Spread between bun halves. Place in 13×9×2″ baking pan; cover with foil. Bake in 350° oven 20 minutes, or until cheese is melted. Makes 8 sandwiches.

Memo to Meal Planner: If everyone in family eats together, bake sandwiches as directed. You can wrap them individually in foil for "late comers," refrigerate and heat 25 to 30 minutes before serving. Choose salad as easy to fix as the sandwiches. Drain a can of green beans; pour on your favorite French dressing and chill several hours. Serve on lettuce. End the meal with cherry crisp made with canned cherry pie filling. Serve the dessert topped with small scoops of vanilla ice cream if you wish to add a fancy note.

KIDNEY BEANS IN RED WINE

Cooking kidney beans in wine enhances their flavor.

2 tblsp. butter or regular margarine	1 (6 oz.) can tomato paste
3 small green onions with tops, chopped	1 c. dry red wine
½ green pepper, chopped	2 (15 oz.) cans kidney beans, drained
1 c. cubed cooked ham	¼ c. chopped bacon ends and pieces

Melt butter in skillet.

Combine onions, green pepper and ham. Add to skillet; cook and stir until ham browns lightly. Stir in tomato paste and wine; cook about 5 minutes.

Blend in kidney beans and turn mixture into greased 2-qt. shallow casserole. Top with chopped bacon. Bake in 350° oven 30 to 35 minutes. Makes 5 servings.

Memo to Meal Planner: Serve this main dish with tomatoes or tomato aspic on lettuce, hot rolls and a make-ahead dessert, such as blueberry cobbler baked alongside casserole.

SAUSAGE WITH SPLIT PEAS

Ideal to serve on a blustery cold day.

1½ c. dry split peas	¼ c. melted regular margarine
1 bay leaf	¼ c. flour
1 qt. water	2 c. reconstituted nonfat dry milk
2 c. sliced peeled carrots	
1 c. chopped onion	1 tsp. salt
1 c. chopped celery	¼ tsp. pepper
1 lb. lean bulk pork sausage	

Wash peas; combine in kettle with bay leaf and water. Bring to a boil; reduce heat. Cover and simmer 20 minutes. Add carrots, onion and celery; simmer 25 minutes. Drain and discard bay leaf.

Cook sausage in skillet until browned; drain on paper toweling.

Combine margarine and flour in saucepan; add milk and cook, stirring constantly, until mixture thickens and bubbles. Add salt and pepper. Combine with vegetables and sausage. Turn into a greased 2½-qt. casserole. Cover and bake in 350° oven 25 minutes. Makes 6 to 8 servings.

Memo to Meal Planner: Serve with stewed tomatoes, your favorite apple salad and if the people who gather around your table will be hungry, have pumpkin pie for dessert.

SAUSAGE/POTATO BAKE

With meat-and-potato fans this dish becomes an instant favorite.

1 lb. bulk pork sausage	½ tsp. salt
1 (10¾ oz.) can condensed cream of chicken or celery soup	¼ tsp. pepper
	4 c. thinly sliced peeled potatoes
⅓ c. milk	½ c. shredded process American cheese (2 oz.)
½ c. finely chopped onion	
2 tblsp. chopped pimiento	

Crumble sausage in skillet and cook until brown. Drain well on paper toweling.

Mix together soup, milk, onion, pimiento, salt and pepper.

Place half the potatoes in greased 2-qt. casserole. Add half the sausage, then half of the soup mixture. Repeat layers. Cover and bake in 350° oven 1 hour 15 minutes. Remove cover and test doneness of potatoes with a fork. If not tender, cover and continue baking until they test done. Remove cover, sprinkle with cheese and bake uncovered 15 minutes, or until cheese is melted. Serves 6.

Memo to Meal Planner: Put a dessert in the oven to bake alongside the sausage casserole. This might be Apple Crisp or Baked Cherry Pudding. Green Bean Salad Bowl is an excellent salad choice (see Index for recipes). If you want to splurge a little, include chilled tomato juice in the menu as an appetizer.

SAUSAGE/CORN SCALLOP

This combination tastes wonderful; it makes a splendid main dish.

¼ c. finely chopped onion
2 tblsp. finely chopped green
  pepper
1 tblsp. regular margarine
1 (1 lb. 1 oz.) can cream style
  corn
1 c. milk
1 egg, beaten

1½ c. coarse cracker crumbs
¾ c. shredded process
  American cheese (3 oz.)
¾ tsp. salt
Dash of pepper
1 tblsp. melted regular
  margarine
1 lb. bulk pork sausage

Cook onion and green pepper in 1 tblsp. melted margarine in saucepan until soft. Add corn, milk, egg, 1 c. cracker crumbs, ½ c. cheese, salt and pepper. Heat, stirring, but do not boil. Pour into 1½-qt. casserole. Toss remaining ½ c. cracker crumbs with 1 tblsp. melted margarine; sprinkle over top. Bake in 350° oven 25 to 30 minutes.

Meanwhile, shape sausage into 6 oblong patties. Cook in skillet until done, browning on both sides.

When corn is baked, top with sausage and sprinkle with remaining ¼ c. cheese. Return to oven about 3 minutes, long enough to melt cheese. Makes 6 servings.

SAUSAGE/SUCCOTASH SCALLOP

The corn makes the sauce for this hearty casserole.

1 lb bulk pork sausage
1 c. chopped onion
2 c. loose-pack frozen lima
  beans
½ tsp. salt
Dash of pepper
4 hard-cooked eggs, sliced

¼ tsp. salt
1 (1 lb. 1 oz.) can cream style
  corn
½ c. cracker crumbs
2 tblsp. melted regular
  margarine

Brown sausage in skillet; remove and drain on paper towels.

Cook onion in drippings in skillet until soft; drain off excess fat.

Meanwhile, cook lima beans as directed on package; drain. Place in greased 2-qt. casserole; sprinkle with ½ tsp. salt and pepper. Top with onions, then with egg slices; sprinkle with ¼ tsp. salt. Layer sausage on top, then the corn.

Toss cracker crumbs with margarine and sprinkle over top. Bake in 350° oven 35 minutes. Makes 6 servings.

Memo to Meal Planner: Lettuce-pickled beet salad adds color and flavor to menu. To make it, cut head lettuce into wedges, put on sides on salad plates and cut slits in lettuce. Insert drained pickled beet slices and bias-sliced celery in slits. Pass your favorite French or other salad dressing.

SAUSAGE POLENTA

Bulk pork sausage assumes the meat role in this Americanized version of polenta.

1½ c. yellow cornmeal
2 tsp. salt
4 c. boiling water
1 lb. bulk pork sausage
1 c. chopped onion
2 cloves garlic, minced
1 (6 oz.) can tomato paste
1 (1 lb. 12 oz.) can tomatoes, cup up
¼ tsp. salt
¼ tsp. dried orégano leaves, crushed
⅛ tsp. pepper
½ c. grated Parmesan cheese

Gradually stir cornmeal and 2 tsp. salt into boiling water in large, heavy saucepan. Reduce heat and cook 20 minutes, stirring frequently. Turn into oiled 9×5×3″ loaf pan. Chill several hours.

Cook pork sausage, onion and garlic in skillet until sausage is browned; drain off excess fat. Add tomato paste, tomatoes, ¼ tsp. salt, orégano and pepper. Simmer uncovered 20 minutes, stirring occasionally.

Cut cornmeal mush into 10 slices. Arrange in bottom of 13×9×2″ baking pan, cutting some of the pieces so that mush covers bottom of pan. Pour tomato mixture over mush; sprinkle with cheese. Bake in 400° oven 30 minutes. Let stand 10 minutes in pan before cutting to serve. Makes 8 servings.

Memo to Meal Planner: Serve buttered Italian beans, tossed salad, crusty bread and a lemon or chocolate dessert with this tasty main dish. For a short-cut version of the hearty main dish, pour the hot mush onto a large platter, cover with the tomato mixture, sprinkle with cheese and carry to the table.

SAUSAGE SCRAPPLE

Serve for supper, lunch, brunch or Sunday breakfast.

1 c. yellow cornmeal	1 lb. bulk pork sausage
¼ c. flour	2 eggs, beaten
1 tsp. salt	2 tblsp. water
2 c. cold water	2 c. corn flake crumbs
4 c. boiling water	Salad oil

Blend cornmeal, flour and salt in bowl. Mix well with 2 c. cold water; gradually add to boiling water, stirring constantly. Reduce heat and cook, stirring frequently, 20 to 25 minutes, or until mush is thickened and bubbling.

Meanwhile, brown sausage in skillet; drain off fat. Stir sausage into mush. Rinse two 8½×4½×2½" loaf pans with cold water; pour in scrapple. Cool, and chill overnight.

To cook, turn scrapple from pans, cut in ½" slices. Dip in eggs mixed with 2 tblsp. water, then in corn flake crumbs. Brown on both sides in hot oil in skillet. Makes about 28 slices.

Memo to Meal Planner: Scrapple is an ideal main dish for a cold day. Serve it with brown sugar, maple-flavored or other table syrup. Add Baked Butter Beans and a big tossed salad with Cottage Cheese Salad Dressing (see Index for recipes) to the supper or lunch menu, scrambled eggs to breakfast or brunch menu.

SAUSAGE/CHEESE SPOON BREAD

Delicious way to serve sausage at women's luncheon.

3½ c. milk	2 eggs, separated
1½ tsp. salt	½ lb. bulk pork sausage
¾ c. cornmeal	1½ c. shredded Cheddar
1 tblsp. butter or regular margarine	cheese (6 oz.)

Scald milk in top of double boiler; add salt and cornmeal, stirring constantly. Continue cooking and stirring until mixture thickens. Add butter. Remove from heat.

Beat egg yolks until thick and lemon colored.

Beat egg whites until stiff peaks form.

Blend yolks into hot cornmeal mixture; gently fold in egg whites. Pour into greased 2-qt. casserole. Bake in 375° oven about 30 minutes.

Meanwhile, cook sausage until slightly browned; drain well and mix with cheese. Sprinkle quickly over top of spoon bread. Continue baking 15 minutes. Serve *immediately*. Makes 6 servings.

Memo to Meal Planner: Serve with your favorite molded cranberry salad and vanilla ice cream, topped with faintly warm applesauce, for dessert. Or serve with Harvard beets, a tossed green salad and have pineapple sherbet for dessert. Remember that the spoon bread will not wait.

Lamb Favorites

If your family enjoys lamb, you are in luck. The trio of recipes that follow transforms less expensive cuts into extra delicious dishes. One lamb stew contains fluffy cornmeal dumplings and Country Lamb Pie has an appealing topping of dill-flavored biscuits. Nutritious lentils are the unusual ingredient in the other lamb stew.

LAMB WITH CORNMEAL DUMPLINGS

Light, feathery dumplings are fine meat stretchers.

1½ lbs. lamb shoulder, cut in 1½″ cubes	¼ tsp. pepper
¼ c. flour	3 medium potatoes, peeled and quartered
2 tblsp. salad oil	2 c. sliced peeled carrots
4 c. water	1 c. chopped celery
3 large onions, quartered	1 c. frozen loose-pack lima beans
2 beef bouillon cubes	Cornmeal Dumplings
2 tsp. salt	
½ tsp. dried orégano leaves	

Shake lamb, a few pieces at a time, in a paper bag with flour. Brown in hot oil in Dutch oven. Add water, onions, bouillon cubes, salt, orégano and pepper. Cover and simmer about 1 hour, until lamb is tender. Add vegetables and simmer 10 minutes.

Meanwhile, prepare dough for Cornmeal Dumplings. Drop by spoonfuls into boiling stew. Cook uncovered over low heat 10 minutes. Cover and cook 10 minutes longer. Makes 8 servings.

Cornmeal Dumplings: In medium bowl, lightly mix with fork 1½ c. all-purpose buttermilk biscuit mix, ½ c. yellow cornmeal and ⅔ c. milk (reconstituted dry milk is thrifty).

LAMB STEW WITH LENTILS

Lamb and lentils are one of the world's oldest and best-liked food teams. The thrifty, dried vegetable is a fine economical source of protein—a tasty way to stretch tender lamb.

1 lb. lamb breast, cut in 1½″ cubes	¼ tsp. pepper
	1 (1 lb.) can tomatoes, cut up
2 tblsp. salad oil	1 c. lentils
2 cloves garlic, minced	½ c. uncooked rice
3 large onions, sliced	2 c. celery, cut in ¾″ pieces
1 tblsp. salt	2 c. sliced peeled carrots
½ tsp. dried orégano leaves, crushed	2½ c. water

Brown lamb cubes in hot oil in Dutch oven. Add garlic, onion, salt, orégano, pepper and tomatoes. Cover and simmer 1 hour and 15 minutes. Wash lentils and add to Dutch oven with rice, celery, carrots and water. Cover and simmer 1 hour, stirring occasionally, adding more water if necessary. Makes 8 servings.

Memo to Meal Planner: Serve this stew with wilted garden lettuce in springtime, tossed green salad at other seasons. For dessert have chocolate or butterscotch sundaes.

COUNTRY LAMB PIE

Lamb stew puts on a new face with Dill Biscuits on top. The main-dish pie contains meat and vegetables, plus bread for the meal.

1½ lbs. boneless lamb shoulder, cut in 1″ cubes	4 carrots, peeled and cut in 1″ pieces
2 tblsp. salad oil	3 potatoes, peeled and quartered
1 clove garlic, minced	
2½ c. water	1 (10 oz.) pkg. frozen peas
2½ tsp. salt	⅓ c. flour
¼ tsp. pepper	½ c. water
1 medium onion, sliced	Dill Biscuits

Brown meat on all sides in hot oil in Dutch oven. Add garlic, 2½ c. water, salt and pepper. Cover and simmer 1½ hours, or until meat is almost tender. Add onion, carrots and potatoes. Simmer about 25 minutes, until tender. Add peas and cook just until separated.

Blend together flour and ½ c. water. Add to stew; cook and stir until thickened and bubbly.

Pour hot stew into 3-qt. casserole. Top with Dill Biscuits. Bake in 425° oven 12 to 15 minutes. Makes 6 servings.

Dill Biscuits: Use homemade Biscuit Mix (see Index for recipe) or commercial biscuit mix. Combine 2 c. mix and 2 tsp. dried dill weed. Prepare biscuits as directed in recipe (or on box) and bake on top of stew as directed.

Memo to Meal Planner: Fruit salad, which answers both for salad and dessert, makes a great companion. If your family insists on ending dinner on a sweet note, serve everyone a big sugar or molasses cookie with or without cocoa. (See Index for Instant Cocoa Mix.)

Ready-to-Eat Sausages

When time is money, consider using prepared sausages that require little or no cooking. Their cost fluctuates, as does their availability. When they are a good buy, you can use them occasionally to add different seasoning to quick dishes and to keep them from getting monotonous. They accomplish the most for the menu maker when the weather is hot and you want to spend less time cooking.

Frankfurters lead, followed by salami, bologna and knockwurst.

FRANK/KRAUT STEW

Surprisingly good—easy, quick, economical, too.

1 lb. frankfurters, cut in thirds	1 (1 lb.) can tomatoes, cut up
2 tblsp. salad oil	1 c. water
1 c. chopped onion	2 tblsp. brown sugar
¼ c. chopped green pepper (optional)	½ tsp. dried basil leaves, crumbled
2 c. sliced peeled carrots	¼ tsp. pepper
3 c. cubed peeled potatoes	
1 (1 lb.) can sauerkraut, drained	

Brown frankfurters in hot oil in large kettle; remove and set aside.

Cook onion and green pepper in drippings in kettle until soft. Add remaining ingredients. Cover and simmer about 35 minutes, until carrots and potatoes are tender. Stir in frankfurters; simmer about 3 minutes, until heated through. Makes 6 servings.

Memo to Meal Planner: Serve with hot rye or Vienna bread. Cut bread in ½″ slices, spread with butter and top each with a thin slice of process American cheese; reassemble loaf, wrap in heavy-duty foil and heat in 400° oven 20 minutes. Have pear sundaes for dessert. Drain chilled canned pears, place a pear half in each serving dish, fill centers with vanilla ice cream and top with chocolate sauce.

SPAGHETTI WITH FRANKS

Easy, quick and popular with youngsters and adults.

1 c. chopped onion	1 tsp. chili powder
2 tblsp. salad oil	¼ tsp. salt
1 (15 oz.) can tomato sauce	½ tsp. Worcestershire sauce
1 lb. frankfurters, bias cut in	1 (8 oz.) pkg. spaghetti
1″ pieces	1 c. shredded process
1 tblsp. prepared mustard	American cheese (4 oz.)

Cook onion in hot oil in skillet until soft. Stir in tomato sauce, frankfurters, mustard, chili powder, salt and Worcestershire sauce. Cover and simmer 30 minutes.

Meanwhile, cook spaghetti as package directs; drain. Put in shallow baking dish. Spoon sauce over the top; sprinkle with shredded cheese. Broil just until cheese melts. Makes 6 servings.

Memo to Meal Planner: Include broccoli or succotash, hot garlic bread and lettuce, or a tossed green salad, in menu. Apple tapioca, rice pudding or other pudding made with milk is a good dessert. If you are food-cost and calorie conscious, use reconstituted dry milk to make it. You may prefer to have a fruited gelatin to end this dinner. A fruit compote is another good choice.

OPEN-FACE CONEYS

Pleasing, easy-to-make variation of an old-time sandwich favorite.

1 lb. frankfurters, cut in ½"
pieces
2 tblsp. butter or regular
margarine
1 c. chopped onion
2 (15 oz.) cans kidney beans,
drained

1 (10¾ oz.) can condensed
tomato soup
1 to 2 tsp. chili powder
2 tblsp. water
1 tsp. vinegar
½ tsp. Worcestershire sauce
10 bias-cut slices French bread

Cook frankfurters in melted butter in skillet until partially browned. Add onion and continue cooking until onions are soft and frankfurters browned.

Stir in remaining ingredients, except French bread. Cover and simmer 15 minutes, stirring 2 or 3 times. Serve over toasted French bread. Makes 10 sandwiches.

Memo to Meal Planner: If you wish, serve frankfurter mixture between split and toasted hot dog buns instead of on French bread. Serve sandwiches with Casserole Bean Salad (see Index). Have canned fruit, such as pineapple slices or peaches and chocolate cupcakes for dessert. Or end the meal with milk shakes and cookies.

SANDWICHES WITH ROLL-UP FILLING

Try this new and exciting way to serve cold cuts.

2 c. finely chopped cabbage
1 peeled carrot, shredded
¼ c. salad dressing
2 tsp. vinegar
1 tsp. sugar

½ tsp. salt
1 (6 oz.) pkg. process Swiss
cheese (long slices)
1 (8 oz.) pkg. sliced salami
8 hot dog buns

Mix together cabbage and carrot.

Thoroughly blend together salad dressing, vinegar, sugar and salt. Stir into cabbage mixture.

Cut cheese slices in halves crosswise. Place 1 slice cheese on top of each salami slice. Spoon ¼ c. coleslaw at one end and roll up salami and cheese. Serve in long hot dog buns. Makes 8 sandwiches.

Memo to Meal Planner: You can add your choice of seasonings to the coleslaw. Try celery seeds and/or finely chopped green onion. Start the summer lunch or supper with hot chicken rice soup. Serve sandwiches with corn on the cob or buttered corn and sliced tomatoes. Chilled melon makes a splendid dessert. You can use other cold cut slices if you prefer them to salami. If you want a more substantial meal, serve fresh peach cobbler for dessert.

MAIN-DISH SANDWICHES

Good supper main dish or teen-age evening snack. The crustiness of French bread in open-face sandwiches provides interesting change from the usual sandwiches made with soft buns.

½ lb. bologna, cut in small strips	½ c. pickle relish
	¼ c. chopped green pepper
2 c. shredded process American cheese (8 oz.)	2 tblsp. chopped onion
	½ c. salad dressing
1 (8 oz.) can kidney beans, drained	12 bias cut 1" slices French bread

Combine all ingredients, except bread.

Toast bread slices on one side. Turn and spread with filling.

Broil just long enough to melt cheese. Makes 3½ cups filling, enough for 12 open-face sandwiches.

Memo to Meal Planner: If you do not wish to broil sandwiches you can spread the filling between split hamburger buns, stack them in a 13×9×2" pan, cover with foil and heat in 350° oven 20 minutes. Heat 10 minutes longer if you make the sandwiches ahead and chill them in the covered pan. Good to serve with this main dish are buttered peas and carrots, banana salad and chocolate chip cookies.

BOILED DINNER, GERMAN STYLE

Interesting boiled dinner to fix in about 35 minutes. Knockwurst give vegetables an exciting flavor. Stick toothpicks through thickest part of cabbage wedges to hold leaves together during cooking. Remove picks before serving.

5 c. water	6 small potatoes, peeled and
3 beef bouillon cubes	cut in halves
6 knockwurst	3 turnips, peeled and cut in
1 tsp. salt	quarters
⅛ tsp. pepper	1 medium head cabbage, cut in
6 carrots, peeled and cut in 1"	6 wedges
pieces	

Combine water and bouillon cubes in large kettle. Bring to a boil. Remove from heat and add knockwurst; cover and let stand 12 minutes. Remove knockwurst. Add salt, pepper and vegetables to kettle. Cover and cook about 20 minutes, until vegetables are done. Add knockwurst, reduce heat and simmer about 5 minutes, just until knockwurst are heated. Makes 6 servings.

Memo to Meal Planner: Pass horseradish if you like. Serve with rye bread and have an apple, blueberry, peach or other fruit cobbler for dessert. For a special dinner, top warm cobbler with ice cream.

BARBECUED GIANT SUBMARINES

Teen-age boys especially like these hearty sandwiches for lunch.

2 loaves French bread	6 slices process Swiss cheese
6 slices chopped ham	6 slices process American
luncheon meat	cheese
6 slices salami	Barbecue Sauce

Cut each bread loaf in thirds. Split each third in half horizontally. Place 1 slice each chopped ham luncheon meat, salami, Swiss cheese and American cheese on half of the bread pieces. Spoon Barbecue Sauce over, adjust tops on sandwiches and wrap in foil.

Bake in 350° oven about 15 minutes, until cheese melts. Makes 6 large sandwiches.

Barbecue Sauce: In saucepan combine 1 c. ketchup, 1 c. wine vinegar, ¾ c. chili sauce, ¾ c. brown sugar, 3 tblsp. steak sauce, 2 tblsp. Worcestershire sauce, 2 tblsp. prepared mustard, ½ tsp. pepper and 2 cloves garlic, minced. Bring to a boil. Reduce heat and simmer 15 minutes. Makes about 3½ cups.

Memo to Meal Planner: Carrot sticks, pickled beets and/or other relishes are fine accompaniments. Glasses of milk and homemade cookies answer eloquently for dessert. Cool, cover and refrigerate leftover Barbecue Sauce. Heat frankfurters in it for another favorite with youngsters. Use it in making Oven-barbecued Chicken (see Index for recipe) and other dishes.

Meat from the Cupboard

A can of corned beef, corned beef hash or luncheon meat in the cupboard insures a good main dish that can be made with little fuss. The price of these foods varies; one year it may be a wise purchase, less economical the next. If you decide the price is not out of line for your budget, do make Reuben Bake and the Corned Beef/Cabbage Scallop. They are two casserole dishes that men praise. Handy corned beef hash is easy and quick—open a can and make Off-the-Shelf Sandwiches, which are dipped in batter and browned in a skillet, like French toast. Speedy Skillet Supper, made with canned luncheon meat, lives up to its name any time, but especially on busy days.

REUBEN BAKE

The taste of Reuben sandwiches dominates this substantial casserole in which noodles extend the corned beef.

6 oz. noodles	1 tblsp. minced dill pickle
2 tblsp. butter or regular margarine	1 tsp. grated onion
1 (1 lb.) can sauerkraut	2 tomatoes, sliced
1 (12 oz.) can corned beef, shredded	2 c. shredded Swiss cheese (8 oz.)
½ c. mayonnaise or salad dressing	½ c. crushed rye crackers
1 tblsp. ketchup	¼ tsp. caraway seeds
	2 tblsp. melted butter or regular margarine

Cook noodles by package directions, drain. Toss with 2 tblsp. butter. Place noodles in bottom of 11×7×1½″ pan; top with sauerkraut, then corned beef.

Thoroughly mix together mayonnaise, ketchup, pickle and onion. Spread over corned beef. Top with tomato slices, then cheese.

Toss rye crackers and caraway seeds with 2 tblsp. butter; sprinkle over top of casserole. Bake in 350° oven 35 minutes. Serves 6.

Memo to Meal Planner: Serve this main dish with buttered green beans and a plate of assorted relishes. End the meal with an apple dessert. It might be Apple Cobbler (see Index for recipe).

CORNED BEEF/CABBAGE SCALLOP

Potatoes join the favorite corned beef-cabbage team.

4 c. sliced peeled potatoes
3 c. boiling water
2 qts. shredded cabbage
1 (10½ oz.) can condensed
   cream of celery soup
⅓ c. milk
1 c. shredded Colby cheese
   (4 oz.)

1 (12 oz.) can corned beef,
   shredded
1 tblsp. instant minced onion
½ tsp. salt
¼ tsp. pepper
½ c. bread crumbs
2 tblsp. melted regular
   margarine

Cook potatoes in boiling water in large kettle 5 minutes. Stir in cabbage; continue cooking 5 minutes. Drain in colander or sieve.

Meanwhile, blend together cream of celery soup and milk in saucepan. Add cheese, corned beef, onion, salt and pepper. Heat to boiling, stirring frequently. Place half the potato-cabbage mixture in greased 2½-qt. casserole. Top with half the corned beef mixture. Repeat layers.

Toss bread crumbs with margarine; sprinkle over top of casserole. Bake uncovered in 350° oven 30 to 35 minutes. Makes 6 servings.

Memo to Meal Planner: Complete supper with hot whole wheat rolls and crushed pineapple-shredded carrot salad, molded in lemon flavor gelatin, if desired.

OFF-THE-SHELF SANDWICHES

Canned corned beef hash makes tasty hot sandwiches.

1 (15 oz.) can corned beef hash	4 eggs, beaten
12 bread slices	½ c. milk
Ketchup	½ tsp. salt
⅓ c. finely chopped onion	Melted butter or regular margarine
6 slices process cheese	

Spread hash on 6 bread slices, pressing it on bread with a knife. Spread ketchup over hash; sprinkle with onion. Top each with cheese slice (whatever kind you wish). Top with remaining bread slices.

Blend together eggs, milk and salt. Dip sandwiches in egg mixture to coat both sides. In 2 large skillets or on griddle, cook sandwiches in a little butter over medium heat until golden brown. Makes 6.

Memo to Meal Planner: These are a splendid choice for lunch on Saturday. Serve them with mugs of hot soup and a simple salad.

SQUAW CORN SKILLET

It takes about 15 minutes from start to finish to make this dish from ingredients you can keep on hand in your kitchen.

1 (12 oz.) can luncheon meat	2 tsp. chopped chives (optional)
1 tblsp. melted butter or regular margarine	¼ tsp. salt
3 eggs, beaten	⅛ tsp. pepper
1 (1 lb. 1 oz.) can cream style corn	

Cut luncheon meat in cubes; brown in butter in skillet.

Combine remaining ingredients. Add to meat and cook over low heat, stirring occasionally, just until eggs are set. Makes 6 servings.

Memo to Meal Planner: Serve this speedy country favorite with scalloped tomatoes, toast or hot biscuits, carrot sticks and canned fruit, such as peaches, pears or applesauce. Cookies, if you have them hidden in the freezer, make the fruit dessert a real treat.

SPEEDY SKILLET SUPPER

Keep makings for this main dish on hand.

1 (12 oz.) can luncheon
   meat, cubed
1 c. chopped onion
½ c. chopped green pepper
   (optional)
3 tblsp. butter or regular
   margarine
4 c. cubed cooked peeled
   potatoes

4 hard-cooked eggs, sliced
1 (10¾ oz.) can condensed
   cream of mushroom soup
½ c. milk
1 tblsp. parsley flakes
¼ tsp. salt
⅛ tsp. pepper

Cook luncheon meat, onion and green pepper in melted butter in 12″ skillet until meat is lightly browned. Add remaining ingredients. Cover and simmer 10 minutes, stirring once. Makes 6 servings.

Memo to Meal Planner: Complete menu with broccoli, applesauce and peanut cookies. Include green pepper if you have one in garden or refrigerator; it contributes much to flavor and adds color. You can freeze green peppers during the growing season to use the rest of the year. Cut them in halves, cut out stem ends and remove seeds. Scald in boiling water 3 minutes, cool in ice water, drain and freeze at once. Or freeze chopped peppers without scalding.

CHAPTER 4

Chicken, Turkey and Fish

Platters piled high with golden, crisp-crusted fried chicken . . . a large, plump turkey roasted to a glistening brown on Thanksgiving Day . . . the family fishermen's "catch" on the dinner table—these are the meals that make traditions in country homes. But there are other delicious ways in which country women use these protein-rich foods frequently to beat the high cost of living.

Recipes for some of their thrifty specials follow: Creamed Turkey with Herbed Stuffing, made with inexpensive ground turkey, captures that wonderful taste of the holiday stuffed bird for a fraction of the cost. Chicken/Noodle Casserole is a homey favorite in Pennsylvania Dutch kitchens. And Tuna Pie with Cottage Cheese Biscuits makes use of that economical canned fish in a delicious way.

These dishes have in common superior flavor, excellent protein and other nutrients and, often, bargain prices. Most supermarkets offer chicken and turkey parts for sale. Whole chickens usually are a better buy than the parts, but not always—so compare costs, remembering that the higher priced breasts contain more meat, less bone and fat per ounce than other parts.

Many women buy whole chickens when on sale and freeze them to save money. They usually cut up some of them (see directions in this chapter) and freeze the like parts together in separate packages. The woman who shares the recipe for Chicken Livers, Chinese Style builds her supply in the freezer until she has a pound of the livers, enough to make this interesting dish.

The larger size of turkeys makes the parts especially advantageous because you can serve dishes made with them more frequently. When you taste thrifty Turkey Drumstick Pie, you will be grateful that its cost makes repetitions desirable. Sweet-sour Turkey rivals other oriental dishes so seasoned. You make it with ground turkey meat available in an increasing number of supermarkets, especially after the holiday season. (Since it is usually ground from frozen turkey, it is a good idea to use it within a couple of days after you bring it home.)

Fresh fish is not readily available in many areas, but frozen fillets are a good substitute and many of the following recipes feature them.

Country women hold tuna, the most abundant canned fish, in high esteem and use it in interesting dishes. Recipes for some of their specials are in this chapter.

Salmon canners struggle to meet the demand for salmon, especially the red kinds, sockeye and blueback, which are scarce and therefore more expensive than pink. Almost half the salmon canned is the pink variety. Pink salmon is small-flaked and excellent for use in many dishes—our New-style Salmon Soufflé, for instance.

Canned mackerel, plain rather than salted, is an inexpensive fish. Be sure to try penny-pinching Mackerel Loaf with Egg Sauce. You will be surprised how good it tastes.

Chicken, turkey and fish help hold down food costs. And menu planners find that they provide interesting variety to meals. You will find some favorite soup recipes featuring them in Chapter 6.

ROAST CHICKEN

When you have roast chicken on the menu, put an extra bird in oven—an easy way to cook chicken to use later.

3 (2½ to 3 lb.) whole broiler-   Salad oil
   fryers

Rinse chicken in cold water, drain and pat dry with paper towels. Tuck wings under back. Tie legs together. Brush with oil. Place on rack in roasting pan or broiling pan. Bake in 375° oven 1 hour. Cut string between legs. Continue roasting 15 to 30 minutes, or until drumsticks move up and down easily and twist easily when grasped in hand and moved. Cool 1 chicken to use later. Keep other 2 chickens warm while you make the gravy. Two chickens make 8 servings. One chicken makes about 3 c. meat when removed from bones.

Memo to Meal Planner: Serve chicken with Giblet Dressing Casserole, Cream Gravy (recipes follow) and mashed potatoes. These are the four important foods for a country chicken dinner. Other additions that make a meal a treat are a green vegetable of your choice and either Vegetable/Cranberry Salad or Beet/Horseradish Molded Salad (see Index for recipes), both of which you make ahead.

GIBLET DRESSING CASSEROLE

Mixture is not stuffed into chicken so it is a dressing. Cook giblets and cube bread a day ahead if more convenient.

Giblets from 3 chickens	2 tblsp. parsley flakes
½ tsp. salt	1½ tsp. rubbed sage
¾ c. chopped onion	1 tsp. salt
¾ c. chopped celery	½ tsp. pepper
¾ c. butter or regular	2 chicken bouillon cubes
margarine	1½ c. giblet broth
12 c. dry bread cubes	

Place giblets, except liver, and necks in saucepan. Add water to cover and ½ tsp. salt. Cover and simmer 1 hour. Add liver and continue simmering 10 minutes. Drain off broth and strain (you will need 1½ c. for this casserole; save the rest for gravy). Chop giblets.

Cook onion and celery in butter until soft. Combine with bread cubes, parsley, sage, 1 tsp. salt and pepper.

Add bouillon cubes to giblet broth and heat until cubes are dissolved. Add broth and giblets to bread mixture and toss. Pile lightly into greased 2½-qt. casserole. Cover and bake in 375° oven 30 minutes; uncover and bake 15 minutes longer. Makes 8 servings.

CREAM GRAVY

Stirring with a wire whisk helps make gravy velvety smooth.

Milk	¼ tsp. pepper
Giblet broth	½ c. drippings (chicken fat)
6 tblsp. flour	2 chicken bouillon cubes
1½ tsp. salt	

Add enough milk to giblet broth to make 3 cups. Place 1½ c. mixture in a jar with tight-fitting lid. Add flour, salt and pepper; shake until mixture is blended.

Place drippings in skillet; add mixture in jar, remaining 1½ c. milk-broth mixture and bouillon cubes. Cook, stirring, until bouillon cubes are dissolved and gravy thickens and is bubbly. Makes 3 cups.

Crisp Oven-fried Chicken

One universal country kitchen custom is to vary familiar, thrifty foods so no one tires of them. Chicken offers a splendid example. Skillet-fried, or old-fashioned fried chicken, never lacks for loyal supporters, but an increasing number of people now switch frequently to oven-fried. One reason is that by changing the coating for the pieces you come up with different and intriguing flavor surprises.

Take the basic oven-fried chicken and instead of using seasoned flour to coat the pieces, substitute crushed potato or corn chips, crisp, ready-to-eat cereals or an herb stuffing and cheese mix. This is an easy and quick way to add interest to the meat on the platter.

Oven-fried chicken also eliminates the worry of spattering hot fat. There's no greasy skillet to wash. You put the chicken in the oven and forget about it. You do not have to stop what you are doing to turn the pieces to get even browning. And oven-fried chicken is lower in calories than the old-fashioned kind. Eliminating the rich gravy removes temptation for weight-conscious people. Anyway, there are times when gravy is out of place, such as when you tote fried chicken to picnics and covered dish suppers.

When the price for a nutritionally valuable food, such as chicken, is favorable, it is good business to serve it often.

OVEN-FRIED CHICKEN

To win an enthusiastic welcome for chicken every time, introduce new flavor variations to complement the meat.

½ c. flour
1 tsp. salt
¼ tsp. pepper
1 (2½ to 3 lb.) broiler-fryer, cut up

⅓ c. melted butter or regular margarine

Combine flour, salt and pepper in paper or plastic bag.

Dip chicken pieces in butter. Shake, a few pieces at a time, in seasoned flour. Place skin side up without touching in foil-lined 15½ × 10½ ×1″ pan. Bake in 375° oven 1 hour, until done. Serves 4.

Variations

Cereal Coating: Substitute 2 c. crushed corn flakes or crushed crisp rice cereal for flour. Roll butter-coated chicken in crumbs; do not shake in a bag.

Potato Chip Coating: Substitute 2 c. crushed potato chips or barbecued potato chips for the flour. Omit salt. Roll butter-coated chicken in crumbs.

Corn Chip Coating: Substitute 2 c. crushed taco-flavored corn or tortilla chips for flour. Omit salt. Roll butter-coated chicken in crumbs.

Herb/Cheese Coating: Substitute ¾ c. packaged herb-seasoned stuffing mix or homemade Stuffing Mix (see Index for recipe), crushed, combined with ½ c. grated Parmesan cheese for the flour. Roll butter-coated chicken in stuffing-cheese mixture.

Memo to Meal Planner: If you wish to double the recipe, you will need 2 large shallow pans. Set each pan on a rack in the oven. After chicken has cooked 30 minutes, move the pan from the bottom to the top rack and vice versa; both pans of chicken brown evenly.

OVEN-BARBECUED CHICKEN

Tastes in barbecue sauce vary greatly from one kitchen to another. If you have a favorite, use it in this chicken dish. Or use the Barbecue Sauce that is spooned over Barbecued Giant Submarines (see Index for recipe). It has many champions and you may become one of them. Pan drippings taste too good to waste. Serve them as sauce.

Legs, thighs and breasts of 2 broiler-fryers	1 onion, sliced and separated into rings
1 tsp. hickory smoked salt	½ c. water
¼ tsp. pepper	1¾ c. barbecue sauce

Place chicken pieces skin side up in 13×9×2″ pan. Sprinkle with hickory smoked salt and pepper. Top with onion rings. Pour water around chicken. Bake uncovered in 375° oven 30 minutes. Pour barbecue sauce (one of your favorites) over chicken; continue baking for 30 minutes. Makes 6 servings.

HOW TO CUT UP A CHICKEN

Using a sharp knife or poultry shears, cut through skin where leg joins the body. Pull the leg away from the body and find the joint. Cut through the joint. Then cut leg into two pieces at the knee joint. Repeat with other leg. Locate the wing joints in the same manner and cut them away from the body. Separate the breast from the back by cutting down both sides just below the ribs. Split back and breast in half along the center and cut each piece in half crosswise.

PLANTATION CHICKEN STEW

Beautifully seasoned chicken-vegetable stew—country style.

1 (3 lb.) broiler-fryer, cut up	1 c. chopped onion
3 c. water	1 (15 oz.) can tomato sauce
1 small onion, cut up	1 (10 oz.) pkg. frozen corn
1 (6″) branch celery	1 tsp. sugar
1 tsp. salt	½ tsp. salt
4 peppercorns	¼ tsp. pepper
2 c. cubed peeled potatoes	⅛ tsp. dried orégano leaves,
1 (10 oz.) pkg. frozen lima	crushed
beans	⅛ tsp. poultry seasoning

Combine chicken, water, cut-up onion, celery, 1 tsp. salt and peppercorns in Dutch oven or large kettle. Cover and simmer about 50 minutes, until chicken is tender. Strain off broth. Cut meat from bones, discarding skin. Skim fat from broth. Simmer broth until it is reduced to 2 cups.

Add potatoes, lima beans and chopped onion to broth in Dutch oven; cover and cook 20 minutes. Add tomato sauce, chicken, corn, sugar, ½ tsp. salt, pepper, orégano and poultry seasoning. Simmer 10 to 15 minutes, or until vegetables are tender. Makes 6 servings.

Memo to Meal Planner: Serve this meal-in-a-dish in soup bowls. It is a greatly simplified version of southern Brunswick stew. Consider rounding out dinner with hot corn bread and a cranberry salad.

CHICKEN LASAGNE FOR COMPANY

You can prepare this gourmet dish several hours ahead and refrigerate it ready to bake 40 minutes before mealtime. To reduce work on company day, cook chicken and make tomato sauce a day ahead.

1 (3 lb.) broiler-fryer, cut up	¼ tsp. dried orégano leaves,
3 c. water	crushed
1 small onion, cut up	1 small bay leaf
1 (6") branch celery, cut up	½ tsp. salt
1 tsp. salt	12 lasagne noodles
4 peppercorns	2 c. small-curd creamed
1 (1 lb. 12 oz.) can tomatoes,	cottage cheese
cut up	2 c. grated mozzarella cheese
1 (6 oz.) can tomato paste	(8 oz.)
1 clove garlic, minced	1 c. grated Parmesan cheese
1 tsp. dried rosemary leaves,	(4 oz.)
crushed	

Place chicken with water, onion, celery, 1 tsp. salt and peppercorns in kettle. Bring to a boil; reduce heat, cover and simmer 50 minutes. Strain off broth and reserve (you will need 1 c.). Cut chicken from bones; discard skin.

To make sauce, combine tomatoes, reserved chicken broth, tomato paste, garlic, rosemary, orégano, bay leaf and ½ tsp. salt in large saucepan. Simmer uncovered 30 minutes; remove bay leaf.

Cook noodles as directed on package. Cover with cold water until noodles can be handled. Lift out, do not drain them.

Spread thin layer of tomato sauce in 13×9×2" baking pan. Arrange 6 noodles lengthwise in pan. Top with half of each: chicken, cottage cheese, mozzarella cheese, tomato sauce and Parmesan cheese. Repeat layers. Bake uncovered in 350° oven 30 minutes (40 minutes if refrigerated). Let stand in pan 10 minutes before cutting. Makes 12 servings.

Memo to Meal Planner: Serve this country-style, praise-winning dish with buttered peas, crusty rolls and Lemon Coleslaw; have a light dessert—fruit or Fruited Pink Whip (see Index for recipes).

CHICKEN/NOODLE CASSEROLE

Unusual, attractive and tasty version of chicken and noodles.

1 (2½ to 3 lb.) broiler-fryer, cut up
4 c. water
1 tsp. salt
2 c. cubed peeled potatoes
1 c. sliced peeled carrots
½ c. chopped celery
½ c. chopped onion
1 (10 oz.) pkg. frozen peas
1 tsp. salt
¼ tsp. pepper
⅓ c. flour
4 oz. noodles
1 tblsp. butter or regular margarine
2 tblsp. dry bread crumbs

Place chicken, water and 1 tsp. salt in kettle or Dutch oven. Cover and bring to a boil; reduce heat and simmer about 50 minutes, until chicken is tender. Strain broth and reserve. Cut up chicken, discarding skin and bones.

Cook potatoes, carrots, celery and onion in 3 c. chicken broth in large saucepan about 15 minutes, until tender. Add frozen peas, 1 tsp. salt and pepper; cook just until peas separate. Stir in chicken.

Blend together flour and 1 c. broth (add water if necessary to make 1 c.). Add to mixture in saucepan and cook, stirring constantly, until mixture comes to a boil.

Meanwhile, cook noodles as directed on package; drain. Toss with butter until noodles are coated.

Place hot chicken mixture in greased 2½-qt. casserole. Top with noodles; sprinkle with bread crumbs. Place under broiler 5″ from heat about 3 minutes, until top is lightly browned. Makes 6 servings.

Memo to Meal Planner: This is an adaptation of an old Pennsylvania Dutch dish. Serve with Stir-fried Broccoli and make-ahead molded Apple/Pineapple Salad (see Index for recipes). The salad takes a double role—it also answers for dessert.

CHICKEN PAPRIKA

Buttermilk substitutes ably for the more costly sour cream.

½ c. flour	1 (8 oz.) pkg. noodles,
2 tsp. salt	cooked and drained
¼ tsp. pepper	¼ c. flour
Legs, thighs and breasts of	2 tsp. paprika
2 broiler-fryers	½ tsp. salt
¼ c. salad oil	⅛ tsp. pepper
½ c. chopped onion	2 c. buttermilk
¾ c. hot water	

Combine ½ c. flour, 2 tsp. salt and ¼ tsp. pepper in plastic or paper bag.

Shake chicken pieces, a few at a time, in seasoned flour. Brown chicken on all sides in hot oil in a large skillet. Add onion and hot water; cover and simmer about 40 minutes, until chicken is tender.

Place hot noodles in large, shallow casserole or baking dish; top with chicken pieces. Keep warm in oven.

Stir together ¼ c. flour, paprika, ½ tsp. salt and ⅛ tsp. pepper; blend in buttermilk. Add to mixture in skillet in which chicken cooked. Cook, stirring constantly, just until mixture is thickened and starts to boil. Pour over chicken and noodles and sprinkle lightly with a little extra paprika. Makes 6 to 8 servings.

Memo to Meal Planner: Build your menu for a company or special occasion chicken dinner around this main dish. Save the bony chicken pieces and giblets to make casseroles, soups and sandwiches.

Chicken Croquettes, New Style

Chicken croquettes are back on the dining table. These are much easier to make than the traditional croquettes fried in deep fat. And they are lower in calories. You can shape and chill them several hours before browning and heating them quickly in a hot oven. If you have leftover cooked chicken, you can utilize it in croquettes, good both in party and family menus.

CHICKEN CROQUETTES, OVEN-BROWNED

They skip the hot fat kettle, bake fast, are less work. Roll them in wheat germ for a good nutritional touch.

1 c. chicken broth	2 tblsp. chopped onion
¼ c. flour	¾ tsp. poultry seasoning or
2 c. cooked white rice	rubbed sage
2 c. diced cooked chicken	¼ c. wheat germ or fine dry
4 tsp. lemon juice	bread crumbs
1 tsp. salt	

Combine chicken broth and flour. Cook, stirring constantly, until sauce is smooth and thick.

Combine rice, chicken, lemon juice, salt, onion and poultry seasoning. Add sauce, a little at a time, to make a soft mixture, but one easily handled. Cool.

Form chicken mixture in 8 balls, cones or other shapes, using a scant ½ c. of mixture for each croquette. Roll in wheat germ to coat evenly. Place in greased 13×9×2″ baking pan. Bake in 400° oven 20 minutes, or until croquettes are golden brown. Makes 8 servings.

Memo to Meal Planner: You can easily cut the recipe in half to make 4 croquettes. And if you have leftover cooked turkey, you can substitute it for the chicken. Serve with creamed peas, buttered carrots or broccoli, hot rolls and your favorite fruit salad. This might be Cranberry/Apple Salad (see Index for recipe).

CHICKEN/SWEET POTATO CASSEROLE

This is a thrifty and delicious dish to serve to a group. To simplify preparation cook the chicken a day ahead.

6 medium sweet potatoes, cooked and peeled	½ c. chopped onion
	¼ c. flour
¼ c. butter or regular margarine	2 c. chicken broth
	1 (10 oz.) pkg. frozen peas
½ tsp. salt	3 c. cubed cooked chicken
¼ c. milk	(2½- to 3-lb. broiler-fryer)
¼ c. chicken fat	

Mash sweet potatoes with butter, salt and milk. (To cook them, scrub sweet potatoes, but do not peel. Cook in a little salted water 30 to 35 minutes, until tender. Drain. Hold on fork and peel.)

Melt chicken fat (add butter if necessary) in large saucepan. Add onion and cook until soft. Blend in flour to make smooth mixture. Add chicken broth and cook, stirring constantly, until mixture comes to a boil. Add peas and cook just until separated. Add chicken and heat until mixture is bubbly.

Turn into greased 3-qt. casserole. Top with fluffy ring of sweet potatoes around the edge. Bake in 350° oven 30 to 35 minutes, until bubbly. Makes 8 servings.

Memo to Meal Planner: Serve with hot rolls, molded Vegetable/ Cranberry Salad with Chocolate Oatmeal Cake for dessert (see Index for recipes). If your budget permits, top cake servings with vanilla ice cream.

Special Scalloped Corn with Chicken

Practically every country kitchen cherishes at least one special recipe for scalloped corn. Often you find surprises in it, such as scraps of leftovers like chicken, ham and cheese. A good example is chicken-corn scallop, a favorite of a Minnesota woman, who calls it Chicken/Corn Hot Dish. In her honor we christened her specialty Minnesota Chicken/Corn Hot Dish. The recipe for it follows.

She uses leftover chicken and either her home-canned or commercially canned corn to make it. When she has ½ c. chicken broth in her refrigerator or freezer, she combines it with an equal amount of milk for the liquid. Otherwise she uses all milk.

MINNESOTA CHICKEN/CORN HOT DISH

What a wonderful treat—corn and chicken scalloped together.

¼ c. finely chopped onion	½ c. chicken broth
2 tblsp. finely chopped green pepper	1 egg, beaten
	1½ c. coarse cracker crumbs
1 tblsp. butter or regular margarine	1½ c. diced cooked chicken
	1 tsp. salt
1 (1 lb. 1 oz.) can cream style corn	Dash of pepper
	1 tblsp. melted butter or
½ c. milk	regular margarine

Cook onion and green pepper in 1 tblsp. butter in saucepan until soft. Add corn, milk, chicken broth and egg. Mix, then add 1 c. cracker crumbs, chicken, salt and pepper. Heat, stirring, but do not boil. Turn into greased 1½-qt. casserole. Toss remaining ½ c. cracker crumbs with 1 tblsp. melted butter. Sprinkle over corn mixture. Bake in 350° oven 25 to 30 minutes. Makes 6 servings.

Memo to Meal Planner: Serve with buttered peas and carrots, hot rolls and your favorite molded cranberry salad. Cranberry/Apple Salad makes an ideal choice. Cottage Cheese Cupcakes are good for dessert (see Index for recipes).

MACARONI AND CHEESE WITH CHICKEN

Two cups cooked chicken, a bit of chicken broth and mixed vegetables from freezer make macaroni and cheese a new dish.

1 (10 oz.) pkg. frozen mixed vegetables	¼ tsp. Worcestershire sauce
	2 c. chopped cooked chicken
⅔ c. chicken broth	1 (7 oz.) pkg. elbow macaroni, cooked and drained
1 (10¾ oz.) can condensed cream of chicken soup	
	½ c. dry bread crumbs
2 c. shredded process American cheese (8 oz.)	2 tblsp. melted butter or regular margarine
¼ tsp. poultry seasoning	

Cook vegetables in chicken broth in saucepan until they can be separated; bring to a full boil. Reduce heat and stir in chicken soup until blended. Add cheese and cook, stirring constantly, until cheese is melted. Stir in poultry seasoning, Worcestershire sauce and chicken.

Combine chicken mixture and cooked macaroni in greased 2-qt. casserole. Toss together crumbs and butter. Sprinkle over top. Bake in 350° oven 30 to 35 minutes. Makes 6 servings.

Memo to Meal Planner: If you have Stuffing Mix on hand, you can crush the cubes and use them instead of the bread crumbs; omit the poultry seasoning in recipe. Serve this main dish with Four-season Bean Salad (see Index for recipes). End the meal with canned fruit and cookies. Wonderful supper for a blustery, cold evening!

Chicken Livers, Chinese Style

Country women, when they put chickens in their freezers, package the livers separately. You can build a supply of chicken livers in a similar way even though you buy and use one chicken at a time. Save out the liver, package it in plastic wrap, drop into a jar, cover and freeze. In kitchens where chicken is a staple food, a pound of chicken livers, required to make this delightful oriental dish, accumulates faster than you might think.

Include hot rice in the menu along with Herbed Scalloped Corn (or buttered corn), molded Country Vegetable Salad and for dessert, lemon-glazed Cottage Cheese Cupcakes (see Index for recipes). All you need to complete the feast is hot tea. Or do you prefer coffee?

CHICKEN LIVERS, CHINESE STYLE

Pineapple and tender-crisp vegetables add color and texture.

1 lb. chicken livers	1 tblsp. soy sauce
⅓ c. flour	3 tblsp. brown sugar
½ tsp. salt	2 tblsp. cornstarch
½ tsp. ground ginger	1 c. bias-sliced celery
3 tblsp. salad oil	½ c. green onions and tops
1 (13¼ oz.) can pineapple	(1″ pieces)
tidbits	1 green pepper, cut in 1″
Water	squares
2 chicken bouillon cubes	Hot cooked rice
3 tblsp. vinegar	

Wash chicken livers; pat dry with paper toweling. Shake in paper or plastic bag with flour, salt and ginger. Brown in hot oil in skillet.

Meanwhile, drain pineapple, saving syrup. Add enough water to syrup to make 1½ c. Heat to boiling; add bouillon cubes and stir until dissolved. Stir in vinegar and soy sauce.

Blend together brown sugar and cornstarch; gradually blend in pineapple liquid.

Add celery, onions, green pepper and pineapple to browned livers. Add sauce and bring to a boil, stirring constantly. Reduce heat, cover and simmer 7 to 10 minutes, until vegetables are tender-crisp. Serve over hot cooked rice. Makes 6 servings.

TURKEY DRUMSTICK PIE

Turkey drumsticks never tasted better. You'll find it easier to remove meat from simmered than from roast turkey. When shopping, consider turkey legs—often an economical buy.

4 turkey legs (about 3 lbs.)	½ c. chopped onion
4 c. water	1 c. frozen loose-pack peas
1½ tsp. salt	⅓ c. flour
¼ tsp. pepper	1 c. water
1½ c. sliced peeled carrots	1 tsp. salt
1 c. cubed peeled potatoes	Biscuit Topping
½ c. chopped celery	

Combine turkey legs, 4 c. water, 1½ tsp. salt and pepper in large skillet. Cover and simmer 2 to 2½ hours, until turkey is tender. Remove turkey from broth; strip meat from bone. Discard skin and bones.

Add water to broth to make 3 cups, if necessary. Add carrots, potatoes, celery and onion; simmer about 15 minutes, until vegetables barely are tender. Add peas and turkey meat.

Blend together flour, 1 c. water and 1 tsp. salt. Add to turkey mixture and cook, stirring constantly, until mixture comes to a boil.

Meanwhile, prepare Biscuit Topping.

Place bubbling, hot turkey mixture in greased 2½-qt. casserole. Top with biscuits. Bake in 450° oven 12 to 15 minutes, until biscuits are golden brown. Makes 8 servings.

Biscuit Topping: Sift together 2 c. flour, 3 tsp. baking powder and 1 tsp. salt. Cut in ¼ c. shortening until mixture resembles coarse crumbs. Stir in ¾ c. milk. Turn out on lightly floured surface. Knead 6 to 8 times. Roll dough to ½" thickness. Cut with floured cutter.

Memo to Meal Planner: Serve this tempting, biscuit-topped pie with winter squash, Apple/Pineapple Salad and a make-ahead dessert, such as Cherry/Cheese Torte or Frosty Lemon Squares (see Index for recipes). If the turkey legs you use weigh more than 3 lbs., you may need to use a larger casserole.

DEVILED TURKEY PIE

Extra-delicious way to salvage leftover turkey or chicken. When you spoon this main dish onto serving plates, the creamy turkey mixture spreads over the Corn Bread Topping. It's really good eating.

¼ c. chopped onion
¼ c. butter or regular
  margarine
¼ c. flour
1 tsp. salt
⅛ tsp. pepper
2½ c. reconstituted nonfat dry
  milk

2 chicken bouillon cubes
1 tblsp. prepared mustard
1 tsp. Worcestershire sauce
3 c. cubed cooked turkey or
  chicken
1 (10 oz.) pkg. frozen peas
  and carrots
Corn Bread Topping

Cook onion in butter until soft. Blend in flour, salt and pepper. Add milk and cook, stirring constantly, until mixture comes to a boil. Add bouillon cubes, mustard, Worcestershire sauce, turkey and peas and carrots. Heat until bubbling; pour into greased 3-qt. casserole.

Meanwhile, prepare batter for Corn Bread Topping. Top casserole with cornmeal batter. Bake in 425° oven 30 to 35 minutes. Makes 6 to 8 servings.

Corn Bread Topping: Sift together 1 c. flour, 2 tblsp. sugar, 4 tsp. baking powder and ¾ tsp. salt. Stir in 1 c. yellow cornmeal. Add 2 eggs, beaten, 1 c. reconstituted nonfat dry milk and ¼ c. shortening. Beat just until batter is smooth (do not overbeat).

Memo to Meal Planner: Good companions are mashed winter squash or sweet potatoes and your favorite apple or cabbage salad.

TURKEY MEAT BALLS

Ground turkey, which contains complete protein at comparatively low cost, appears in some supermarkets many times during the year, especially after the holidays. It is made with frozen turkey. The key to success in making delicious dishes with it is to provide moisture. The turkey is very lean; it can be dry if not handled properly. We give you two main dishes calling for the thrifty ground turkey balls— Sweet-sour Turkey and Turkey Pilaf. Experiment, and find other delicious ways to include them in your recipes.

1½ lbs. ground turkey	¾ c. fine dry bread crumbs
½ c. milk	1½ tsp. salt
2 eggs, beaten	Dash of pepper

Thoroughly combine turkey, milk, eggs, bread crumbs, salt and pepper. Using 1 tblsp. mixture at a time, roll into small balls. Use as recipe directs. Makes 36 to 40.

SWEET-SOUR TURKEY

Sweet-sour, pineapple-soy sauce complements bland turkey that goes glamorous in this delicious oriental-type dish. Serve it to company.

1 recipe Turkey Meat Balls	¼ c. vinegar
¼ c. brown sugar, firmly packed	1 tblsp. soy sauce
	1 chicken bouillon cube
3 tblsp. cornstarch	1 onion, thinly sliced and separated into rings
¼ tsp. salt	
1 (1 lb. 4 oz.) can pineapple chunks	1 green pepper, cut in narrow strips
1½ c. water	Hot cooked rice

Place Turkey Meat Balls close together, but not touching, in greased 15½ × 10½ × 1″ pan. Bake in 375° oven 25 minutes.

Meanwhile, blend together brown sugar, cornstarch and salt in saucepan. Drain pineapple, reserving syrup. Add syrup to brown sugar mixture and blend thoroughly. Stir in water, vinegar, soy sauce and bouillon cube. Cook over medium heat, stirring constantly, until mixture comes to a boil and is clear.

Place pineapple chunks and Turkey Meat Balls in large skillet. Pour sauce over. Simmer 20 minutes. Add onion rings and green pepper strips; cover and cook 2 minutes longer, or until onion and pepper are tender-crisp. Serve over hot rice. Makes 6 servings.

Memo to Meal Planner: You can bake the Turkey Meat Balls ahead, cool and refrigerate them for a few days or freeze them to use weeks later. Then when you want to fix Sweet-sour Turkey, all you have to do is add them to the sweet-sour mixture and simmer 20 minutes, 25 to 30 minutes if frozen, while the rice cooks. Green peas are a pleasing accompaniment, as is a tray of relishes. Crisp home-baked almond cookies and tea answer for dessert eloquently.

TURKEY PILAF

One of the best ways to serve economical ground turkey.

1 recipe Turkey Meat Balls
1½ c. uncooked rice
¼ c. butter or regular
   margarine
1 green pepper
1 c. chopped onion
1 (10¾ oz.) can condensed
   cream of chicken soup

⅓ c. milk
1 (13¾ oz.) can chicken
   broth (1¾ c.)
1½ tsp. salt
¼ tsp. pepper

Place Turkey Meat Balls in greased 2½-qt. casserole.

Cook rice in butter in skillet until golden. Spoon over turkey balls.

Cut green pepper in half crosswise. Cut one half in rings and re-serve; chop the other half. Put onion, chopped green pepper and cream of chicken soup in skillet. Blend in milk. Then blend in chicken broth, salt and pepper; heat to boiling. Pour over rice and turkey in casserole; stir gently to mix well. Cover and bake in 375° oven 45 minutes. Uncover; top with green pepper rings. Bake 10 minutes longer. Makes 8 servings.

CREAMED TURKEY WITH HERBED STUFFING

Ground turkey and tasty stuffing outwit the food budget. A way for your family to enjoy turkey and stuffing with little work and at a low cost. While it is not the same as the Thanksgiving roast turkey with stuffing, it makes mighty good eating.

Herbed Stuffing:

1 c. chopped celery
½ c. chopped onion
¼ c. butter or regular margarine
3 qts. dry bread cubes (14 slices cut in ½″ cubes)
1½ tsp. salt
½ tsp. rubbed sage
¼ tsp. pepper
¼ tsp. dried rosemary leaves, crushed
¼ tsp. dried thyme leaves, crushed

2 eggs, beaten
1 (13¾ oz.) can chicken broth

Creamed Turkey:

1 lb. ground turkey
¼ c. butter or regular margarine
¼ c. flour
1¼ c. milk
1 c. frozen loose-pack peas
1 tblsp. parsley flakes
1 tsp. salt
⅛ tsp. pepper

To make stuffing, cook celery and onion in butter until soft. Combine in large bowl with bread cubes, salt, sage, pepper, rosemary and thyme.

Blend together eggs and 1 c. chicken broth. Reserve remaining ¾ c. broth to use in creamed turkey. Stir egg-broth mixture into bread cubes. Turn into greased 8″ square pan. Bake in 350° oven 45 minutes.

Meanwhile, prepare creamed turkey. Lightly brown ground turkey in butter in skillet. Blend in flour and cook 1 minute. Add reserved ¾ c. chicken broth and milk. Cook, stirring, until mixture comes to a boil. Stir in peas, parsley, salt and pepper. Simmer 3 to 5 minutes, or until peas are cooked. (Peas may be omitted, but the creamed turkey is colorless without them; they also add flavor).

To serve, cut stuffing into 6 pieces. Top with creamed turkey. Makes 6 servings.

Memo to Meal Planner: Among the vegetables that make a good companion to the turkey are broccoli, carrots, winter squash and sweet potatoes. If you serve broccoli or carrots, either of which provides the daily serving of a green or yellow vegetable, you can end the feast with pumpkin, squash or sweet potato pie.

A True Fish Story

Many homemakers living in inland regions and wives of meat-and-potato men are experts with meats, but lack experience in handling packages of frozen fish fillets. First, keep the fish frozen in its original wrapper until ready to use. Then thaw it, without unwrapping, in the refrigerator for an hour or two, or, if in a big hurry, in cold water (still unwrapped). Thaw it only until the fillets or pieces separate easily. Cook at once.

Fish, unlike meat, is tender before you cook it. The purpose of cooking is to bring out flavor, improve texture and coagulate the protein as you coagulate the whites when you poach eggs. To poach fish cook it in water or other liquid. In First-choice Fish Loaf, you poach the fillets before you combine them with the other ingredients. This takes from 5 to 10 minutes. Then bake the mixture; you have a superb platter treat that even the most ardent meat fans praise.

Cook fish only until it flakes easily, or until it comes up in layers when you insert a fork and lift it. It then is opaque or has a milky-white color. Overcooking spoils both flavor and texture.

BAKED FISH FILLETS WITH CHEESE

This will sell fish to those who claim they don't care for it.

2 lbs. fresh sole fillets, or frozen fillets, thawed	3 tblsp. butter or regular margarine
3 tblsp. melted butter or regular margarine	3 tblsp. flour
	¾ c. milk
1 tsp. salt	1 c. shredded Cheddar cheese
1 tsp. seasoned salt	(4 oz.)
⅛ tsp. pepper	Paprika
½ c. milk	

Coat both sides of fish fillets with melted butter. Place in 12×7× 2″ baking dish. Sprinkle with salt, seasoned salt and pepper. Pour ½ c. milk over fillets. Bake in 350° oven 25 minutes, or until fish flakes with a fork.

Meanwhile, melt 3 tblsp. butter in saucepan. Blend in flour. Add

¾ c. milk and cook, stirring constantly, until mixture comes to a boil. Reduce heat and stir in cheese. Continue cooking and stirring until cheese is melted.

Remove fish from oven and pour off pan liquid. Stir ½ c. liquid into cheese mixture. Pour cheese sauce over fish; sprinkle with paprika. Broil until sauce is bubbly. Makes 6 to 8 servings.

Memo to Meal Planner: For accompaniments, serve your favorite coleslaw, Homemade Stewed Tomatoes, and Lemon Crisp Supreme for dessert. Since men like potatoes with fish, you may wish to add them to the menu in some form. If you have Frozen Hashed Brown Potatoes on hand, they will help make this fish dinner memorable (see Index for recipes).

GOLDEN BROILED FLOUNDER

A good way to cook both frozen and fresh fish fillets.

2 lbs. flounder or other fish fillets, frozen or fresh	2 tblsp. finely chopped onion
⅓ c. salad oil	1 tblsp. parsley flakes
1 tsp. salt	½ c. mayonnaise or salad dressing
¼ tsp. pepper	2 egg whites, stiffly beaten
2 egg yolks, beaten	

Thaw fish fillets if frozen. Skin if necessary and cut in serving-size pieces.

Combine oil, salt and pepper.

Combine egg yolks, onion, parsley and mayonnaise; fold in egg whites.

Place fish on oiled broiler pan; brush with half of oil mixture. Broil about 3″ from source of heat 3 to 4 minutes. Turn carefully and brush with remaining oil mixture. Broil 3 to 4 minutes or until fish flakes easily when tested with a fork. Top fish with mayonnaise mixture and broil 5″ from source of heat 1 to 3 minutes, or until golden brown. Serve immediately. Makes 6 servings.

Memo to Meal Planner: For a delicious fish dinner, serve with buttered broccoli, Creamed Potatoes with Dill and Baked Cherry Pudding (see Index for recipes). Bake pudding before you start grilling fish.

FISH/MACARONI CASSEROLE

Marvelous way to stretch 1 lb. fish fillets to serve 8. Two kinds of cheese contribute flavor and boost the protein.

1 lb. fish fillets, fresh or frozen, thawed
3 tblsp. butter or regular margarine
1 tblsp. parsley flakes
1 tsp. onion salt
1 (7 oz.) pkg. elbow macaroni
1 (10¾ oz.) can condensed cream of mushroom soup

1½ c. creamed cottage cheese
¼ c. milk
1 c. frozen peas
1 tsp. instant minced onion
⅛ tsp. pepper
1 c. shredded process American cheese (4 oz.)

Spread fish fillets with mixture of butter, parsley and onion salt. Roll up.

Meanwhile, cook macaroni as directed on package; drain.

Combine soup, cottage cheese, milk, peas, onion and pepper. Heat to boiling. Stir in drained macaroni. Place half of macaroni mixture in greased 2-qt. casserole.

Cut fish rolls into 1″ slices. Arrange on top of macaroni in casserole. Top with remaining macaroni mixture. Bake in 350° oven about 40 minutes, until bubbly. Remove from oven and sprinkle with cheese. Return to oven about 3 minutes, just to melt cheese. Serves 8.

Memo to Meal Planner: Serve with Molded Tomato Salad or sliced tomatoes if in season. If a dessert is desired, consider Old-fashioned Cottage Pudding with Lemon Sauce (see Index for recipes). The pudding and casserole bake at the same temperature.

BAKED FISH WITH STUFFING

The lemon in stuffing gives this main dish superior flavor.

2 (1 lb.) pkgs. frozen fish fillets
½ c. finely chopped celery
¼ c. finely chopped onion
3 tblsp. butter or regular
    margarine
4 c. dry bread cubes
1 tblsp. parsley flakes
½ tsp. salt

⅛ tsp. pepper
½ tsp. grated lemon peel
2 tblsp. lemon juice
1 tblsp. melted butter or regular
    margarine
¼ tsp. salt
Paprika

Partially thaw fish (about 2 hours at room temperature).

Cook celery and onion in 3 tblsp. butter until soft. Combine with bread cubes, parsley, ½ tsp. salt, pepper, lemon peel and juice.

Slice each block of partially thawed fish in half through the center, making 4 thin rectangular pieces about ½" thick. Place 2 pieces side by side in greased 11×7×1½" baking pan. Top with stuffing, then with remaining 2 pieces of fish. Brush with 1 tblsp. melted butter and sprinkle with ¼ tsp. salt. Bake in 350° oven 25 to 30 minutes, or until fish flakes easily with fork. Sprinkle with paprika. Makes 6 servings.

Memo to Meal Planner: The stuffing is on the dry side. If you prefer a moist stuffing, add a little hot water. Serve with Cabbage Skillet, creamed peas and Refrigerator Vegetable Salad or Molded Tomato Salad. If you wish to serve a dessert, Cherry Crisp is a happy selection. Bake it ahead and reheat in oven after it is turned off and fish is removed for serving. The dessert will be faintly warm by the time to serve it. (See Index for recipes.)

BAKED PERCH FILLETS

Fish bakes fast—in about 15 minutes. It tastes wonderful.

2 lbs. perch fillets, fresh or
    frozen, thawed
½ c. Italian salad dressing

1 c. crushed potato chips
½ c. shredded Cheddar cheese
    (2 oz.)

Roll fillets in salad dressing. Place skin side down in a single layer in 15½×10½×1" baking pan.

Combine potato chips and cheese; sprinkle over fish fillets. Bake in 500° oven 10 to 15 minutes, or until fish flakes easily with a fork. Makes 6 servings.

Memo to Meal Planner: For a quick, praiseworthy meal, give this fast-fix fish the spotlight. Team it with Creamed Potatoes with Dill and a tossed green or gorgeous Vegetable/Orange Salad. If you want to serve a second hot vegetable, it could be Stir-fried Broccoli or green beans. Extra-easy Cherry Crisp makes the perfect dessert (see Index for recipes). Dovetail the preparation of these dishes and you will get dinner in less than an hour. Bake the dessert first and set aside to keep warm. Meanwhile, put the potatoes on to cook and get the salad ready to toss. Start cooking the green beans or broccoli and put fish in oven. You will love sharing this dinner with friends.

FIRST-CHOICE FISH LOAF

Distinctive way to serve cod fillets, and one of the best.

1 lb. frozen cod fillets, thawed	½ tsp. dried tarragon leaves,
Water	crushed
¼ c. chopped onion	⅛ tsp. pepper
¼ c. chopped green pepper	2 egg yolks, slightly beaten
¼ c. chopped celery	½ c. milk
1 c. fine bread crumbs	⅓ c. melted butter or regular
1 tblsp. parsley flakes	margarine
½ tsp. salt	2 egg whites, stiffly beaten

Cover fillets with water. Bring to a boil, reduce heat, cover and simmer 5 to 10 minutes, until fish flakes easily. Cool and flake.

Combine fish with onion, green pepper, celery, bread crumbs, parsley, salt, tarragon and pepper.

Combine egg yolks, milk and melted butter. Stir into fish mixture. Fold in egg whites. Turn into well-greased 9×5×3″ loaf pan.

Set in pan of hot water. Bake in 375° oven about 40 minutes, until set. Makes 6 servings.

Memo to Meal Planner: For a fish dinner to make you proud, spoon creamed peas, made with 1 (1 lb.) can peas and 1 c. medium white sauce, over slices of fish loaf. Have a pineapple-cottage cheese salad (mounds of cottage cheese with shredded carrots on canned pineapple slices), cake for dessert and milk to drink. If you want an appetizer, serve chilled tomato juice.

PAN-FRIED FISH

If your family likes fried fish best, you'll prize this recipe.

2 lbs. frozen haddock fillets, thawed
½ tsp. salt
½ c. instant mashed potatoes (not reconstituted)
6 tblsp. salad oil

1 (13¾ oz.) can chicken broth
2½ tblsp. instant mashed potatoes (not reconstituted)
2 tsp. parsley flakes
1 tsp. instant minced onion
1 tblsp. lemon juice

Separate fish fillets; cut in serving-size portions.

Combine salt and ½ c. instant mashed potatoes. Roll fish fillets in potatoes to coat well. Brown half the fillets on both sides in half the oil in large skillet. Arrange in deep ovenproof platter or shallow casserole and keep warm in low oven.

Brown remaining fillets in remaining oil. Place on platter with other fillets and return to oven.

Combine remaining ingredients in skillet; stir until mixture comes to a boil. Pour hot sauce over fish. Makes 6 servings.

Memo to Meal Planner: Complete the menu with Scalloped Corn Supreme or Herbed Scalloped Corn and your favorite salad containing tomatoes. You cannot surpass Fresh Vegetable Relish Salad for this meal during the garden season. For a dessert that pleases, consider Grandmother's Orange Cake or Speedy Chocolate Cake made with our Homemade Cake Mix (see Index for recipes).

CORNHUSKER FISH STEW

This stew is too thick to be called soup. If your family is not enthusiastic about fish stews, pass Parmesan cheese to sprinkle over the individual servings. It often is the trick that pleases.

1½ c. chopped celery	½ tsp. paprika
1 c. chopped onion	½ tsp. chili powder
1 clove garlic, minced	¼ tsp. pepper
¼ c. butter or regular margarine	1 (7 oz.) pkg. elbow
1 (1 lb. 12 oz.) can tomatoes,	spaghetti
cut up	3 c. boiling water
1 (15 oz.) can tomato sauce	2 lbs. frozen fish fillets, thawed
2 tsp. salt	and cut in 1″ pieces

Cook celery, onion and garlic in butter in large kettle or Dutch oven until soft. Add tomatoes, tomato sauce and seasonings. Cover and simmer 15 minutes. Add uncooked spaghetti and boiling water. Cover and cook slowly about 10 minutes, or until spaghetti is tender. Add fish and cook 10 minutes or until fish flakes easily when tested with a fork. Makes 8 servings.

Memo to Meal Planner: Serve this hearty main dish with a colorful salad, such as Lemon Coleslaw or Beet/Horseradish Molded Salad (see Index for recipes) and toasted French bread slices. Bake your favorite fruit crisp for dessert.

Two Great Tuna Pies

Tuna/Egg Pie and Tuna Pie with Cottage Cheese Biscuits are alike in two important ways: Both taste wonderful and both feature the obliging canned fish so handy on the shelf.

Tuna/Egg Pie comes from the oven as a one-crust pie to cut in wedges for serving. Tuna Pie with Cottage Cheese Biscuits bakes in a pan without an undercrust. It is topped with unusual biscuits that turn a beautiful brown on top during the baking. Keep both of these fish pies in mind when planning a meatless meal, remembering that fish, like meat, contains complete protein.

TUNA PIE WITH COTTAGE CHEESE BISCUITS

Tempting, tasty, nutritious main dish for a no-meat dinner.

2 c. cubed peeled potatoes	1 (9¼ oz.) can tuna, drained
½ c. chopped celery	and flaked
½ c. chopped onion	½ tsp. salt
Water	¼ tsp. pepper
1 (10 oz.) pkg. frozen mixed	Cottage Cheese Biscuits
vegetables	
2 (10¾ oz.) cans condensed	
cream of celery soup	

Cover potatoes, celery and onion with water in large saucepan; cook until barely tender. Add frozen mixed vegetables and cook until they can be separated. Drain; reserving liquid. Add water to make ½ c. cooking liquid, if necessary. Stir soup, tuna, salt, pepper and cooking liquid into vegetables. (Make Cottage Cheese Biscuits at this point.)

Heat vegetable-tuna mixture until boiling; pour into greased 13×9×2″ baking pan. Top with Cottage Cheese Biscuits. Bake in 425° oven 15 to 18 minutes. Makes 6 servings.

Cottage Cheese Biscuits: Sift together 2 c. sifted flour, 3 tsp. baking powder and ½ tsp. salt. Stir in 1 tblsp. parsley flakes. Cut in ⅓ c. shortening until mixture resembles coarse crumbs. Combine ½ c. small curd creamed cottage cheese and ½ c. milk; stir into flour mixture. Turn onto lightly floured surface; knead lightly 6 to 8 times. Cut with biscuit cutter.

Memo to Meal Planner: It is not necessary to serve a hot vegetable with the tuna pie, but if you want one for a special-occasion meal, try Orange Beets. Include Winter Bean Salad Bowl, an unusual tossed salad to step up the protein in the meal (see Index for recipes). End with milk shakes and cookies. To make milk shakes, for each serving, add a scoop of vanilla ice cream to ¾ c. reconstituted nonfat dry milk or skim milk. Blend until smooth. (If you do not have a blender, use a rotary beater.) A half banana, mashed, added to the milk and blended with it and the ice cream, offers a variation. A good way to salvage bananas that are ripening too soon.

TUNA/EGG PIE

Good enough for a supper party, easy enough for everyday.

Unbaked 9″ pie shell
6 eggs
¼ c. milk
1 (7 oz.) can tuna, drained and flaked
2 c. grated mozzarella cheese, (8 oz.)
½ tsp. dried orégano leaves, crushed
½ tsp. dried basil leaves, crushed
¼ tsp. salt
¼ tsp. pepper

Beat eggs and milk together until blended. Stir in remaining ingredients. Spoon into pie shell. Bake in 425° oven 35 to 40 minutes, until lightly browned. Serve hot. Makes 6 servings.

Memo to Meal Planner: Good accompaniments are buttered peas and carrots and a lettuce or cabbage salad. Consider having Peach-pudding Parfait for dessert (see Index for recipe).

TUNA LOAF

A good, moist fish loaf that really requires no sauce, but for company you may want to serve one just to dress it up.

2 (7 oz.) cans tuna
1 (10¾ oz.) can condensed cream of celery soup
3 egg yolks, slightly beaten
1 c. fine cracker crumbs
⅓ c. finely chopped onion
1 tblsp. parsley flakes
1 tblsp. lemon juice
⅛ tsp. pepper
3 egg whites, stiffly beaten

Combine tuna, soup, egg yolks, crumbs, onion, parsley, lemon juice and pepper. Fold in egg whites. Turn into a very well-greased 8½×4½×2½″ loaf pan. Bake in 350° oven 45 minutes or until center of loaf is firm. To serve, invert on platter. Makes 6 servings.

Memo to Meal Planner: Good foods to serve with the fish loaf are hashed brown potatoes, Homemade Stewed Tomatoes and Cabbage/ Cottage Cheese Salad. If you use Frozen Hashed Brown Potatoes (see Index for recipes), you can get them ready days or weeks ahead for last minute browning.

SEAFOOD/MACARONI BAKE

Canned cream of shrimp and celery soups and tuna add a happy change to this version of macaroni and cheese.

1 (8 oz.) pkg. elbow macaroni
½ c. chopped onion
1 tblsp. butter or regular
   margarine
1 (10¾ oz.) can condensed
   cream of shrimp soup
1 (10¾ oz.) can condensed
   cream of celery soup

⅔ c. milk
2 (7 oz.) cans tuna, drained
   and flaked
1½ c. shredded process sharp
   American cheese (6 oz.)

Cook macaroni as directed on package; drain.

Meanwhile, cook onion in butter in small skillet until soft. Combine onion mixture, soups, milk, tuna, macaroni and 1 c. of the cheese in greased 2½-qt. casserole. Bake in 350° oven 30 to 35 minutes, until mixture is hot and bubbly. Sprinkle with remaining cheese. Return to oven 3 minutes, until cheese melts. Serves 6.

COMPANY TUNASAGNE

There are many kinds of lasagne. Tuna makes one of the best.

1 c. chopped celery
½ c. chopped onion
½ c. chopped green pepper
½ c. butter or regular margarine
½ c. flour
1 tsp. salt
¼ tsp. pepper
1 qt. reconstituted nonfat dry
   milk

12 lasagne noodles
2 (7 oz.) cans tuna, drained
2 c. grated Colby or Cheddar
   cheese (8 oz.)
1 c. dry bread crumbs
3 tblsp. melted butter or regular
   margarine

Cook celery, onion and green pepper in ½ c. butter until soft, but not browned. Blend in flour, salt and pepper. Add milk and cook, stirring constantly, until mixture comes to a boil and is thickened. Remove from heat.

Meanwhile, cook noodles by package directions. Cover with cold water until noodles can be handled. Lift out, do not drain them. Place 4 noodles in bottom of greased 13×9×2″ pan. Top with ⅓ of each: tuna, cheese and sauce. Repeat layers two times. Toss bread crumbs with 3 tblsp. butter. Sprinkle over top.

Bake in 350° oven 35 minutes. Let stand in pan 10 minutes before cutting. Makes 12 servings.

Memo to Meal Planner: For 6 servings, cut recipe in half. To lower cost, use canned grated tuna.

EXCEPTIONAL TUNA PATTIES

These browned fish cakes contain soybean protein—nutritious.

⅔ c. textured vegetable protein
⅓ c. water
2 (7 oz.) cans tuna, drained
    and flaked
3 slices bread, torn in small
    pieces
½ c. finely chopped celery

¼ c. finely chopped onion
½ tsp. salt
⅛ tsp. pepper
3 eggs, beaten
2 tblsp. milk
3 tblsp. salad oil

Mix textured vegetable protein with water; stir until water is absorbed. Mix in tuna, bread, celery, onion, salt, pepper, eggs and milk. Shape mixture into patties about 3″ in diameter and ½″ thick. Brown in hot oil over medium heat 6 to 8 minutes, turning once. Makes 10 patties.

Memo to Meal Planner: Mothers who try to feed their families with foods rich in protein, especially favor this tasty, quick and inexpensive main dish. Serve for dinner with baked or other potatoes, Tender-crisp Carrots and Broccoli Salad (see Index for recipes). Skip dessert.

TASTY TUNABURGERS

If you need more than 4 sandwiches, just double the recipe.

1 egg
1 (7 oz.) can tuna, drained
½ c. dry bread crumbs
½ c. mayonnaise or salad
    dressing
2 tblsp. chopped onion

2 tblsp. sweet pickle relish
1 tblsp. melted butter or regular
    margarine
4 hamburger buns
Lettuce
4 tomato slices

Beat egg; stir in tuna, bread crumbs, mayonnaise, onion and pickle relish. Form into 4 patties. Brown on both sides in butter in skillet. Serve between split buns, topping each tuna patty with lettuce and a tomato slice. Makes 4 servings.

Memo to Meal Planner: Select a firm, ripe tomato to slice and crisp lettuce leaves to insert in these sandwiches. The flavor and color of the tomatoes and the texture of the lettuce deserve considerable credit for the enthusiastic reception the burgers get. When frost cuts off the supply of home-grown tomatoes, increasing their cost, or for a variation at any season, make open-face sandwiches with the patties and bun halves. Spoon creamed peas over them, and presto, you have tempting hot knife-and-fork sandwiches.

WISCONSIN HOT DISH

For a tasty change substitute 1 c. cooked chicken for tuna.

½ c. uncooked rice
1 (12 oz.) can whole kernel corn, drained
1 (7 oz.) can tuna, drained
1 c. shredded process American cheese (4 oz.)
1 (10¾ oz.) can condensed cream of mushroom soup
1 c. small curd creamed cottage cheese
1 c. Stuffing Mix (see Index) or dry bread crumbs
¼ c. melted butter or regular margarine

Cook rice by package directions; drain. Combine with corn, tuna, shredded cheese, mushroom soup and cottage cheese. Turn into greased 1½-qt. casserole.

Crush Stuffing Mix and toss with butter, sprinkle over top. Bake in 350° oven about 35 minutes, until bubbly. Makes 6 servings.

Memo to Meal Planner: Serve this Sunday-best casserole with a green vegetable or scalloped tomatoes and rye bread.

COTTAGE TUNA SANDWICHES

Pronounced tuna and mild cottage cheese flavors complement each other in these sandwiches. Vegetables add crispness.

1 (7 oz.) can tuna, drained and flaked	½ c. chopped celery
	¼ c. chopped green onion
1 c. creamed cottage cheese	6 red radishes, sliced
½ c. mayonnaise or salad dressing	6 hamburger buns, split and toasted

Combine tuna, cottage cheese, mayonnaise and vegetables. Serve between toasted bun halves. Makes 6 sandwiches.

Memo to Meal Planner: Serve with cups of hot chicken soup and sliced tomatoes for lunch.

NEW-STYLE SALMON SOUFFLÉ

With the demand for salmon greater than the supply, this is a good way to keep it in your menus. Cottage cheese extends the fish.

1 (7¾ oz.) can pink salmon	½ tsp. salt
2 tblsp. butter or regular margarine	¼ tsp. dill weed
	⅛ tsp. pepper
¼ c. finely chopped onion	3 egg yolks, beaten
2 tblsp. flour	1 c. creamed cottage cheese
¾ c. milk	3 egg whites, stiffly beaten

Place salmon with liquid in bowl; remove bones. Mash salmon into liquid.

Melt butter in saucepan; add onion and cook until soft. Blend in flour. Add milk and cook, stirring constantly, until mixture comes to a boil. Stir in salt, dill weed and pepper.

Beat together egg yolks and cottage cheese; stir in hot mixture and salmon. Fold in egg whites. Turn into a 1½-qt. casserole. Bake in 300° oven 60 to 70 minutes, or until knife inserted halfway between center and edge comes out clean. Makes 5 or 6 servings.

Memo to Meal Planner: The soufflé is a great dish, but be ready to serve it when you take it from the oven. It is a good idea to have a made-ahead dessert ready to serve. Choose from Orange County

Rice Pudding, Pink Grapefruit Pie or Lemon Crisp Supreme (see Index for recipes). Include hot rolls, a relish plate and buttered peas and carrots in the menu.

MACKEREL LOAF WITH EGG SAUCE

You'll be surprised at the tastiness of this budget fish loaf.

1 (15 oz.) can mackerel	2 tblsp. chopped onion
1½ c. coarse cracker crumbs	2 eggs, beaten
¾ c. milk	2 tblsp. melted butter or regular
½ c. chopped gherkins or sweet	margarine
pickle relish	Egg Sauce

Drain mackerel; reserve liquid for Egg Sauce. Flake mackerel.

Combine mackerel with crumbs, milk, gherkins, onion, eggs and butter. Spoon into greased 9×5×3″ loaf pan; pack tightly. Bake in 350° oven 50 minutes. Spoon Egg Sauce over servings of mackerel loaf, or pour into pitcher and pass with loaf. Makes 6 servings.

Egg Sauce: Make sauce while fish loaf bakes. Melt 3 tblsp. butter in saucepan; blend in 3 tblsp. flour to make a smooth paste. Add enough milk to reserved liquid drained from mackerel to make 1½ c. Stir milk mixture into saucepan and cook, stirring constantly, until sauce comes to a boil. Stir in ¼ tsp. salt and 2 hard-cooked eggs, chopped; heat. Serve with mackerel loaf.

Memo to Meal Planner: The pickle adds interesting flavor to the fish loaf, the eggs dress up the sauce. Compare the cost of mackerel with other canned fish and you will know why it is a bargain in good eating. Serve with buttered peas, tomato or cabbage salad and a lemon dessert. For an elegant meal ending that glorifies the entire meal, have Lemon Crisp Supreme (see Index for recipe).

CHAPTER 5

Eggs and Cheese

The higher cost of living and the increased demand for protein-rich foods is giving eggs and cheese new importance in menus.

The recipes in this chapter show what happens when you give country women eggs and cheese, a little time in the kitchen and the determination to hold food prices in line without sacrificing the quality of their meals.

Creative cooks usually start by taking tried and true favorite dishes and adding their own touches. Deviled Eggs with Broccoli and Deviled Egg Casserole, two main dishes you will want to make, are good examples. And so is Chili with Cheese Soufflé, a casserole of Mexican-type chili with cheese soufflé baked on top. Egg salad departs from its traditional role as a sandwich filling to win acclaim as Egg Salad Casserole, a hearty main dish that requires only 30 minutes in the oven to heat thoroughly. Be sure to try Eggs in Vinaigrette Sauce to extend the platter of cold meats.

Cottage cheese, relatively low-cost, is combined with somewhat higher priced and more flavorful cheeses in the Egg Lasagne recipe—a delicious dish you will enjoy serving to company as well as the family. Spaghetti Supper Special is another two-cheese special that wins praise.

With sandwiches assuming a more impressive role as the main dish for lunch or supper, it is natural that eggs and cheese provide tasty, nutritious fillings. People of all ages praise Egg Salad Toast-wiches hot off the griddle. Broiled Cheese on Rye sandwiches are especially popular in summer when fresh tomatoes are in season.

With millions of people around the world hungry for more protein in their meals, American country women are developing new ways to serve eggs and cheese, as this collection of their favorite recipes reflects. You will find more recipes using eggs and cheese as ingredients in other chapters of this book as well.

DEVILED EGG CASSEROLE

Appetizing main dish for supper any time—great for spring.

8 hard-cooked eggs	2 tblsp. flour
¼ c. mayonnaise or salad dressing	1⅓ c. milk
1 tsp. vinegar	1 (10¾ oz.) can condensed cream of chicken soup
½ tsp. salt	½ c. shredded process American cheese (2 oz.)
½ tsp. paprika	
½ tsp. curry powder (optional)	1 c. dry bread crumbs
2 tblsp. melted butter or regular margarine	2 tblsp. melted butter or regular margarine

Cut eggs in halves lengthwise; remove yolks and mash. Blend together mayonnaise, vinegar, salt, paprika and curry powder. Mix with egg yolks. Refill egg whites with mixture. Place in a 10×6×1½″ baking dish.

Combine 2 tblsp. butter and flour in saucepan. Blend in milk and soup. Cook, stirring constantly, until mixture comes to a boil. Add cheese; stir until cheese melts. Pour sauce over eggs.

Toss bread crumbs with 2 tblsp. butter; sprinkle over top of eggs. Bake in 350° oven about 25 minutes, until mixture is bubbly. Makes 6 to 8 servings.

Memo to Meal Planner: To complete the supper menu, have buttered peas, Apple Coleslaw and Chocolate Oatmeal Cake (see Index for recipes). If it's a lovely, cool spring evening, substitute wilted garden lettuce for the coleslaw.

DEVILED EGGS WITH BROCCOLI

A pleasing way to include a green vegetable in the day's meals! Teamed with eggs and cheese sauce, the main dish is as nutritious as it is appealing.

6 hard-cooked eggs	2 tblsp. flour
3 tblsp. mayonnaise or salad dressing	½ tsp. dry mustard
1 tsp. vinegar	¼ tsp. salt
⅛ tsp. salt	1 c. milk
⅛ tsp. dry mustard	1 (8 oz.) pkg. process Swiss cheese, diced
2 (10 oz.) pkgs. frozen chopped broccoli	Paprika
2 tblsp. butter or regular margarine	

Slice eggs lengthwise in halves; remove yolks. Mash yolks and blend with mayonnaise, vinegar, ⅛ tsp. salt and ⅛ tsp. dry mustard. Spoon into egg whites.

Cook broccoli in a little salted water just until pieces separate.

Meanwhile, melt butter in saucepan; blend in flour, ½ tsp. dry mustard and ¼ tsp. salt. Add milk and cook over medium heat, stirring, until mixture comes to a boil. Stir in cheese and continue to stir until melted. Remove from heat.

Place broccoli in greased 1½-qt. casserole. Top with eggs. Pour cheese sauce over and sprinkle with paprika. Bake in 350° oven 20 to 25 minutes, until heated through. Makes 6 servings.

Memo to Meal Planner: Buttered toast and fruit salad are delightful accompaniments. Have chocolate pudding or cake for dessert.

EGG SCALLOP WITH PEAS

Great supper dish to make with foods kept on hand in kitchen.

⅓ c. butter or regular
  margarine
⅓ c. flour
2½ c. milk
1½ tsp. salt
⅛ tsp. pepper
⅛ tsp. paprika
2 tsp. grated onion

½ c. grated process American
  cheese (2 oz.)
9 hard-cooked eggs, sliced
1 (1 lb.) can peas, drained
½ c. fine dry bread crumbs
2 tblsp. melted butter or regular
  margarine

Melt ⅓ c. butter in skillet; blend in flour. Add milk all at once and cook, stirring, until mixture thickens. Stir in salt, pepper, paprika, onion and cheese. Cook, stirring, over low heat until cheese is melted. Add eggs and peas; heat. Turn into 2-qt. casserole.

Toss together crumbs and 2 tblsp. melted butter; sprinkle over top of casserole. Bake in 400° oven 25 to 30 minutes, until mixture is bubbly. Makes 6 servings.

Memo to Meal Planner: Serve this main dish with buttered carrots, chilled canned pears topped with cubes of jellied cranberries and spicy cookies for a delightful supper that children especially enjoy. If you have White Sauce Mix (see Index) in your refrigerator, omit ⅓ c. butter and flour from recipe for Egg Scallop with Peas. Reduce salt to ½ tsp. Place 1½ c. White Sauce Mix in large saucepan; add milk and cook, stirring, until sauce thickens. Add the seasonings and other ingredients in the scallop and bake as recipe directs.

EGG/CLAM SCRAMBLE

Clams add a new and especially flavorful note to scrambled eggs. Serve with tomato juice.

8 eggs
1 (8 oz.) can minced clams
1 tblsp. parsley flakes
⅛ tsp. pepper

1 tblsp. lemon juice
2 tblsp. chopped onion
3 tblsp. butter or regular
  margarine

Beat eggs. Drain clams, reserving liquid. Add clams and 3 tblsp. clam juice, parsley, pepper and lemon juice to eggs.

Cook onion in butter in skillet until soft. Add egg mixture; reduce heat to low. As egg mixture starts to set on bottom and sides, lift and fold over with wide spatula so uncooked portion goes to the bottom. Cook until eggs are set throughout but still are glossy and moist. Serve like scrambled eggs or in buns for supper sandwiches. Makes 6 servings.

EGG/CLAM CHOWDER SKILLET

Surprisingly good sandwich filling—also serves as supper dish.

8 eggs, slightly beaten	⅛ tsp. pepper
1 (10¾ oz.) condensed	2 tblsp. butter or regular
Manhattan-style clam	margarine
chowder	

Combine eggs with soup and pepper.

Melt butter in 10″ skillet. Add egg mixture and cook, stirring occasionally, until eggs are just set. Makes 6 servings.

Memo to Meal Planner: Serve as filling for whole wheat sandwiches or in toasted buns if you like. Or spoon onto buttered whole wheat toast for a supper main dish. Sliced tomatoes are a good accompaniment when available; other seasons serve with tomato juice or hot tomato soup. For dessert, consider Chocolate Drop Cookies (see Index for recipe).

Famous Eggs Foo Yung

One of the quickest ways to lift your cooking out of a rut is to experiment with some world-famous dishes in your own kitchen. People in most countries do not have the abundance of food available in America. Necessity teaches them to develop intriguing ways to stretch the foods they have, especially those rich in top-quality protein.

Eggs Foo Yung is a classic example. These Chinese omelets make a little leftover cooked meat count. Even eggs, the major ingredient, have the support of less expensive vegetables—are extended by them. One difference between Chinese omelets and the fluffy kind most Americans make is their adaptability. You can cook them at mealtime, or, if you wish, make them ahead. If you liked the eggs foo yung you ate in a Chinese restaurant, or if you wish to introduce change in meals without running up the grocery bill, you will want to try the recipe that follows.

EGGS FOO YUNG

You can make these Chinese omelets several hours ahead and chill.

6 eggs	¾ c. finely chopped cooked ham
½ tsp. salt	or pork (optional)
1 tblsp. soy sauce	2 tblsp. finely chopped green
1 (1 lb.) can bean sprouts,	pepper
drained	Salad oil
1 c. finely chopped onion	Chinese Sauce

Beat eggs with salt and soy sauce. Stir in bean sprouts, onion, ham and green pepper.

Pour a little oil in small skillet. Drop 2 tblsp. egg mixture in center, spreading vegetables evenly with back of spoon. Cook over medium heat until browned on under side, 2 to 3 minutes. Turn and repeat. (You can make several omelets at a time in a large skillet, but their shape will be less attractive. To speed production, use more than one small skillet.) Drain omelets on paper toweling and keep warm in 250° oven. To serve, place on a warm platter and pour warm Chinese Sauce over. Makes 28 to 30.

Chinese Sauce: Blend together 4 tsp. cornstarch, 4 tsp. soy sauce, 2 tsp. dark molasses and 2 tsp. vinegar in small saucepan. Stir in 1 c. water and 1 chicken bouillon cube. Cook, stirring constantly, until mixture comes to a boil and bouillon cube is dissolved. Remove from heat. Serve hot. (If you make the sauce before you cook the omelets, reheat it before serving.)

Memo to Meal Planner: If you make the omelets ahead and refrigerate them, reheat in 300° oven 10 minutes before serving. Plan your menu as you would if serving regular omelets. A crisp lettuce salad is a good accompaniment and chilled pineapple chunks or pineapple sherbet ends the supper or brunch pleasantly.

EGG LASAGNE

The economy of this lasagne depends on the price of eggs.

1 c. chopped onion
1 clove garlic, minced
2 tblsp. salad oil
1 (1 lb.) can tomatoes, cut up
1 (15 oz.) can tomato sauce
1½ tsp. dried basil leaves, crushed
1 tsp. dried orégano leaves, crushed
1 tsp. salt
1 bay leaf
8 oz. lasagne noodles (about 10)
2 c. creamed cottage cheese
1 egg, slightly beaten
1 tblsp. parsley flakes
1 tsp. salt
¼ tsp. pepper
½ c. grated Parmesan cheese
10 hard-cooked eggs, sliced
12 oz. mozzarella cheese, thinly sliced

For sauce, cook onion and garlic in salad oil in large saucepan until soft. Add tomatoes, tomato sauce, basil, orégano, 1 tsp. salt and bay leaf. Simmer uncovered 30 minutes; stir occasionally. Remove bay leaf.

To prepare casserole, cook noodles according to package directions. Add cold water until noodles can be handled. Lift out; do not drain them.

Combine cottage cheese, 1 egg, parsley, 1 tsp. salt, pepper and Parmesan cheese.

Spread a third of sauce in greased 13×9×2" baking pan. Top with half of each: noodles, cottage cheese mixture, sliced hard-cooked eggs and mozzarella cheese slices. Add a third of sauce. Repeat layers. Bake in 350° oven 35 to 40 minutes. Let stand in pan 10 minutes before cutting. Makes 8 to 10 servings.

Memo to Meal Planner: Consider this different, distinctive and flavorful lasagne for a company supper. Compare its cost with that of Beef Lasagne in Chapter 3. Egg prices fluctuate and greatly affect the cost of Egg Lasagne. Serve whichever lasagne you choose with crusty bread or rolls, and make-ahead Refrigerator Vegetable Salad (see Index), an American interpretation of a mixed Italian salad. Fruit or ice cream for dessert, or chilled canned purple plums are a fine selection, too.

EGG SALAD CASSEROLE

Your family doesn't like egg salad in sandwiches? They'll like this.

8 hard-cooked eggs, chopped
1 c. frozen loose-pack peas
½ c. chopped celery
2 tblsp. chopped pimiento
2 tblsp. chopped onion
1 c. cracker crumbs
1 c. mayonnaise or salad
   dressing

⅓ c. milk
½ tsp. garlic salt
¼ tsp. pepper
½ c. cracker crumbs
2 tblsp. melted butter or regular
   margarine

Combine eggs, peas, celery, pimiento, onion, 1 c. cracker crumbs, mayonnaise, milk, garlic salt and pepper; turn into 1-qt. casserole.

Toss together ½ c. cracker crumbs and butter; sprinkle over top of casserole. Bake in 400° oven 30 minutes. Makes 6 servings.

Memo to Meal Planner: Serve for supper on a spring evening with whole wheat rolls, Green Limas with Cheese and Rhubarb Cobbler for dessert (see Index for recipes). Include a tray of little red radishes, green onions and carrot sticks in the menu. The casserole and dessert bake together.

EGG SALAD TOASTWICHES

Please youngsters and grownups alike by grilling egg salad sandwiches like French toast. Rush them hot to the table.

6 hard-cooked eggs, chopped
⅓ c. finely chopped celery
¼ c. sweet pickle relish
1 tblsp. parsley flakes
¼ c. mayonnaise or salad
   dressing
¾ tsp. salt

½ tsp. dry mustard
⅛ tsp. pepper
12 bread slices
2 eggs, slightly beaten
½ c. milk
½ tsp. salt

Combine chopped eggs, celery, pickle relish, parsley, mayonnaise, ¾ tsp. salt, mustard and pepper. Spread mixture on 6 slices of bread; top with remaining bread slices.

Blend beaten eggs, milk and ½ tsp. salt. Dip each sandwich on both sides in mixture. Cook on hot greased griddle until brown on one side; gently turn and brown other side. Serve hot. Makes 6.

Memo to Meal Planner: Feature these sandwiches in a meal without meat. If you have fresh parsley, chop and use 2 tblsp. of it instead of the instant kind. You can use the egg salad filling for cold sandwiches, but the hot, browned toastwiches are especially welcome in spring when served with garden lettuce and cups of hot potato, tomato or other soup.

EGGS IN VINAIGRETTE SAUCE

Marvelous, easy way to make hard-cooked eggs a special treat.

3 tblsp. salad oil	½ tsp. garlic salt
1½ tblsp. vinegar	⅛ tsp. pepper
2 tsp. pickle relish	6 hard-cooked eggs, peeled and
2 tsp. chopped parsley	halved
2 tsp. finely chopped onion	

Combine salad oil, vinegar, pickle relish, parsley, onion, garlic salt and pepper. Chill at least 1 hour. Shake well to mix. Spoon over hard-cooked egg halves. Makes 6 servings.

Memo to Meal Planner: Serve as a relish on the buffet table, as a salad on shredded lettuce or on a plate of cold cuts to extend meat.

DOUBLE CHEESE BAKE

Cottage cheese adds a sour cream taste that is delicious in this baked fondue.

1 tblsp. butter or regular margarine	4 egg yolks, beaten
1¼ c. milk, scalded	1 tsp. salt
2 c. small soft bread cubes	⅛ tsp. pepper
1 c. shredded process American cheese (4 oz.)	½ tsp. prepared mustard
1 c. creamed cottage cheese	½ tsp. Worcestershire sauce
	4 egg whites, stiffly beaten

Stir butter into hot milk until melted. Mix in bread cubes, American and cottage cheeses. Combine with egg yolks, salt, pepper, mustard and Worcestershire sauce. Fold in egg whites. Pour into greased 1½-qt. casserole. Set in pan of hot water and bake in 325° oven 1 hour, or until knife inserted in center comes out clean. Makes 6 servings.

Memo to Meal Planner: For luncheon serve the casserole with crusty bread or rolls or with rye bread, and a relish tray including carrot sticks. For dessert have Pineapple Rice Custard (see Index for recipe). You will have a meal to share with company.

CHEESE SPAGHETTI WITH EGGS

Quick-to-make spaghetti dish with bacon and eggs.

1 (1 lb.) pkg. spaghetti, broken up
½ c. chopped bacon ends and pieces
2 c. chopped onion
½ c. chopped green pepper (optional)

6 eggs, slightly beaten
1 tsp. salt
⅛ tsp. pepper
1 c. cubed process cheese spread (Velveeta, 4 oz.)

Cook spaghetti as directed on package; drain.

Meanwhile, cook bacon in 12″ skillet until crisp. Remove with slotted spoon and drain on paper toweling.

Cook onion and green pepper in bacon drippings until soft. Add spaghetti and toss until well mixed. Stir in eggs, salt, pepper and cheese. Cook until cheese is melted and eggs are set. Sprinkle reserved bacon on top just before serving. Makes 6 servings.

Memo to Meal Planner: For a family supper, serve this unusual substantial spaghetti dish containing eggs, as well as cheese, and flavored with just enough bacon to add its smoky flavor but not too much to the cost. Serve a vegetable salad. It might be Lemon Coleslaw, prepared in advance and refrigerated. If you choose this salad, omit the green pepper from the spaghetti main dish. How about Extra-easy Cherry Crisp (see Index for recipe) for dessert. Such a meal makes youngsters happy and guarantees no one will leave the table hungry.

CHEESE/SPAGHETTI LOAF

Spaghetti takes on a new look. The loaf slices like a charm.

2 c. elbow spaghetti	¾ tsp. salt
2 c. shredded process American cheese (8 oz.)	1 tblsp. parsley flakes
	1 tblsp. grated onion
1 (14½ oz.) can evaporated milk	1 (10¾ oz.) can condensed tomato soup
2 eggs, beaten	¼ c. milk

Cook spaghetti as directed on package; drain.

Melt cheese in evaporated milk in heavy saucepan over low heat, stirring frequently. Slowly stir into eggs. Stir in salt, parsley, onion and spaghetti. Spoon into greased 9×5×3″ loaf pan.

Bake in pan of hot water in 325° oven 45 to 50 minutes, until set. Let stand 10 minutes, then turn out of pan and slice.

Heat soup with ¼ c. milk. Serve with spaghetti loaf. Serves 8.

Memo to Meal Planner: Serve with a cabbage salad—it might be October Coleslaw. For dessert have Winter Fruit Cobbler made with the canned fruit you have (see Index for recipes).

Chili with Cheese Soufflé

Chili con carne is called simply "chili" in this book and in the area across Texas to the Pacific Ocean where it rates as one of the most important economical main dishes. To speak of chili *con carne* there marks you as a stranger.

Chili with Cheese Soufflé is a company version. If your family and friends like the chili powder taste, *you* will give thanks for the following recipe.

CHILI WITH CHEESE SOUFFLÉ

Chili goes high hat: A fluffy cheese mixture bakes on top.

1 lb. ground beef
½ c. chopped onion
2 tblsp. flour
1 tsp. salt
1 tsp. chili powder
⅓ c. butter or regular
   margarine

⅓ c. flour
1 tsp. salt
1½ c. milk
2 c. shredded process American
   cheese (8 oz.)
4 egg yolks, slightly beaten
4 egg whites, stiffly beaten

Cook beef and onion in skillet until onion is soft; do not brown. Stir in 2 tblsp. flour, 1 tsp. salt and chili powder. Place mixture in bottom of greased 2-qt. casserole.

Melt butter in saucepan. Stir in ⅓ c. flour and 1 tsp. salt. Add milk and cook, stirring constantly, until mixture comes to a boil. Add cheese and cook over low heat, stirring, until cheese melts. Blend a little of the hot mixture into egg yolks. Add to cheese mixture and blend thoroughly. Fold mixture into egg whites. Spoon lightly over chili. Bake in 350° oven 55 to 65 minutes. Makes 6 servings.

Memo to Meal Planner: Serve with a tossed salad and French bread. You may wish to select a special dessert. A good candidate is Pink Grapefruit Pie (see Index for recipe).

TWO-CHEESE/NOODLE CASSEROLE

For a meatless meal, this protein rich, two-cheese casserole makes an ideal selection. It is hearty, satisfying and flavorful.

3 eggs, beaten
2 c. cottage cheese
¼ c. milk
1½ c. shredded Cheddar cheese
   (6 oz.)
1 (10 oz.) pkg. frozen chopped
   spinach, thawed

8 oz. noodles, cooked and
   drained
½ tsp. salt
⅛ tsp. pepper
½ c. fine bread crumbs
2 tblsp. melted butter or
   regular margarine

Combine eggs and cottage cheese. Stir in milk and Cheddar cheese.

Press all liquid out of spinach and stir into cheese mixture. Stir in noodles, salt and pepper. Turn into greased 2-qt. casserole.

Toss together crumbs and butter; sprinkle over top of cheese mixture. Bake in 350° oven about 45 minutes, until set in center. Makes 6 servings.

Memo to Meal Planner: To complete the menu, have rye bread, buttered carrots and a tossed green or cabbage salad.

SPAGHETTI SUPPER SPECIAL

Every woman needs at least a few speedy substantial dishes to hurry to the table when she is busy right up to mealtime and the youngsters think they are starving. This spaghetti dish is a good example of such a wonder worker. The spaghetti package contains a packet of seasoning mix and the Parmesan cheese as well as the spaghetti. You furnish the can of tomato paste, eggs and mozzarella cheese. When the time is short, fix this fast main dish for supper.

1 (8 oz.) pkg. Italian-style spaghetti dinner	2 eggs, beaten
1 (6 oz.) can tomato paste	1 (6 oz.) pkg. sliced mozzarella cheese

Prepare spaghetti and sauce, using tomato paste, as directed on package. Combine eggs and grated Parmesan cheese from packet; add to spaghetti. Layer half of spaghetti and mozzarella cheese slices in a 9″ pie pan; repeat layers. Bake in 350° oven 10 minutes. Cut into wedges. Serve with spaghetti sauce. Makes 6 servings.

Memo to Meal Planner: If you know in advance you will have this main dish for supper, make a refrigerator salad in the morning to bring out at mealtime. Molded Country Vegetable Salad (see Index for recipe) is a super-fine choice.

BROILED CHEESE ON RYE

Sandwiches are not big—you may want to double recipe.

6 thin slices onion	¼ tsp. dried basil leaves, crushed
2 tblsp. butter or regular margarine	Seasoned salt
6 slices dark rye bread, toasted	1½ c. shredded Colby cheese (6 oz.)
6 tomato slices	

Cook onion slices in butter until soft. Divide over toasted rye bread. Top each with a tomato slice. Sprinkle lightly with basil and seasoned salt; top with cheese. Broil until cheese melts. Makes 6.

Memo to Meal Planner: The size of the rye bread loaf determines how big the sandwiches are. When the summer day is warm, serve with potato or macaroni salad and have a fruit dessert. If the price of fresh blueberries is not prohibitive, try Versatile Blueberry Kuchen (see Index for recipe.)

Cottage Cheese/Dill Bread—A Leader

One clever woman, who counts pennies when she entertains as well as for family meals, likes to feature one dish, so distinctive and delicious that it carries the rest of the menu with it to an enthusiastic reception. She calls such dishes her leaders.

She reports that this cottage cheese bread is an especially successful attention-getter in salad luncheons. Like other batter breads, this one has a deeper brown and somewhat thicker crust than kneaded yeast breads. Its texture is apt to be less even and a trifle coarser, but its nutlike taste with a miraculous mingling of dill, onion and yeast flavors is its triumph.

Having a "leader" in family meals also pays off, according to this homemaker. She frequently chooses a dessert everyone really likes, which, like the bread, is not costly and does not defeat her efforts to hold down the grocery bill.

COTTAGE CHEESE/DILL BREAD

Try these brown-beauty loaves of no-knead bread expertly sea-soned and enriched in protein by cottage cheese. Cottage Cheese/Dill Bread, like all no-knead, quick yeast breads, tastes best the day you bake it. But, it is usually good on the second day when sliced and toasted. You can use small loaf pans of a slightly differ-ent size from the one specified in the recipe; the important point is to fill them no more than half full of dough and let the dough rise only until doubled.

1 pkg. active dry yeast	2 tblsp. sugar
¼ c. warm water (110 to 115°)	2 tsp. dill seeds
2 tblsp. finely chopped onion	1 tsp. salt
2 tblsp. butter or regular margarine	¼ tsp. baking soda
	1 egg
1 c. large curd creamed cottage cheese	2½ c. flour (about)
	Melted butter (optional)

Sprinkle yeast on warm water; stir to dissolve.

Cook onion in 2 tblsp. butter until soft; do not let brown.

Heat cottage cheese over low heat or in double boiler until luke-warm. (Do not let it get warmer or the protein in the cheese will harden.) Place cottage cheese in large mixer bowl. Beat in sugar, dill seeds, salt, soda and egg. Beat well. Add onion and yeast. Beat to mix thoroughly.

Gradually add 1 c. flour, beating well after each addition. With a spoon beat in enough remaining flour, a little at a time, to make a soft dough. Place in lightly greased bowl, invert dough and let rise in a warm place (80 to 85°) until doubled. (Do not let rise more than double or the bread may fall slightly after baking. If it does rise too much, stir down and let rise a second time.) Stir down dough; it will be sticky. Turn onto lightly floured surface, cut in half and spread in 2 well-greased 8½ ×4½ ×2½″ loaf pans. Let rise in warm place only until doubled. Bake in 350° oven 40 to 50 minutes. Turn loaves onto racks. Spread tops with butter. Makes 2 loaves.

CHAPTER 6

Hearty Main-dish Soups

Hearty, main-dish soups are back in high favor. They have always been popular in country kitchens, but the higher cost of living is contributing to their general popularity. For soup-sandwich and soup-salad lunch menus, the quick soups are ideal.

Slow-cooking, substantial soups produce marvelous flavor. Inexpensive dry beans, lentils and peas—excellent sources for vegetable protein—often team with a little meat to make the soups nutritious as well as thrifty. These sturdy soups simmer to perfection with little attention. And by making enough soup for more than one meal, you will have a main dish ready to heat for serving at a later time. You will notice that some of the recipes that follow yield large amounts. Most of these soups keep successfully a few days in the refrigerator, several weeks in the freezer.

The slow-cooking soups, such as Country Split Pea, Hoosier Bean or Chicken/Corn Soup are simply delicious and filling. They are merely examples of many other soups in our collection for which recipes follow.

If you are busy at home or outside on a job, you will welcome the new, quick-cooking but hearty soups. Hamburger Soup, for instance—you can take to the table in a little more than a half-hour. This meat-vegetable soup is a perfect choice for the one-dish meal and is a bargain in cost and in good nutrition, too. A pound of ground beef will give you more for your money than a soup bone.

You can make Tuna/Vegetable Chowder, another thrifty, fast-cooking soup, in less than 30 minutes. Speedy Saturday Potato/Cheese Soup adds milk to meals, as does Egg/Corn Chowder. You can use either fresh or reconstituted nonfat dry milk in them, but the dry kind cuts costs without sacrificing food values.

Our grandmothers, experts in economy, made chicken soups with stewing hens culled from their flocks. Our recipes call for broiler-fryers because they are more widely available and contain less fat. They cook more quickly, cutting down time spent in soup making.

Be sure to make Turkey/Vegetable Soup after Thanksgiving Day or any time you have roast turkey. It not only tastes marvelous, but it also salvages the leftovers.

Notice that some of the recipes call for flavor boosters. Keep beef and chicken bouillon cubes and instant bouillon on hand. Use them discreetly as recipes suggest and you will produce flavorful soups.

Soup and homemade bread go together like strawberries and cream. This may explain why the custom evolving today in many country kitchens is to bake bread and make soup on the same day. Corn bread and muffins are among the favored quick breads. Home baking of yeast breads—even of homemade sour dough bread, is increasing.

Anyone who ever stepped into a country kitchen when the aroma from a bubbling soup kettle mingles with the fragrance of yeast bread understands why members of the family drift to the kitchen and ask: "Mom, when do we eat?"

This chapter provides your soup recipes. Look in the Index for breads.

HAMBURGER SOUP

This soup is almost as thick as a stew. Serve it once and you will make it again and again by family request.

1 lb. ground beef	3 c. water
1 (1 lb.) can tomatoes, cut up	3 beef bouillon cubes
3 medium carrots, peeled and sliced	1½ tsp. salt
	¼ tsp. pepper
2 medium potatoes, peeled and cubed	¼ tsp. dried orégano leaves, crushed
1 medium onion, chopped	1 c. frozen green beans
½ c. chopped celery	

Brown ground beef in a kettle; drain off excess fat. Add remaining ingredients, except green beans. Bring to a boil; reduce heat, cover and simmer 15 minutes. Add green beans and continue simmering 15 minutes more. Makes 6 servings.

Memo to Meal Planner: For an inexpensive one-dish meal, it is difficult to duplicate the economy, ease of preparation and taste pleasure this soup brings to the menu. One time serve your favorite fruit salad with it and skip dessert. Next time, eliminate salad and have a dessert. Consider alternating Apple/Pineapple Salad and Apple/Orange Coffee Bread (see Index for recipes).

AMERICAN-STYLE BORSCH

Beef and beets unite in a famous color-bright soup.

3 lbs. cross-cut beef shanks
2 c. chopped onion
2 qts. water
3 c. shredded raw beets
3 c. shredded cabbage
1 (15 oz.) can dry lima beans, drained
2 c. sliced peeled carrots

1 medium potato, peeled and diced
1 (8 oz.) can tomato sauce
1 tblsp. sugar
1 tblsp. salt
⅛ tsp. pepper
3 tblsp. vinegar

Simmer beef shanks and onion in water in large kettle about 2 hours, until meat is tender. Remove shanks, cut up meat and discard bones. Return beef to kettle. Add remaining ingredients. Cover and simmer about 35 minutes, or until vegetables are tender. Serve hot. Makes 4 quarts.

Memo to Meal Planner: You can substitute 2 (1 lb.) cans whole beets for fresh beets. Be sure to use canned *dry* lima beans; they contain much more protein than the fresh and other canned limas. If your food budget permits, top each serving of hot soup with a spoonful of dairy sour cream, the traditional topping for beet soups in Russia and other East European countries. Serve with dark rye bread and a deviled egg-lettuce salad. End dinner with raisin pie.

SAUSAGE/VEGETABLE SOUP

Sausage provides an interesting flavor. The recipe is big, but you can freeze the surplus if there is one.

1 lb. Polish sausage, sliced
4 c. shredded cabbage
3 c. cubed peeled potatoes
2 c. chopped celery and leaves
2 c. sliced peeled carrots
1 c. chopped onion
2 qts. water

1 (8 oz.) can tomato sauce
2 tblsp. vinegar
1 tblsp. salt
½ tsp. dried thyme leaves, crushed
½ tsp. pepper
4 beef bouillon cubes

Combine all ingredients in large kettle. Bring to a boil; reduce heat, cover and simmer 35 to 45 minutes, until vegetables are tender. Makes about 4 quarts.

Memo to Meal Planner: Serve grilled cheese sandwiches as an accompaniment to this Polish-style vegetable soup. They not only complement the soup's flavor but also boost the amount of body-building protein in the meal. Sprinkle shredded cheese on buttered bun halves or French bread slices; broil just until cheese is melted. Have cupcakes for dessert. You can bake them ahead and freeze.

All-American Bean Soups

Scarcely had the Indians introduced beans to colonists living along the Eastern seashore before thrifty women were making sturdy soups with them. Salt pork, then a common meat, was used for seasoning.

As settlers moved to Midwestern farms, economical women salvaged ham bones by teaming them with dry beans in soup kettles. Now that ham bones are not plentiful, we substituted cooked cubed ham, ham hocks or fresh (uncured) pork hocks, beef neck bones and smoked sausages in the soup recipes that follow. You will like the delicious results.

HOOSIER BEAN SOUP

Substantial Saturday supper special—good any day. The savory soup does not deteriorate when supper is delayed or someone arrives too late to eat with the family. You can reheat it quickly.

1 c. dry Great Northern beans	¼ tsp. pepper
2½ qts. water	¼ tsp. dried orégano leaves, crushed
2 c. cubed cooked ham	
1 c. chopped onion	1 (1 lb.) can tomatoes, cut up
½ c. chopped celery	½ c. (1″) pieces spaghetti
2 cloves garlic, minced	1 tblsp. parsley flakes
2 tsp. salt	Grated Parmesan cheese

Wash beans. Combine beans and water in kettle. Bring to a boil over high heat; boil 2 minutes. Remove from heat; let stand 1 hour. Add ham, onion, celery, garlic, salt, pepper, orégano and tomatoes. Bring to a boil. Reduce heat, cover and simmer 1½ hours, or until beans are tender.

Add spaghetti and parsley; simmer 15 minutes longer. Serve sprinkled with Parmesan cheese. Makes 2¾ quarts.

Memo to Meal Planner: Great Northern beans break down in cooking and produce a thicker soup than the pea or navy beans favored in New England, but you can use either kind. Round out the meal with molded perfection salad and streusel apple pie.

HAM/BEAN SOUP

Tomatoes enhance flavor and looks of soup. Check salt before serving—ham hocks, which are more available than the ham bones our grandmothers used to make bean soup, vary in saltiness.

1 c. dry Great Northern or pea beans	¼ tsp. dried basil leaves, crushed
2½ qts. water	1 (1 lb.) can tomatoes, cut up
1½ lbs. ham hocks	1 c. sliced peeled carrots
1 c. chopped onion	1 c. chopped celery
1 tsp. salt	1 c. shredded cabbage
¼ tsp. pepper	2 tsp. parsley flakes, crumbled

Wash beans. Combine beans and water in large kettle. Bring to a boil and let boil 2 minutes. Remove from heat; let stand 1 hour. Add ham hocks, onion, salt, pepper, basil and tomatoes; simmer 2 hours.

Remove ham hocks; cut off meat and return it to soup kettle. Add carrots and celery; simmer 20 minutes. Add cabbage and parsley and continue simmering 10 minutes. Check salt. Makes 3½ quarts.

Memo to Meal Planner: Serve soup with hot corn bread and tossed lettuce salad; have baked apples for dessert.

CHICKEN/LIMA BEAN SOUP

Big recipe makes a hearty, two-meal, three-season main dish. Store the portion not used for its first appearance in the refrigerator for a few days, or put it in the freezer where it will keep in prime condition for several weeks. Broiler-fryers cook more quickly, contain less fat and are more widely available than stewing chicken.

2 c. dry lima beans	1 c. chopped celery
2½ qts. water	4 tsp. salt
1 (3 lb.) broiler-fryer, cut up	1 tblsp. parsley flakes
1 c. sliced peeled carrots	¼ tsp. pepper
1 c. chopped onion	

Wash beans; combine with water in a large kettle. Bring to a boil; boil 2 minutes. Remove from heat; let soak 1 hour. Add remaining ingredients; cover and simmer about 1 hour, until chicken and beans are tender.

Take chicken from soup; remove meat from bones. Discard bones and skin and add chicken to soup. Serve hot. Makes 3¼ quarts.

Memo to Meal Planner: In spring serve a garden lettuce salad, crusty bread and rhubarb crisp with this thrifty main-dish soup. Send a platter of sliced, red-ripe tomatoes to the autumn table with the soup. Gingerbread (see Index for our Gingerbread Mix to use in making it) and applesauce make a great dessert. For a winter meal, serve soup with hot corn bread or muffins, coleslaw, and pineapple or other fruit upside-down cake.

SAUSAGE/LIMA BEAN SOUP

Make this substantial, country-style soup on a blustery, snowy or rainy day when your family and friends will welcome its come-hither aroma and satisfying taste. Smoked sausage lends a delightful flavor.

1 c. dry lima beans	½ lb. smoked pork sausages, cut
2 qts. water	in 1″ pieces
1 (1 lb.) can tomatoes, cut up	¼ c. barley
8 beef bouillon cubes	1 tsp. salt
1½ c. chopped onion	¼ tsp. pepper

Wash beans. Combine beans with water in large kettle. Bring to a boil and boil 2 minutes. Remove from heat; let stand 1 hour.

Add tomatoes, bouillon cubes and onion. Cover and simmer about 1½ hours, until beans are tender. Mash part of the beans, leaving the remainder whole.

Add sausages, barley, salt and pepper. Simmer 30 minutes more. Makes 2½ quarts.

Memo to Meal Planner: Serve with hot golden corn bread or crusty corn sticks and shredded carrot-cabbage slaw. For dessert bring on homemade chocolate cake or applesauce and raisin-oatmeal cookies.

COUNTRY SPLIT PEA SOUP

Beef is the unusual ingredient in this hearty soup. It is a big recipe; freeze the surplus for another meal. Today's dry split peas, unlike dried beans, require no pre-soaking. They cook usually in 45 minutes. The peas contain a goodly amount of body-building protein.

1½ lbs. beef neck bones	2 c. dry split green peas (1 lb.)
1 bay leaf	2 c. cubed peeled potatoes
1 tblsp. salt	1½ c. chopped onion
¼ tsp. pepper	1½ c. chopped celery with tops
2½ qts. water	

Combine beef neck bones, bay leaf, salt, pepper and water in large kettle. Cover and simmer about 2 hours, until beef is tender. Discard bay leaf. Remove neck bones.

Wash peas, and add to soup kettle; cover and simmer 20 minutes.

Meanwhile, remove meat from bones. Cut up meat; discard bones. Add meat, potatoes, onion and celery to soup kettle. Continue simmering, covered, 30 minutes, or until vegetables are tender. Makes 3¼ quarts.

Memo to Meal Planner: Using the thrifty beef cut in making this soup provides good flavor, but you can use ham bone if you have one.

NORTH-OF-THE-BORDER PEA SOUP

Polish sausage gives this soup its distinctive flavor.

2 c. dry split yellow or green peas (1 lb.)	¼ tsp. pepper
	1 c. chopped onion
2½ qts. water	1 c. chopped peeled carrots
1 tblsp. salt	1 c. chopped celery
½ tsp. dried marjoram leaves, crushed	½ c. diced turnips
	1 (12 oz.) ring Polish sausage

Wash peas. Combine peas, water, salt, marjoram and pepper in large kettle. Bring to a boil and simmer 20 minutes.

Add remaining ingredients and simmer about 30 minutes, until vegetables are tender. Remove sausage ring from soup; slice, removing casing if necessary. Return sausage to soup. Makes 3 quarts.

Memo to Meal Planner: You can use ¾ lb. regular Polish sausage or 1 (12 oz.) ring garlic bologna instead of the ring Polish sausage if you like. Serve with a green salad, or, if tomatoes and cucumbers are in season, make a salad with them. If you have vanilla ice cream in the freezer and canned applesauce in the cupboard, serve applesauce à la mode for dessert. Freeze the leftover soup for another meal.

PORK/LENTIL SOUP

Making lentil soup in old-time kitchens awaited an available ham bone. Today's soup makers often use the easier-to-find ham hocks. Uncured pork hocks also are a good choice. They give this soup a delicate, delicious flavor. Since the recipe is large and the soup freezes successfully, you are cooking for more than one meal.

1½ lbs. uncured pork hocks	2 c. lentils (1 lb.)
3 qts. water	1 c. chopped onion
1 tblsp. salt	1 c. chopped celery
¼ tsp. pepper	1 c. sliced peeled carrots
¼ tsp. dried thyme leaves, crushed	

Combine pork hocks, water, salt, pepper and thyme in large kettle. Bring to a boil; cover and simmer 2 hours, or until meat is tender. Remove hocks; cut meat from bones, discarding fat and bones. Return meat to soup.

Wash lentils. Add lentils, onion, celery and carrots to soup. Continue simmering about 30 to 35 minutes, until vegetables are tender. Makes 3 quarts.

Memo to Meal Planner: Serve pumpernickel or other rye bread, wilted leaf lettuce or spinach, your favorite fruit cup and peanut cookies with this different and distinctive soup.

CHICKEN/CORN SOUP

Adaptation of the famous, old-time Pennsylvania Dutch soup by the same name made with fresh corn cut from the cob. This recipe uses the quicker cooking broiler-fryer, packaged ready-to-cook noodles and frozen corn, unknown in old-time kitchens.

1 (2½ to 3 lb.) broiler-fryer, cut up	⅛ tsp. pepper
7 c. water	¼ c. chopped onion
4 chicken bouillon cubes	¼ c. chopped celery
2 tsp. salt	1 (10 oz.) pkg. frozen corn
½ tsp. sugar	4 oz. noodles
	¼ tsp. chopped parsley

Place chicken, water, bouillon cubes, salt, sugar, pepper, onion and celery in large kettle or Dutch oven. Bring to a boil. Reduce heat, cover and simmer about 50 minutes, until chicken is tender. Remove chicken; cool slightly. Cut up chicken, discarding skin and bones.

Add chicken to broth, and bring to a boil. Add remaining ingredients, cover and simmer 15 minutes. Makes about 9 cups.

Memo to Meal Planner: Molded Vegetable/Cranberry Salad (see Index for recipe) is an excellent accompaniment, as are tomato salads. Corn muffins are ideal with the soup. Leftover corn muffins, split, buttered and toasted lightly, are especially good.

CHICKEN/VEGETABLE SOUP

Soup is thick with vegetables, tasty with chicken flavor.

Backs, wings, necks and giblets from 2 broiler-fryers	¾ c. sliced peeled carrots
1 qt. water	⅔ c. sliced celery
1½ tsp. salt	¼ c. chopped onion
1 (8 oz.) can tomatoes, cut up	1 tblsp. uncooked rice

Place chicken, except livers, in kettle with water; add salt. Bring to a boil; reduce heat, cover and simmer 45 minutes. Add livers and continue simmering 15 minutes. Strain broth; skim off fat. Cut chicken from bones, discarding skin. Chop giblets.

Return chopped chicken and giblets to broth; add remaining ingredients. Simmer about 25 minutes, until vegetables and rice are tender. Makes 1½ quarts.

Memo to Meal Planner: Team this invigorating soup, made with the bony chicken pieces, with crackers or toast and a mixed fruit salad for a satisfying light supper. Use the legs, thighs and breasts of the broiler-fryers in other dishes, such as Oven-barbecued Chicken (see Index for recipe).

TURKEY/VEGETABLE SOUP

In the home of the woman who shares this favorite recipe, the thrifty soup is called After-Thanksgiving Turkey Soup. That's because it is made with the bones of the holiday bird. It is a heart-warming, hearty main-dish soup worth the time and effort involved in making it. It contains enough turkey meat to serve four people that otherwise is wasted. If the carcass is that of a smaller turkey, reduce the other ingredients in soup proportionately. Freeze the portion of the soup not served the first time. The noodles give a true country flavor.

1 carcass of a 20-lb. roasted turkey	1 c. sliced peeled carrots
Water to cover (about 6 qts.)	1 c. chopped celery
3 tblsp. salt	2 tblsp. parsley flakes
½ tsp. pepper	2 c. Homemade Noodles, broken up (see Index)
1 c. chopped onion	1 c. frozen lima beans

Cut meat from turkey carcass, leaving bits that stick to the bones and any stuffing that clings to inside cavity. Cut body cavity in half lengthwise through ribs. Place bones in large kettle; cover with water. Add salt and pepper. Cover and simmer 3 hours.

Remove bones from broth. When bones are cool, pick off pieces of turkey meat; return meat to broth. Add onion, carrots, celery and parsley; simmer 20 minutes. Add Homemade Noodles and lima beans and continue simmering about 20 minutes, until noodles are tender. Makes 5¾ quarts.

EGG/CORN CHOWDER

Guaranteed to appease hunger and warm cold, wintry days.

1 c. cubed peeled raw potatoes
1 c. thinly sliced peeled carrots
¼ c. chopped celery
½ small onion, sliced and
　separated into rings
1 (13¾ oz.) can chicken broth
2 tblsp. flour
¼ c. water
2 c. reconstituted nonfat dry
　milk

1 (1 lb. 1 oz.) can whole
　kernel corn with liquid
1 tsp. parsley flakes
½ tsp. salt
⅛ tsp. pepper
½ c. diced process sharp
　American cheese (2 oz.)
5 hard-cooked eggs, chopped
Butter or regular margarine
　(optional)

Cook potatoes, carrots, celery and onion in chicken broth in large kettle about 15 minutes, until vegetables are almost tender.

Blend flour with water to make a smooth paste.

Add milk, corn, parsley, salt, pepper, cheese and flour mixture to vegetables. Cook, stirring, until cheese is melted and mixture is slightly thickened. Add eggs and reheat. Serve each bowl of chowder topped with a small pat of butter, if desired. Makes about 2 quarts.

Memo to Meal Planner: This soup of vegetables, milk, cheese and eggs is a meal in itself, but crisp crackers and homemade pickles, if you have them in your fruit closet, are good flavor companions. If you want to serve a dessert, Cottage Cheese Cupcakes (see Index for recipe) and applesauce fill the bill in an admirable way.

Saturday Potato/Cheese Soup

You can serve bowls of this invigorating soup any day of the week you choose, but with so many activities claiming the attention of youngsters on Saturday during the school year, the noon meal often is hurried and neglected. This hearty, piping hot soup fits admirably in the lunch menu on the week's seventh day. It is an easy-to-fix and easy-to-eat main dish that appeals to teen-agers who think they scarcely have time for lunch.

SATURDAY POTATO/CHEESE SOUP

Cheese makes this a main-dish soup, bacon helps flavor it. You can use 2 cups rather than 1 cup of cheese in making it. The larger measurement doubles the amount of wonderful protein so important in the diet of youngsters and adults.

4 c. cubed peeled potatoes	½ c. chopped onion
2 c. water	3 c. reconstituted nonfat dry
2 tsp. salt	milk
¼ tsp. dry mustard	1 c. shredded Cheddar cheese
⅛ tsp. pepper	(4 oz.)
4 slices bacon, chopped	1 tblsp. parsley flakes

Cook potatoes with water, salt, dry mustard and pepper in large saucepan until soft; do not drain. Mash potatoes.

Meanwhile, cook bacon and onion in small skillet until bacon is lightly browned and onion is soft. Add to potato mixture along with remaining ingredients. Cook over low heat, stirring frequently, until thoroughly heated and cheese is melted; do not boil. Makes 2 quarts.

Memo to Meal Planner: Serve the soup with toast and set out peanut butter and jelly to spread on it, if desired. Pickled beets and carrot sticks make a relish tray that adds cheerful color and interesting flavors. No dessert is required, but if you have cookies, they will get an enthusiastic welcome.

CHEESE/VEGETABLE SOUP

Country women consider this an ideal main dish for lunch or supper on a busy winter day. It is easy and quick to fix. With frozen vegetables in the freezer and canned soup and broth in the cupboard, ingredients for the soup are ready. All you need is a loaf of French bread and cheese. The cheese supplies complete protein and, combined with the vegetables, produces an adequate main dish.

1 (10 oz.) pkg. frozen mixed vegtables	2 c. chicken broth, or 1 (13¾ oz.) can chicken broth
1½ c. water	12 (1″) slices French bread
½ tsp. salt	1 (8 oz.) pkg. sliced process
1 tblsp. parsley flakes	American cheese
2 (10½ oz.) cans condensed turkey-vegetable soup	

Cook frozen vegetables with water, salt and parsley in large sauce-pan until vegetables are tender. Add soup and chicken broth; heat until it simmers.

Place bread slices on broiler rack; toast on one side and turn over. Top with cheese slices, cutting them in halves or quarters if neces-sary to cover bread. Broil about 2 minutes, just until cheese melts.

Ladle soup into soup plates; float 2 pieces of cheese toast in each. Or serve the soup in bowls, and pass the cheese toast instead of serv-ing pieces in the soup. Makes 6 servings.

CHEESE/BROCCOLI SOUP

One of the best-tasting hearty soups ever made. It's a main dish packed with good nutrition and fine flavor.

2 tblsp. chopped onion	1 c. grated process American
2 tblsp. melted butter or regular	cheese (4 oz.)
margarine	2 c. chicken bouillon cubes
3 tblsp. flour	1½ c. boiling water
½ tsp. salt	1 (10 oz.) pkg. frozen chopped
¼ tsp. pepper	broccoli
2 c. milk	

Cook onion in butter in 3-qt. saucepan until soft. Blend in flour, salt and pepper. Add milk and cook, stirring constantly, until mix-ture comes to a boil and is thickened. Add cheese and stir until melted; remove from heat.

In another saucepan dissolve bouillon cubes in boiling water. Add frozen broccoli; cover and cook until broccoli is tender. Add broccoli and cooking liquid to cheese mixture. Heat to serving temperature. Makes 5½ cups, or 5 servings.

Memo to Meal Planner: With peanut butter sandwiches and a fruit salad, this rich, nutritious soup makes a splendid supper or luncheon. Serve the soup in cups or small bowls.

TUNA/VEGETABLE CHOWDER

Quick, inexpensive main dish and a favorite with tuna fans.

2 tblsp. salad oil	1 tsp. salt
1 small onion, minced	¼ tsp. pepper
1 c. chopped celery	1 (10 oz.) pkg. frozen mixed
1 clove garlic, minced	vegetables
1 (10½ oz.) can condensed	2 (7 oz.) cans tuna
chicken broth	Grated Parmesan cheese
1 soup can tomato juice	(optional)
1 tsp. dried thyme leaves,	
crushed	

Heat oil in saucepan. Add onion, celery and garlic; cook until soft. Add undiluted chicken broth, tomato juice, thyme, salt, pepper, frozen vegetables and tuna. Bring to a boil; reduce heat, cover and simmer 10 minutes. Sprinkle Parmesan cheese over servings of the chowder. Makes 6 servings.

Memo to Meal Planner: Serve with crackers or toast and fruit salad. It might be Peach Salad with French Celery Seed Dressing (see Index for recipes). Skip dessert or have cookies and milk.

FISH CHOWDER

Use whatever kind of fish is available at the most reasonable price in your supermarket. This supper or lunch is nourishing and satisfying. Serve steaming bowls of it after the lights go on when the evening is chilly and rainy; contentment will abound around the table.

2 slices bacon, chopped	1 tsp. salt
½ c. chopped onion	¼ tsp. pepper
½ c. chopped celery	2 c. reconstituted nonfat dry
2 c. diced peeled potatoes	milk
1 lb. fish fillets, cut in 1″ pieces	1 tblsp. butter or regular
(fresh or frozen, thawed)	margarine
1½ c. boiling water	

Cook bacon in large saucepan until crisp; remove bacon bits and set aside.

Cook onion and celery in bacon drippings until soft. Add bacon, potatoes, fish, water, salt and pepper. Cover and simmer 20 minutes, or until vegetables are tender. Add milk and butter; heat to serving temperature. Makes 6 servings.

Memo to Meal Planner: Serve the chowder with crisp carrot sticks and other relishes you have on hand—pickles, for instance. An apple dessert—baked apples or apple pie—ends the meal in good form.

MIDWESTERN FISH CHOWDER

Serve with crisp crackers and sliced Cheddar or other cheese.

1 lb. frozen fish fillets
¼ c. chopped bacon ends and
   pieces
1 c. chopped celery
½ c. chopped green pepper
½ c. chopped onion
2 c. cubed peeled potatoes
1 tsp. salt
¼ tsp. pepper
¼ tsp. dried thyme leaves,
   crushed
3 c. tomato juice
2 c. water

Thaw fish fillets; skin and cut in ½" pieces.

Cook bacon, celery, green pepper and onion in large kettle or Dutch oven until bacon is lightly browned. Add fish and remaining ingredients; bring to a boil. Reduce heat; cover and simmer about 20 minutes, until potatoes are tender. Makes about 2 quarts.

Memo to Meal Planner: To complete the meal, serve carrot sticks and pickles and for dessert Cherry Crisp (see Index for recipe).

CHAPTER 7

Vegetables—Nutritious and Necessary

Juicy, vine-ripened tomatoes, chilled and sliced, and sweet corn only minutes away from the garden before it arrives steaming hot on the dinner table—these are famous country vegetable specials. Their season is limited; how do you serve them the remainder of the year? Recipes in this chapter provide an answer.

No one wisely can dismiss the importance of vegetables in meals. Take a look at the chart "Nutrients the body needs"—you'll find it when you open the front cover of this book. The emphasis on vegetables is impressive. This guide is the foundation on which to base the intelligent selection and buying of foods to make well-balanced meals.

When the cost of living, including the price of food, is high, vegetables can help you provide superior meals while you practice economy. They are the mainstay in the diet of millions of people in places where meat, fish, poultry, eggs and cheese are scarce. Vegetables stretch these complete protein foods. Americans are more fortunate in having larger amounts of the animal proteins, but the challenge is to make the most of vegetables week after week for what they can contribute.

Some people think country women have an advantage with vegetables because so many of them can grow their own to eat fresh and to can and freeze. True, but these women also fully appreciate the time and work involved to provide vegetables at their best as well as to save cash outlay. They are rightfully proud of what their efforts earn.

But country kitchens do not entirely escape vegetable problems. The major one is to serve these foods in ways that please the family. This calls for imagination and cooking skills and the recipes that follow are a sampler of successful efforts. We perfected these family favorites in our Test Kitchens and pass them on to you.

Be sure to read the "Memo to Meal Planner" that follows many of the recipes. You will find suggestions of foods to serve with the vegetable dish and many other helpful ideas.

If you believe the bean family gets more than its share of attention in this chapter, remember that beans are traditional country favorites.

Try our economical, tasty, protein-rich dry bean dishes, such as Maple Baked Beans, Lima Beans with Tomatoes, Lima Bean/Apple Skillet and Baked Butter Beans (using canned dry beans). You'll find others in the chapters on Economical Meat Dishes, Thrifty Salads, Homemade Mixes and Hearty Main-dish Soups (see Index for the recipes). Lentils have the same qualifications as dry beans. Even if you never have cooked them, be adventurous and try Baked Lentils Supreme. This vegetable has maintained great prestige from biblical times until today—it deserves wider acceptance in America.

Cabbage and carrots are standard fare, next after potatoes, in country kitchens. Try Scalloped Carrots for a change. And make Cabbage Noodles and Ranch-style Cabbage to see how delicious and economical common cabbage can be.

Scalloped corn continues to rate as a great Midwestern dish to take to picnics, to family reunions and to serve frequently in family meals at home. There are two versions in this chapter.

The wise menu planner keeps in mind the vitamins and minerals that vegetables add to meals, along with their attractive colors that give eye appeal.

ASPARAGUS SCALLOP

The cream of asparagus soup not only strengthens the asparagus taste, but it also, along with the rice, stretches the asparagus, which is not one of the less expensive canned vegetables.

1½ c. cooked rice	2 hard-cooked eggs, sliced
1 (15 oz.) can cut-up asparagus	¼ tsp. salt
	Dash of pepper
1 (10¾ oz.) can condensed cream of asparagus soup	¼ c. dry bread crumbs
⅓ c. milk	1 tblsp. melted butter or regular margarine

Place half the rice in bottom of greased 1-qt. casserole. Top with half the asparagus.

Blend together soup and milk. Spread half of mixture over asparagus. Arrange sliced eggs over top; sprinkle with salt and pepper. Add a second layer of remaining rice, asparagus and soup mixture.

Toss together bread crumbs and butter; sprinkle over top of casserole. Bake in 350° oven 30 minutes. Makes 6 servings.

Memo to Meal Planner: As an escort to chicken, this casserole is not easily surpassed. Include hot rolls and cranberry or other fruit salad.

Ranch Kitchen Green Beans with New Potatoes

When midsummer reaches the fertile valleys of Colorado, ranch women make an occasion of cooking a kettle of green garden beans with new potatoes. For a short season in mountain country this vegetable specialty is an important part of many fried chicken dinners. Mature tubers are later substituted and the recipe that follows calls for them. But if you have new spuds fresh from the earth, be sure to use them.

Women today cook this vegetable combination, accented with bacon, in their convenient kitchens. In the old days a big iron kettle held them over coals in the yard. Memories of those former gatherings of ranchers and their families shed a luster over today's company dinners and picnics that mountain people sense and appreciate. This feeling and the superior taste of the vegetable dish explains its continued popularity.

RANCH KITCHEN GREEN BEANS WITH NEW POTATOES

What a treat—succulent green beans and little new potatoes.

4 slices bacon, chopped	½ c. chopped onion
4 c. tender green beans, cut up (1 lb.)	2 c. water
	1 tsp. salt
2 c. cut peeled potatoes (6 new cut in halves, or 3 medium potatoes, cut in eighths)	¼ tsp. pepper

Cook bacon in large saucepan until lightly browned. Add remaining ingredients. Cover and cook about 20 to 25 minutes, until vegetables are tender. Check to see that there is enough liquid during the last part of the cooking. Makes 6 servings.

Memo to Meal Planner: If you use new potatoes that are very small, leave them whole. While green beans and potatoes cooked together taste wonderful in chicken dinners, they also are a splendid accompaniment for beef. Include a cabbage salad in the menu and end the meal with a fruit cobbler of your choice.

GOURMET GREEN BEANS

This dish demonstrates how easy, quick and inexpensive it is to give fresh green beans a delightful, new taste. Seasonings, including the herbs, deserve credit for promoting them to gourmet status.

1½ lbs. green beans, sliced	¼ tsp. pepper
¼ c. chopped onion	¼ tsp. dried basil leaves,
¼ c. chopped celery	crushed
¼ c. butter or regular margarine	¼ tsp. dried marjoram leaves,
1 tblsp. parsley flakes	crushed
1 tsp. salt	

Cook beans, onion and celery in a small amount of water in large saucepan until beans are just tender; drain. Add remaining ingredients. Heat just until butter is melted, stirring often. Serves 6.

SWEET-SOUR GREEN BEANS

Onion, vinegar, sugar and a bit of bacon take the taste of spring's wilted lettuce to summer's green beans. A little bacon delivers a lot of flavor in deference to food budgets.

2 slices bacon, chopped	¼ tsp. pepper
¼ c. chopped onion	1 tblsp. vinegar
1 tblsp. sugar	4 c. cooked cut-up green beans
½ tsp. salt	

Cook bacon in a small skillet; remove from pan. Add onion to skillet and cook just until soft. Add onion with bacon drippings, bacon, sugar, salt, pepper and vinegar to hot beans. Serves 6.

Memo to Meal Planner: This vegetable dish is best served hot. You can quickly reheat it after combining all the ingredients if necessary. Serve with chicken and cheese dishes.

MAPLE BAKED BEANS

When the need for a dish to take to a picnic arises on short notice, or when the request comes for you or some member of the family to bring a covered dish to a social gathering, this easy-to-fix dish deserves consideration. You can keep the ingredients for it in your kitchen ready to use. The beans require 2 hours in the oven, but you need not watch them. Maple-flavored syrup gives them a new taste, on the sweet side, which recommends them to many people.

2 (1 lb. 15 oz.) cans pork and beans with tomato sauce	1 tblsp. instant minced onion
	½ c. ketchup
1 c. maple-blended syrup	2 tsp. dry mustard

Stir together beans, syrup and onion. Blend together ketchup and mustard; stir into beans. Turn into greased 2½-qt. casserole. Bake uncovered in 400° oven 2 hours. Makes 8 servings.

LIMA BEAN/APPLE SKILLET

It's traditional in country kitchens to team thrifty dry limas and apples in taste-rewarding dishes. The custom gets more attention today with food costs not so low as they once were. Here is a way to fix a bean-fruit special to serve as a vegetable or a hearty main dish.

2 c. dry lima beans	¼ c. brown sugar, firmly packed
6 c. water	
1 tsp. salt	1 tsp. salt
2 onions, sliced and separated into rings	¼ tsp. pepper
	1 tblsp. vinegar
¼ c. butter or regular margarine	
4 unpeeled apples, cored and sliced	

Wash and sort limas. Place beans in a large kettle, cover with water and add 1 tsp. salt. Bring to a boil and boil 2 minutes. Remove from heat and let stand 1 hour. (Or if more convenient, soak the beans overnight and skip the preboiling.) Bring beans to a boil, reduce heat and simmer 40 to 50 minutes, until beans are tender. Drain beans, reserving liquid.

Meanwhile, cook onion rings in butter in large skillet until soft.

Combine beans, ¾ c. reserved bean liquid (add water if necessary to make ¾ c.), onion mixture, apples, brown sugar, 1 tsp. salt, pepper and vinegar. Simmer about 20 minutes, until apples are tender. Makes about 2 quarts.

Memo to Meal Planner: If you wish to serve this bean-apple special for a main dish, include a cottage cheese salad in the menu to increase the amount and quality of protein. It might be simple Cottage Cheese/Vegetable Salad, Cabbage/Cottage Cheese Salad or Cottage Cheese Salad Dressing spooned over wedges of head lettuce. Hot corn bread makes a splendid accompaniment. Lima Bean/Apple Skillet also rises to the occasion for a side dish when served with ham dishes, such as Baked Ham/Cheese Sandwiches, or with a platter of cold meats. (See Index for recipes.)

GREEN LIMAS WITH CHEESE

You'll never discover an easier-to-fix vegetable dish than this one in which cheese delightfully seasons lima beans.

2 (10 oz.) pkgs. frozen lima
   beans

4 slices process American
   cheese

Cook beans as directed on package. Drain, reserving cooking liquid. Return ¼ c. liquid to beans. Lay cheese over the top. Cover and let stand off heat about 5 minutes. Stir to blend cooking liquid, cheese and beans. Makes 6 servings.

Memo to Meal Planner: While this lima bean dish is excellent with chicken, it also tastes wonderful with pork and ham.

LIMA BEANS WITH TOMATOES

Use limas to add variety to baked bean dinners and to please the family. Faint chili powder taste in this dish keeps everyone guessing what it is.

2½ c. dry baby lima beans
1½ qts. water
½ c. chopped bacon ends and
   pieces, or bacon
1 (1 lb.) can tomaoes, cut up

½ c. chopped onion
¼ c. brown sugar, firmly packed
2 tsp. salt
¼ tsp. chili powder
1 tblsp. vinegar

Wash beans; combine with water in large kettle and simmer about 1½ hours, until beans are tender. Drain.

Meanwhile, cook bacon; remove from skillet and reserve.

Combine beans, bacon drippings and remaining ingredients. Simmer 25 minutes, or until slightly thickened. Sprinkle with reserved bacon just before serving. Makes 1½ quarts, about 6 servings.

Memo to Meal Planner: Include a cottage cheese salad in the menu, or fold finely diced carrot, onion and green pepper into the cheese and serve it in a bowl. Piping hot corn or whole wheat muffins lift the meal out of the commonplace.

BAKED BUTTER BEANS

Bake a pot of budget-stretching lima beans. The seasonings in our recipe make the dish an out-of-the-ordinary one. It's easy to tote.

¼ c. chopped onion
2 tblsp. chopped green pepper
2 tblsp. butter or regular margarine
1 (10¾ oz.) can condensed tomato soup

¼ c. water
1 tblsp. brown sugar
2 tblsp. vinegar
1 tsp. prepared mustard
3 (15 oz.) cans butter beans, drained

Cook onion and green pepper in butter in saucepan until soft. Add soup, water, brown sugar, vinegar and mustard; simmer 5 minutes.

Place beans in greased 1-qt. casserole; pour sauce over. Bake uncovered in 350° oven 1 hour. Makes 6 servings.

Memo to Meal Planner: You can cook dry butter beans until tender, but using the canned vegetable saves time if you are in a hurry. As an accompaniment to hamburgers or frankfurters, these beans are not easily surpassed.

ORANGE BEETS

Including color is doubly important in menus when you try to cut food costs. It contributes eye appeal and influences the reactions people have to meals. This dish brightens dinner plates and adds interesting flavor. The orange marmalade, which might be a leftover, provides a subtle, intriguing touch that makes the vegetable special. The beets have a tangy, sweet-sour taste with orange overtones.

3 tblsp. butter or regular margarine
⅓ c. orange marmalade
2 tsp. cornstarch
¼ tsp. salt

1½ tblsp. vinegar
2 (1 lb.) cans sliced beets, drained, or 3 c. sliced cooked beets

Melt butter in saucepan; stir in orange marmalade.

Blend together cornstarch, salt and vinegar; stir into marmalade mixture. Heat, stirring, to boiling. Add beets and heat thoroughly, stirring occasionally. Makes 6 servings.

LEMON-BUTTERED BROCCOLI

Lemon juice gives broccoli its piquant flavor. Your family and guests will think the green vegetable never tasted better.

1½ lbs. broccoli
3 tblsp. lemon juice
2 tblsp. butter

¾ tsp. salt
Dash of pepper

Wash broccoli; trim off stem ends. Remove flowerets. Cut stems in ¼″ diagonal slices; place in saucepan with 1″ boiling water. Cover and cook 5 minutes. Add flowerets and continue cooking 5 minutes. Drain.

Add lemon juice, butter, salt and pepper, and toss gently to distribute. Makes 6 servings.

STIR-FRIED BROCCOLI

Also cook frozen green beans and spinach this Chinese way. The results win acceptance, yielding big flavor dividends with little work.

1 tblsp. butter or regular margarine
1 (10 oz.) pkg. frozen chopped broccoli, thawed
¼ tsp. salt

2 tblsp. finely chopped onion
1 chicken bouillon cube
¼ c. boiling water
1 tsp. cornstarch
1 tblsp. cold water

Melt butter in 10″ skillet. Add thawed broccoli and cook 3 minutes, stirring constantly. Add salt, onion and bouillon cube dissolved in ¼ c. boiling water. Cover and cook 3 to 5 minutes, until broccoli is tender-crisp.

Combine cornstarch and 1 tblsp. water; add to broccoli. Cook and stir until mixture comes to a boil. Makes 4 servings. (You can double recipe for 8 servings.)

RANCH-STYLE CABBAGE

Since cabbage is an all-year vegetable, you cannot have too many ways to use it. This is one of the good, old-fashioned dishes that continues to please—it's delicious with hamburgers.

¼ c. butter or regular margarine
½ tsp. salt
⅛ tsp. pepper

8 c. shredded cabbage
¼ c. milk

Melt butter in a 10″ skillet. Add salt, pepper and cabbage. Cover and cook over medium-high heat 5 to 6 minutes, stirring several times. Add milk; cook 1 to 2 minutes longer. Makes 6 servings.

CABBAGE SKILLET

This is one version of what is known in some country kitchens as fried cabbage—it disappears like magic. The secrets to success with this vegetable specialty are to shred the cabbage fine and cook it slowly (over low heat) until it is tender-crisp.

2 slices bacon	¼ tsp. pepper
8 c. shredded cabbage	2 tblsp. vinegar
¾ tsp. salt	2 tblsp. water

Cook bacon in large skillet until crisp. Remove and reserve.

Add remaining ingredients to drippings in skillet. Cover tightly and cook over low heat, stirring occasionally, about 20 minutes, until cabbage is tender-crisp. Serve in bowl; top with bacon. Serves 6.

CABBAGE NOODLES

Cabbage cut the shape of noodles flavors this interesting dish.

5 oz. medium noodles	1½ tsp. salt
¼ c. butter or regular margarine	⅛ tsp. pepper
½ onion, cut in thin strips	
6 c. cabbage strips (cut the width of noodles), lightly packed	

Cook noodles by package directions; drain.

Melt butter in 12″ skillet; add onion and cook until soft. Add cabbage. Cook gently until tender-crisp. Mix in noodles, salt and pepper. Reheat if necessary. Makes 8 servings.

Memo to Meal Planner: For a hearty dinner, serve with Baked Pork Steaks with Stuffing and have Baked Cherry Pudding for dessert (see Index for recipes). They cook together in the oven, making good use of the oven's heat. Carrot sticks add a colorful note to the menu.

MINT-GLAZED CARROTS

Carrots have many charms that wise menu makers recognize. They almost always are available, are good for you, and add bright color.

9 medium carrots	3 tblsp. sugar
3 tblsp. butter or regular margarine	½ tsp. mint flakes, crushed, or 1 tblsp. chopped fresh mint

Peel carrots; cut in halves crosswise, then in halves lengthwise. Cook in boiling salted water until almost tender. Drain.

Melt butter in skillet; add carrots and sprinkle with sugar and mint. Cook until carrots are glazed, turning occasionally. Serves 6.

Memo to Meal Planner: For a company dinner, combine the vegetable at serving time with briefly cooked and buttered frozen peas. The two vegetables are great flavor partners and they make an appealing color picture. Excellent with lamb, pork and ham dishes.

SCALLOPED CARROTS

Celery soup makes sauce for and helps season thrifty carrots.

4 c. sliced peeled carrots	¼ tsp. salt
1 (10¾ oz.) can condensed cream of celery soup	⅛ tsp. pepper
⅓ c. milk	½ c. dry bread crumbs
1 tblsp. parsley flakes	2 tblsp. melted butter or regular margarine

Cook carrots in boiling salted water until barely tender; drain.

Blend together soup, milk, parsley, salt and pepper. Stir in carrots. Turn into greased 1½-qt. casserole.

Toss together crumbs and melted butter; sprinkle over top of casserole. Bake in 350° oven 30 minutes, until bubbly. Serves 6.

Memo to Meal Planner: You can assemble ingredients in casserole in the morning, cover and refrigerate until time to get dinner. If you refrigerate it, bake 40 minutes instead of 30. Or you can prepare this tasty vegetable dish at the last minute and heat it in a saucepan on top of the range, but save the buttered bread crumbs to sprinkle over carrots just before serving. Take your choice of the cooking methods for one of the most nutritionally valuable vegetables.

TENDER-CRISP CARROTS

Follow the age-old Chinese custom of cooking carrots until almost, but not quite, tender. It's the hint of crispness that makes them so good. They have subtle sweet undertones with a faint onion flavor.

2 tblsp. butter or regular margarine	1 small onion, shredded
3 c. coarsley shredded peeled carrots	1 tblsp. brown sugar ½ tsp. salt

Melt butter in 10″ skillet. Add carrots, onion, brown sugar and salt; cover and cook over medium-high heat about 5 minutes, until carrots are tender-crisp. Makes 6 servings.

SCALLOPED CORN SUPREME

When high prices attempt to shatter the food budget, many old-fashioned dishes refresh memories and kindle hope. Scalloped corn is a splendid example. Every country kitchen once had a cherished recipe for this dish. Country Scalloped Corn Supreme typifies them.

¼ c. finely chopped onion	1 c. milk
¼ c. finely chopped green pepper	1 egg, beaten
1 tblsp. melted butter or regular margarine	1½ c. coarse cracker crumbs ½ tsp. salt
1 (1 lb. 1 oz.) can cream style corn	Dash of pepper 1 tblsp. melted butter or regular margarine

Cook onion and green pepper in 1 tblsp. butter in saucepan until soft but not brown. Add corn, milk, egg, 1 c. cracker crumbs, salt and pepper. Heat, stirring, but do not boil. Turn into greased 1½-qt. casserole.

Toss together remaining ½ c. cracker crumbs and 1 tblsp. butter; sprinkle over corn mixture. Bake in 350° oven 25 to 30 minutes. Makes 6 servings.

Memo to Meal Planner: If you have scraps of cheese on hand, stir ¼ c. of it into the corn mixture. It's a time-honored way of salvaging food that otherwise might be wasted. The practice is thrifty today.

And if green pepper is beyond the reach of the pocketbook, take a tip from grandmothers who recall substituting for it the taste and bright color of canned pimiento.

HERBED SCALLOPED CORN

This recipe originated in an Iowa home where three teen-age boys champion it with superlatives. They hold that it is the best vegetable dish in existence. The herb-flavored stuffing mix deliciously seasons the corn. It vies with old-fashioned scalloped corn for popularity.

2 eggs, beaten
2 (1 lb. 1 oz.) cans cream
    style corn
½ c. milk
¼ c. melted butter or regular
    margarine

1 tblsp. instant minced onion
½ tsp. salt
¼ tsp. pepper
2 c. stuffing mix (homemade or
    commercial), crushed

Combine eggs, corn, milk, butter, onion, salt and pepper. Place half of mixture in greased 2-qt. casserole. Sprinkle crushed stuffing mix over top. *Carefully spoon* remaining corn mixture over top (it is very soft). Do not try to spread. Let stand 10 minutes.

Bake in 325° oven 1 hour, or until center is set but still slightly soft. Cool on wire rack 10 minutes. Makes 6 to 8 servings.

CORN WITH CRISP TOPPING

The seasonings in the stuffing mix enhance the flavor of corn.

1 (20 oz.) bag or 2 (10 oz.)
    pkgs. frozen corn

1 c. stuffing mix, crushed
¼ c. butter or regular margarine

Cook corn in boiling salted water until tender; drain.

Meanwhile, lightly brown stuffing mix crumbs in butter. Turn corn into serving dish; scatter crumbs over the top. Makes 6 servings.

Memo to Meal Planner: Use homemade Stuffing Mix (see Index for recipe). This is an inexpensive and tasty way to introduce a flavor change. You can use commercial stuffing mix, but it costs more.

AUTUMN EGGPLANT BAKE

Even people who are not fond of eggplant like this tasty dish.

1 medium eggplant, peeled and cubed	1 tsp. dried orégano leaves, crushed
1 large onion, sliced	½ tsp. salt
1 green pepper, cut in strips	1½ c. garlic croutons (see Index
1 small clove garlic, minced	for Cheese-seasoned
¼ c. butter or regular margarine	Croutons)
1 (15 oz.) can tomato sauce	¼ c. grated Parmesan cheese

Cook eggplant in boiling salted water 3 minutes; drain. Turn into greased 10×6×2″ baking dish.

Cook onion, green pepper and garlic in butter in skillet until soft. Add tomato sauce, orégano and salt; bring to a boil. Pour over eggplant. Bake in 350° oven 45 minutes, stirring several times. Remove from oven; top with croutons and cheese. Continue baking 15 minutes. Makes 6 servings.

Memo to Meal Planner: Go Italian when you make this and have Spaghetti Supper (see Index for recipe), tossed salad and end the meal with fruit. If pears are in season, they are a fine choice.

BAKED LENTILS SUPREME

Since dry lentils are an excellent source of vegetable protein and less expensive than many vegetables, treasure this recipe and use it. Baked with other vegetables and expertly seasoned, this one-dish meal is a splendid choice. The crown of cheese, added at the end of the baking, not only contributes flavor, but also adds complete protein. The casserole is a gold mine of good nutrition.

2 c. lentils	1½ c. chopped onions
2¼ c. water	2 cloves garlic, minced
2½ tsp. salt	1 (1 lb.) can tomatoes, cut up
¼ tsp. pepper	2 c. thinly sliced peeled carrots
⅛ tsp. dried marjoram leaves, crushed	1 c. thinly sliced celery
	½ c. chopped green pepper
⅛ tsp. dried thyme leaves, crushed	2½ c. shredded process sharp cheese (10 oz.)
1 bay leaf	

Combine lentils, water, salt, pepper, marjoram, thyme, bay leaf, onions, garlic and tomatoes in 13×9×2″ baking dish. Cover tightly with foil. Bake in 375° oven 30 minutes. Uncover; stir in carrots, celery and green pepper. Cover and continue baking about 40 minutes, until vegetables are tender. Remove cover and discard bay leaf. Sprinkle cheese over top. Return to oven just long enough to melt cheese. Makes 8 servings.

OKRA/TOMATO TREAT

Expand the serving season for this long-time favorite from southern gardens by combining frozen okra with canned tomatoes.

1 c. chopped onion	1 (10 oz.) pkg. frozen okra
2 tblsp. melted butter or regular margarine	½ tsp. salt
	¼ tsp. pepper
1 (1 lb.) can tomatoes, cut up	

Cook onion in butter in saucepan until soft but not brown. Add remaining ingredients. Cook uncovered over medium heat 15 to 20 minutes, until okra is tender and mixture thickens. Stir occasionally. Makes 6 servings.

Memo to Meal Planner: This winter version of a famous vegetable combination complements ham, pork and chicken dishes and also is good with cheese, egg and fish casseroles.

CREAMED POTATOES WITH DILL

Good way to fix all potatoes but extra special for new ones.

6 medium potatoes, peeled	½ tsp. salt
2 tblsp. melted butter or regular margarine	¼ tsp. dill weed
	1 c. milk
1 tblsp. flour	

Cook potatoes in boiling salted water until tender; drain.

Meanwhile, blend together butter and flour in small saucepan. Add salt, dill weed and milk. Cook, stirring constantly, until mixture comes to a boil. Pour over hot potatoes. Makes 6 servings.

Memo to Meal Planner: The potatoes make a splendid accompaniment to fish, such as Golden Broiled Flounder or Tuna Loaf. Include your favorite lettuce salad or molded Carrot/Cabbage Salad, and consider Peach-pudding Parfait for dessert. (See Index for recipes.)

BUTTER-BAKED POTATOES

Bake sliced potatoes this way and no one will miss gravy.

2 qts. potato slices (¼" thick) ¼ tsp. paprika
1 tsp. salt ¼ c. butter or regular margarine
¼ tsp. pepper

Place half the potatoes in 2-qt. casserole. Top with half the seasonings; dot with half the butter. Repeat layers. Cover and bake in 350° oven 1 hour, or until potatoes are tender. Makes 8 servings.

Memo to Meal Planner: These delicious potatoes fit into many menus, but they are especially good to serve with meat loaves. They bake at the same temperature. Team them with Beef/Bean Loaf and a baked dessert, such as Old-fashioned Cottage Pudding. Include Homemade Stewed Tomatoes in the meal (see Index for recipes).

MAPLED SWEET POTATO BAKE

This recipe also tells you how to freeze sweet potatoes.

6 medium sweet potatoes, 2 tblsp. water
   cooked and peeled ¼ c. butter or regular margarine
½ c. maple-blended syrup 1 tsp. salt

Cut sweet potatoes in ½" slices. Place in 10×6×2" baking dish.
Combine remaining ingredients in small saucepan; heat until mixture comes to a boil and butter is melted. Pour over sweet potatoes. Bake in 350° oven 45 minutes; baste four or five times. Serves 6.
Sweet Potatoes for Freezing: Since sweet potatoes are not good keepers, salvage the surplus when they are plentiful and least expensive by freezing. Scrub them and bake in 400° oven 40 to 45 minutes, until tender. Cool potatoes, place in plastic bags and freeze. To use, thaw at room temperature, peel and heat. (If you are baking sweet potatoes to serve right away without freezing, you can bake them in a 350° oven about 1 hour, until tender. Baked at this temperature, they fit well into oven meals.)

Memo to Meal Planner: Team delicious Mapled Sweet Potato Bake with a main dish and dessert that can bake in the oven alongside to make economical use of oven heat. Consider having Pork/Cabbage Casserole and either Baked Cherry Pudding or Applesauce Bread Pudding for dessert (see Index for recipes). Serve carrot sticks and other relishes you have on hand.

SPINACH SPECIAL

You can get spinach ready ahead, chill and bake at mealtime.

2 (10 oz.) pkgs. frozen chopped spinach	1 c. milk
¼ c. finely chopped onion	½ c. shredded process American
2 tblsp. butter or regular margarine	cheese (2 oz.)
2 tblsp. flour	½ c. dry bread crumbs
¼ tsp. salt	2 tblsp. melted butter or regular margarine

Cook spinach according to package directions; drain thoroughly.

Meanwhile, cook onion in 2 tblsp. butter in small saucepan until soft. Blend in flour and salt. Add milk and cook, stirring constantly, until mixture comes to a boil. Add cheese and stir until melted.

Place half the spinach in greased 1-qt. casserole. Top with half the cheese sauce. Repeat layers.

Toss bread crumbs with 2 tblsp. melted butter. Sprinkle over top of casserole. Bake in 350° oven about 20 minutes, until bubbly (add 10 minutes if you make it ahead and chill). Makes 6 servings.

Memo to Meal Planner: This casserole is a nice way to dress up spinach—it makes a fine teammate for hamburgers or Tasty Tunaburgers and Homemade Stewed Tomatoes. Have fruit and slices of Carrot Bread with a beverage for dessert. (See Index for recipes.)

ACORN SQUASH WITH APPLESAUCE

The flavor combination of squash and apples is perfection!

3 acorn squash	⅓ c. raisins
¾ tsp. salt	1 tblsp. lemon juice
2 c. applesauce	2 tblsp. butter or regular
⅓ c. brown sugar, firmly packed	margarine

Cut squash in halves; remove seeds and place cut side down in 15½×10½×1" pan. Add enough boiling water to cover bottom of pan. Bake in 400° oven 45 minutes. Remove from oven and turn squash over. Sprinkle each cavity with salt.

Combine applesauce, brown sugar, raisins and lemon juice. Spoon into squash. Dot with butter. Return to oven and bake 30 minutes longer, or until squash is tender. Makes 6 servings.

Memo to Meal Planner: Choose a main dish and dessert to bake in the oven with the squash. This might be Beef/Corn Pie or Baked Ham/Cheese Sandwiches; serve also either Fresh Vegetable Relish Salad or Lemon Coleslaw (see Index for recipes). Thick applesauce is especially good to add to the squash.

BAKED BUTTERNUT SQUASH

You can cook and season other kinds of winter squash this way.

1 butternut squash (about 3 lbs.)	1 tblsp. butter or regular margarine
3 tblsp. butter or regular margarine	¼ c. brown sugar, firmly packed
½ tsp. salt	¼ c. light corn syrup

Cut squash in pieces; peel and seed. Cook in boiling salted water until tender; drain. Add 3 tblsp. butter and salt, and mash. Turn into greased 1½-qt. casserole.

Melt 1 tblsp. butter in small saucepan. Blend in brown sugar and corn syrup. Drizzle over top of squash. Bake in 350° oven 25 minutes. Makes 6 servings.

Memo to Meal Planner: Let this vegetable, a rich source of vitamin A, escort pork or chicken dishes, such as Pork Dinner Bake or Oven-fried Chicken (see Index for recipes). Include a relish plate in the menu and have a fruit cup with oatmeal cookies for dessert.

ZUCCHINI WITH TOMATOES

Try this simple recipe when zucchini comes to the kitchen from the garden in great abundance. Tomatoes add color and flavor.

6 small zucchini, sliced	¾ tsp. salt
1 (1 lb.) can tomatoes, cut up	¼ tsp. pepper
2 tblsp. finely chopped onion	2 tblsp. butter or regular
2 tblsp. finely chopped green	margarine
pepper	1 slice bread, torn in small
2 tsp. sugar	pieces

Combine zucchini, tomatoes, onion, green pepper, sugar, salt and pepper in saucepan. Cover and cook until zucchini is tender. Stir in butter and bread. Makes 8 servings.

Memo to Meal Planner: Complete the menu with Beef-stuffed Buns, carrot sticks and a dessert everyone likes. It might be Chocolate/ Banana Upside-down Cake or Chocolate Drop Cookies (see Index).

HOMEMADE STEWED TOMATOES

Everyone who taste-tested canned tomatoes prepared this way preferred them to canned stewed tomatoes from the supermarket.

1 (1 lb.) can tomatoes, cut up	½ tsp. green pepper flakes
1 tblsp. sugar	½ tsp. celery flakes
1 tsp. instant minced onion	

Combine all ingredients in saucepan; bring to a boil. Cover and simmer 10 minutes. Makes 3 or 4 servings. (Double the recipe for 6 to 8 servings.)

BEAN-STUFFED TOMATOES

Try this different, interesting way of serving canned beans.

1 (31 oz.) can pork and beans	2 tblsp. brown sugar
in tomato sauce	¼ tsp. dry mustard
½ c. chopped green pepper	6 tomatoes
2 tblsp. chopped onion	2 slices bacon, cut in thirds

Combine beans, green pepper, onion, brown sugar and dry mustard in saucepan. Simmer uncovered 10 minutes, stirring frequently.

Slice tops off tomatoes. Scoop out insides (save these for use in soups or casseroles, or combine with cucumber and onions in a salad). Fill tomatoes with bean mixture. Place in shallow baking pan. Top each with a piece of bacon. Bake in 350° oven 25 minutes. Makes 6 servings.

Memo to Meal Planner: Serve with Carrot/Cabbage Salad (see Index) and have gingerbread topped with applesauce for dessert.

CHAPTER 8

Thrifty Salads

Salads . . . tossed, molded, hot, cold, light, substantial, tart, sweet —you'll find recipes for all of them in our collection. Economy is their common denominator. No fancy frills, but superior flavor.

Farm women tend to include some protein foods in salad bowls to help give the family adequate amounts of this body builder. Often you can rely on a salad to boost the protein in meals short of meat.

You'll find cottage cheese an ingredient in a great variety of these salads. It not only provides top-quality protein, but normally is a good buy. And it frequently gives the salad a subtle taste like that of sour cream—which costs more and has more calories. Many of the simple salads taste remarkably good and brighten meals. In our Tossed Carrot Salad, for example, cubes of red-skinned apples join with creamy cottage cheese and shredded carrots. Molded Tomato Salad is second in flavor only to vine-ripened tomatoes.

Lemon Coleslaw, another typically economical salad, contains lemon flavor gelatin but does away with the fuss of unmolding. This time-saver keeps several days in the refrigerator for quick serving.

Who would dream of making chef's salad one day to serve guests the next? The secret in our Overnight Tossed Salad is the salad dressing spread over the ingredients in the bowl. This keeps the air out and prevents wilting during the chilling.

Relish salads again are in vogue. Several of our recipes include vegetables always available, such as kidney and pinto beans, garbanzos (chick-peas) and lentils, rich in good, economical vegetable protein.

We include a few recipes for salad dressings that are special. Look in the Homemade Mixes chapter for others.

The vegetables and fruits in salads contribute important vitamins and minerals to meals, in addition to appealing flavor and texture contrasts. The salad recipes that follow also meet the test of being thrifty at least during the peak season, and some, any time of year.

Old-time Relish Salads

Some of the best-liked country salads contain neither salad oil nor prepared dressings. The right combination of vinegar and sugar produces a delightful sweet-sour taste that blends deliciously with natural vegetable juices. This type of salad has long been popular with country women in the summer season when gardens yielded plenty of tomatoes, cucumbers and onions. Cabbage and root vegetables stored over winter and canned vegetables provided makings when lettuce and other greens were not available.

Today's relish salads include some that are updated. Four examples follow: Fresh Vegetable Relish Salad, a summer specialty, Cornhusker Bean/Corn Salad, Green Bean Salad Bowl and Lentil Salad Bowl, which are around-the-year treats.

While you can serve these excellent homey salads in bowls or on plates lined with lettuce, you can cut costs by eliminating the greens. You will avoid the common waste that occurs when family—and guests—do not eat the lettuce "liners" anyway. Often these same people enjoy tossed salads. You can save money by buying lettuce when you wish to make a splash with it by tossing a salad in which it takes the spotlight.

FRESH VEGETABLE RELISH SALAD

When summer blossoms over the countryside, fresh, succulent vegetables from the garden unite in marvelous relish salads. Remember this all-American treat when you plan food for the next picnic or family reunion. It's a great companion to fried chicken.

3 tomatoes, peeled	½ c. sugar
2 small zucchini	1 tsp. salt
2 large branches celery	½ tsp. mustard seeds
1 cucumber	¼ tsp. pepper
1 large green pepper	½ c. cider vinegar
6 green onions	

Dice tomatoes in ¼ to ½″ square pieces.

Cut zucchini, celery, cucumber, green pepper and onions in pieces about the same size as tomatoes. Put vegetables in salad bowl. Combine with sugar, salt, mustard seeds, pepper and vinegar. Cover and chill 4 hours or overnight.

Serve in bowl for a relish or on lettuce for a salad. Makes 2 quarts.

CORNHUSKER BEAN/CORN SALAD

No-wilt relish salad makes its own dressing as it chills. Great to tote to picnics and potluck suppers. It's filling—and good.

1 (1 lb.) can cut green beans, drained	¼ c. chopped onion
	1 tblsp. sugar
1 (15 oz.) can kidney beans, drained and rinsed	½ tsp. salt
	⅛ tsp. pepper
1 c. corn relish	1 tblsp. vinegar

Combine all ingredients. Cover and refrigerate at least 4 hours. Salad will keep a few days in the refrigerator. Makes 1 quart.

Memo to Meal Planner: If you have homemade corn relish in your cupboard, use it in this salad. Serve it in a bowl or in individual small bowls. The salad is just right with ham or pork and it is a great companion for chicken and hamburgers.

GREEN BEAN SALAD BOWL

A pretty make-ahead salad that reduces the last minute mealtime rush. Yellow and white hard-cooked egg garnish glamorizes this homespun country dish. You can use a commercial pickle relish, but if you have a homemade one cut costs by using it.

2 (1 lb.) cans cut green beans	⅛ tsp. pepper
½ c. sweet pickle relish	½ c. liquid from sweet pickle relish
½ c. chopped celery	
¼ c. finely chopped onion	Lettuce
½ tsp. salt	1 hard-cooked egg, sieved

Combine green beans, relish, celery, onion, salt, pepper and liquid drained from relish in salad bowl. Stir gently to mix. Cover and refrigerate at least 8 hours, or overnight. Stir occasionally. Serve in lettuce-lined bowl. Sprinkle egg over top. Makes 6 servings.

LENTIL SALAD BOWL

Lentils are one of the world's oldest and most used foods. They have proved their worth since ancient days. Even so, they still are strangers in many American kitchens. Due to their relatively low cost and nutritional merits, today's wise meal planners try to help their families and friends acquire a liking for them. This salad offers a golden opportunity to do just that.

1 c. lentils	¼ c. chopped green pepper
1 c. chopped onion	1½ tsp. garlic salt
1 small bay leaf	¼ tsp. pepper
2 c. water	⅛ tsp. dried orégano leaves,
1½ c. sliced celery	crushed
2 tomatoes, chopped	Grated Parmesan cheese
¾ c. grated peeled carrot	

Combine lentils, ½ c. onion, bay leaf and water in large saucepan. Bring to a boil. Reduce heat; cover and simmer 30 minutes, or until tender. Remove bay leaf; drain and chill.

Combine chilled lentils, remaining ½ c. onion, celery, tomatoes, carrot, green pepper, garlic salt, pepper and orégano in bowl. Chill at least 1 hour. Serve in lettuce-lined bowl or on lettuce-lined plates. Sprinkle with cheese before serving. Makes 8 servings.

PICKLED BEET RELISH FOR SALADS

Mounds of cottage cheese on lettuce serve eloquently as salad when you spoon this relish over them. It takes the place of dressing and transforms the salad into a red and white picture on greens. The relish also makes a good topping for lettuce and tossed salads. The beets have a sweet-sour flavor, which is not surprising, for they are an American adaptation of a Chinese favorite.

⅓ c. sugar	Dash of salt
1 tblsp. cornstarch	4 whole cloves
⅓ c. vinegar	1 (1 lb.) can chopped cooked
1 tblsp. ketchup	beets
1 tblsp. salad oil	

Combine sugar and cornstarch in large saucepan. Blend in vinegar. Add ketchup, oil, salt and cloves.

Drain beets, reserving liquid. Add beets and ⅓ c. liquid drained from them to the saucepan. Cook and stir until mixture comes to a boil and thickens. Makes about 2 cups.

Salads That Dress Themselves

You can save minutes and money by serving some salads that make their own dressings. Add the seasonings and a little salad oil and vinegar when you combine the vegetables. This takes only about as long as it does to pour prepared salad dressing from a bottle and you are pennies ahead.

Two excellent salads of this nature are Hearty Hot Bean Salad and Mixed Vegetable Salad with Basil Dressing. Both salads taste good. And both of them contain garbanzos, or chick-peas as they are often called. These creamy yellow beans have a nutlike flavor and texture; they mix well with other vegetables. Garbanzos are favorites in Spain and Portugal and they are gaining popularity in America. You will find them in cans on your supermarket shelves.

HEARTY HOT BEAN SALAD

Versatile—garnish determines if salad is a main or side dish.

1 c. thinly sliced celery	¼ tsp. dry mustard
1 small onion, sliced and separated into rings	1 (15 oz.) can kidney beans
	1 (15 oz.) can pinto beans
⅓ c. salad oil	1 (15 oz.) can garbanzos
¼ c. wine vinegar	(chick-peas)
1 tsp. parsley flakes	3 hard-cooked eggs, sliced, or
½ tsp. garlic salt	2 tomatoes, cut in wedges
¼ tsp. pepper	

Place celery and onion in heatproof bowl.

Shake together oil, vinegar, parsley, garlic salt, pepper and dry mustard until well mixed; pour over celery and onion, and toss.

Combine beans and garbanzos in saucepan; bring to a boil. Reduce heat and simmer about 5 minutes, until vegetables are heated through. Add to vegetables in bowl and toss gently. Serve hot. Garnish with hard-cooked eggs if salad is the main dish, with tomato wedges if a side dish. Makes 6 servings.

Memo to Meal Planner: For a summer ranch-style feast, serve the tomato-garnished salad with grilled hamburgers.

MIXED VEGETABLE SALAD WITH BASIL DRESSING

Herbs give extra zest to many salads—this time it's basil. The salad is good to tote to community and other co-operative suppers.

2 (10 oz.) pkgs. frozen French-
   style green beans, thawed
   and drained
1 (15 oz.) can garbanzos
   (chick-peas), drained
1 c. thinly sliced celery
⅓ c. chopped onion
½ tsp. salt

½ tsp. dried basil leaves,
   crushed
¼ tsp. pepper
¼ c. wine vinegar
¼ c. salad oil
1 clove garlic, minced or
   pressed

Combine green beans, garbanzos, celery and onion in salad bowl. Sprinkle with salt, basil and pepper. Add vinegar, salad oil and garlic. Cover and refrigerate at least 1 hour before serving. Serves 8.

Memo to Meal Planner: Serve this casual salad with lasagne and other main dishes containing cheese. Have it for lunch with steaming tomato soup and buttered toast sprinkled with grated cheese.

WINTER BEAN SALAD BOWL

A blender makes fast work of the salad dressing containing butter beans, but you can mix it by hand. Men especially show an interest in this new, hearty salad. Since the pattern of vegetables in the bowl displays the salad so attractively, it is a good idea to toss and serve it at the table. At least try to do this the first time you make the salad. This gives everyone a chance to admire the design of the lettuce, garbanzos, butter beans and onion rings before tossing.

6 c. lettuce, torn in bite-size
   pieces
1 (15 oz.) can garbanzos
   (chick-peas), drained and
   rinsed
1 (15 oz.) can butter beans,
   drained and rinsed
1 small onion, thinly sliced and
   separated into rings

⅓ c. salad oil
¼ c. vinegar
1 clove garlic
2 tsp. sugar
½ tsp. dry mustard
½ tsp. salt
¼ tsp. pepper

Place lettuce in salad bowl. Spoon garbanzos in circle around the top. Pile 1 c. butter beans in center. Scatter onion rings over all.

Combine remaining butter beans, salad oil, vinegar, garlic, sugar, dry mustard, salt and pepper in blender container. Blend until smooth and thick. Pour over salad just before serving. Toss gently. Makes 6 servings.

Molded Salads

Molded salads continue to have prestige in country kitchens. Busy women like the make-ahead aspect. They also appreciate their sparkling beauty—Vegetable/Cranberry Salad, for instance, is a good holiday special. Be sure to try thrifty Country Vegetable Salad in which orange and vegetable flavors blend deliciously and cottage cheese is an ingredient.

CRANBERRY/APPLE SALAD

If you belong to an organization that has a co-operative dinner, this salad carries successfully in cold weather and can be made a day ahead. Few apple salads equal this ruby-red treat.

2 c. cranberry juice cocktail	1 c. chopped unpeeled apple
1 (3 oz.) pkg. cherry flavor gelatin	½ c. chopped celery
Dash of salt	¼ c. nuts (optional)

Heat 1 c. cranberry juice cocktail to boiling. Dissolve gelatin in hot liquid; stir in remaining 1 c. cranberry juice cocktail and salt. Chill until thickened to the consistency of egg whites. Add remaining ingredients to gelatin.

Pour into individual molds or 8″ square pan. Chill until set. Makes 6 servings.

Memo to Meal Planner: This salad jewel is a worthy candidate for the holiday turkey dinner. You can easily double the recipe.

APPLE/PINEAPPLE SALAD

Ginger ale gives the fruit salad an appetizing fresh zip.

1 (8¾ oz.) can pineapple
   tidbits
Water
1 (3 oz.) pkg. lemon flavor
   gelatin

1 c. ginger ale
1½ c. chopped unpeeled red
   apples

Drain pineapple, reserving juice. Add enough water to juice to make
1 c. Heat to boiling. Remove from heat and stir in gelatin; continue
stirring until gelatin is dissolved. Add ginger ale. Chill until mixture
is the consistency of egg whites. Fold in apple and pineapple. Chill.
Makes 6 servings.

Memo to Meal Planner: Serve this refreshing salad with beef, pork,
chicken and cheese main dishes, such as Beef/Corn Pie, Pork/Cab-
bage Casserole, Chicken Croquettes, Oven-browned and Wisconsin
Hot Dish (see Index for recipes). Or if you prefer, assign the
dessert role to the delicious molded fruits. If you use a 12-oz. can of
ginger ale you can salvage the leftover beverage by adding it to a
fruit cup or pouring it over canned pears.

VEGETABLE/CRANBERRY SALAD

*Cranberry sauce gives this easy, one-step molded vegetable salad a
new taste. It is a near relative of a much-appreciated old-time friend,
perfection salad, and is especially good with chicken dishes.*

1 envelope unflavored gelatin
½ c. cold water
⅛ tsp. salt
1 tblsp. vinegar
1 (1 lb.) can jellied cranberry
   sauce

1 c. finely shredded cabbage
½ c. diced celery
½ c. shredded peeled carrots

Soften gelatin in water. Add salt; cook and stir over low heat until
gelatin is dissolved. Add vinegar.

In a bowl break up cranberry sauce with a fork. Beat with rotary
beater until smooth. Stir into gelatin mixture. Fold in vegetables.
(Do not chill gelatin mixture before adding vegetables.) Spoon into
individual molds or 8″ square pan. Chill until set. Makes 6 servings.

BEET/HORSERADISH MOLDED SALAD

Lively, colorful salad points up the best flavors in other foods. Keep a few cans of beets in the kitchen to rescue meals that otherwise would be colorless; the habit will pay off.

1 (1 lb.) can diced beets	½ tsp. salt
3 tblsp. vinegar	¾ c. chopped celery
1 (3 oz.) pkg. lemon flavor	2 tblsp. prepared horseradish
gelatin	1 tblsp. finely chopped onion

Drain beets, reserving liquid. Set beets aside. Add enough water to beet liquid to make 1½ c. Heat liquid and vinegar; add gelatin and stir until dissolved. Add salt. Chill until mixture thickens to the consistency of egg whites. Fold in celery, horseradish, onion and beets.

Spoon into individual molds or 8" square pan. Chill until set. Makes 6 servings.

Memo to Meal Planner: This thrifty salad, which has a tart note lacking in some gelatin salads, tastes good with almost all meats, chicken, fish, egg and cheese main dishes. The horseradish accent pleases almost everyone who tastes the salad.

MOLDED TOMATO SALAD

Canned tomatoes and cottage cheese combined with good seasoning result in a wonderful salad. The Wisconsin woman who shares this recipe says her family considers it her best winter salad. Since all the ingredients for it are available the year around you may want to make it in every season.

1 (1 lb.) can tomatoes	1 tblsp. vinegar
1 tsp. salt	1 c. creamed cottage cheese
Dash of pepper	1 c. shredded cabbage
1 small bay leaf	¼ c. chopped celery
3 whole cloves	¼ c. chopped green pepper
3 tblsp. chopped onion	⅓ c. mayonnaise or salad
1 (3 oz.) pkg. lemon flavor	dressing
gelatin	

Combine tomatoes, salt, pepper, bay leaf, cloves and onion in saucepan. Cover and simmer 20 minutes. Remove bay leaf and cloves. Force tomatoes through a sieve or food mill.

Dissolve gelatin in hot tomato mixture. Add vinegar and chill until mixture thickens to the consistency of egg whites.

Combine remaining ingredients and fold into gelatin. Pour into individual molds or 8" square pan. Chill until firm. Makes 6 servings.

Memo to Meal Planner: If you have home-canned tomatoes, use 2 c. of them to make this expertly seasoned aspic that holds cottage cheese and vegetables. Serve it with hot corn muffins for a main dish at lunch or supper. Or place individual servings of it on salad plates for the meat-and-potato dinner, or to go with a hearty bean soup.

MOLDED VEGETABLE/COTTAGE CHEESE SALAD

Take this distinctive tomato aspic to covered dish luncheons.

3 c. tomato juice	1½ c. creamed cottage cheese
2 bay leaves	1 c. shredded cabbage
1 (6 oz.) pkg. lemon flavor gelatin	½ c. shredded carrots
	½ c. chopped celery
⅔ c. water	⅓ c. chopped green pepper
¼ c. vinegar	¼ c. chopped green onion and
½ tsp. salt	tops

Combine tomato juice and bay leaves in saucepan. Bring to a boil and simmer a few minutes. Remove bay leaves.

Dissolve gelatin in hot tomato juice. Stir in water, vinegar and salt. Chill until mixture is the consistency of egg whites.

Fold cottage cheese and vegetables into gelatin mixture. Pour into 12×7½×2" pan. Chill until firm. Makes 12 servings.

Memo to Meal Planner: A good way to complete the menu and lower the cost of a women's group luncheon is for everyone to bring her own sandwich. Share the cost of the salad and coffee.

COUNTRY VEGETABLE SALAD

This is not a usual molded salad; the combination of orange and a medley of vegetable flavors has something to do with its superior taste. So does the creamy richness of cottage cheese and mayonnaise.

1 (3 oz.) pkg. orange flavor gelatin	½ c. grated peeled carrots
1 c. boiling water	½ c. chopped celery
1 c. mayonnaise or salad dressing	2 tblsp. finely chopped onion
½ c. drained cottage cheese	2 tblsp. finely chopped green pepper
	Dash of salt

Dissolve gelatin in boiling water. Gently beat in mayonnaise with rotary beater. Chill until mixture is the consistency of egg whites.

Fold remaining ingredients into gelatin. Turn into 8″ square pan or 4-c. mold. Chill until set. Makes 6 servings.

Memo to Meal Planner: Chill the salad in a fancy mold for company. All the garnish you will need is a touch of lettuce. The family will like the salad just as much if you chill it in a pan and cut into squares for serving. Omit the green pepper during seasons when its cost is high, but do add it when available at a reasonably low price.

SUMMER GREEN SALAD MOLD

In this lovely green and white salad lime flavor gelatin holds succulent vegetables, cottage cheese and salad dressing. When the salads are on individual salad plates, frame them with a few shreds of crisp green lettuce. If you have space in the refrigerator, chill the plates before placing the salad on them.

1 (3 oz.) pkg. lime flavor gelatin	1 c. chopped cucumber
1 c. hot water	½ c. chopped celery
½ c. cold water	1 c. creamed cottage cheese
½ c. mayonnaise or salad dressing	⅓ c. chopped green pepper
	1 tblsp. grated onion

Dissolve gelatin in hot water. Add cold water and chill to the consistency of egg whites. Slowly beat in mayonnaise with rotary beater just until blended. Fold in remaining ingredients. Pour into 8″ square baking dish. Chill until set. Makes 6 servings.

CARROT/CABBAGE SALAD

When high food prices threaten food budgets, alert country women begin to search for tasty salads that capitalize on the color, economy and availability of humble cabbage and carrots. The orange-flavored recipe that follows comes from a Mississippi hostess who considers the salad equal to the most special occasions, including holiday dinners. She uses homemade pickles and some of the breakfast orange juice to make her specialty. The success of the make-ahead salad, she says, is the harmonious blending of orange and vegetable flavors—simply wonderful.

1 (6 oz.) pkg. orange flavor gelatin	1 c. shredded cabbage
2 c. hot water	1 c. shredded peeled carrots
1½ c. reconstituted frozen orange juice concentrate	½ c. chopped celery
2 tblsp. vinegar	¼ c. minced sweet pickle
2 tblsp. sweet pickle juice	2 tblsp. minced green or white onion

Dissolve gelatin in hot water. Add orange juice, vinegar and pickle juice; chill until mixture is the consistency of egg whites. Fold in remaining ingredients. Turn into 11×7½×2″ baking dish. Chill until set. Makes 8 to 10 servings.

Memo to Meal Planner: For a company luncheon, serve this color-bright salad with chicken, tuna or toasted cheese sandwiches and a hot beverage. Or take it to the neighborhood covered dish supper.

TUNA SALAD MOLD

If time is precious, chill this salad in a serving bowl. You skip the time required to unmold before serving.

2 envelopes unflavored gelatin	2 (7 oz.) cans tuna, drained and flaked
½ c. cold water	
1 (10¾ oz.) can condensed cream of celery soup	1 c. chopped celery
¼ c. lemon juice	¾ c. chopped cucumber
1 tblsp. prepared mustard	¼ c. chopped green pepper
1 tsp. salt	2 tblsp. chopped onion
1 c. mayonnaise or salad dressing	

Soften gelatin in cold water. Heat soup just until boiling, stirring frequently. Add gelatin and stir to dissolve. Mix in lemon juice, mustard and salt. Chill until thickened to the consistency of egg whites. Stir in mayonnaise. Fold in remaining ingredients. Turn into 1½-qt. mold or serving bowl. Chill until set. Serves 6.

Memo to Meal Planner: If you serve this tasty main-dish salad right from a serving bowl, scatter sprigs of parsley over the top. Excellent accompaniments are buttered carrots and peas and hot rolls. For dessert have fruit and oatmeal cookies. Scotia Oat Squares are a nutritious choice (see Index for recipe).

Main-dish Salads

Substantial and economical salads, some hot and others cold, increasingly serve as main dishes in suppers and lunches. They are appetizing and full of good nutrition.

Oriental Rice Salad is one of our Test Kitchen favorites. It contains, among other things, slender strips of ham, plump mandarin orange sections and chopped unpeeled red apples.

The Utah mother who shares the recipe for Matador Salad, topped with crisp corn chips, says her three sons really "dig" it.

HOSTESS CHICKEN/RICE SALAD

Distinctive salad for a women's group luncheon. Rice cuts costs by extending chicken. Salad is filling, tasty and pretty with garnishes.

1 c. uncooked rice	⅓ c. chopped green pepper
3 c. cubed cooked chicken	½ c. French dressing
2 c. finely chopped celery	½ c. mayonnaise or salad
1 c. frozen peas, thawed	dressing
½ c. sweet pickle relish	½ tsp. salt

Cook rice by package directions. Combine with chicken, celery, peas, pickle relish and green pepper.

Blend together French dressing, mayonnaise and salt; stir into salad. Chill at least 2 hours before serving. Makes 9 servings.

Memo to Meal Planner: Attractive garnishes for salad are hard-cooked egg slices and tomato wedges. Unless you like a fairly sweet salad, use a tart French dressing, such as our Basic French Dressing (see Index for recipe). Good accompaniments are spiced fruits—peaches, pears or apples—and hot rolls. For dessert, if your guests are calorie watchers, Frosty Lemon Squares are a splendid choice. If they favor luscious desserts, even though rich, consider Cherry/Cheese Torte. Both desserts are make-ahead specials (see Index).

HOT CHICKEN SALAD

Peanuts are the new touch in this flavorful baked salad.

1 (2½ to 3 lb.) broiler-fryer, cut up	⅛ tsp. pepper
3 c. water	1 c. mayonnaise or salad dressing
1 small onion, cut up	2 tblsp. lemon juice
1 (6″) branch celery	2 c. thinly sliced celery
1 tsp. salt	¾ c. Spanish peanuts
4 peppercorns	¼ c. chopped onion
1 c. reserved chicken broth	2 tblsp. chopped pimiento (optional)
2 tblsp. flour	1 c. crushed potato chips
¼ tsp. salt	

Combine chicken, water, cut-up onion, celery branch, 1 tsp. salt and peppercorns in large kettle. Bring to a boil. Reduce heat, cover and simmer 50 minutes. Strain broth and reserve. Cut meat from bones. Discard skin and bones.

Slowly blend 1 c. reserved broth into flour in saucepan. Add ¼ tsp. salt and pepper. Cook, stirring constantly, until mixture comes to a boil. Remove from heat and blend in mayonnaise and lemon juice.

Combine chicken, celery, peanuts, chopped onion and pimiento. Stir in mayonnaise mixture. Turn into greased 2-qt. casserole. Sprinkle with potato chips. Bake in 350° oven 25 minutes. Serves 8.

Memo to Meal Planner: Serve this interesting main dish for a guest luncheon or supper, or for family meals, along with buttered broccoli, green beans or peas, spiced fruit or pickles and hot rolls. If you wish to serve a dessert, consider Chocolate/Banana Upside-down Cake, which you can bake alongside the salad.

MATADOR SALAD

If your family and friends enjoy tacos, the increasingly popular Mexican sandwich, they will praise this new, hearty summer salad.

1 lb. ground beef
¼ c. chopped onion
1 (15 oz.) can pinto beans, drained
1 c. tomato juice
2 to 3 tsp. chili powder
1 tsp. salt
5 c. shredded lettuce

⅓ c. sliced green onions
⅓ c. chopped green pepper
1 large tomato, peeled and chopped
1 c. shredded Cheddar cheese (4 oz.)
1 (6 oz.) pkg. corn chips, crushed

Cook ground beef and ¼ c. onion in skillet until beef is browned; drain off excess fat. Add pinto beans, tomato juice, chili powder and salt. Cover and simmer 10 minutes.

Meanwhile, combine lettuce, green onions, green pepper, tomato and cheese in large bowl. Toss gently to mix. Place on individual plates. Spoon on meat mixture; top with corn chips. Serves 6.

Memo to Meal Planner: For tasty accompaniments to this main-dish salad have buttered zucchini and for dessert, fresh fruit.

HOT BOLOGNA SALAD

Quick, easy, different main dish for a summer lunch or supper.

1 lb. bologna, diced
6 hard-cooked eggs, chopped
1½ c. sliced celery
½ c. chopped onion
½ c. sweet pickle relish

1½ c. mayonnaise or salad dressing
1 tblsp. prepared mustard
1 c. crushed potato chips

Combine all ingredients, except potato chips. Turn into a greased 2-qt. casserole. Top with potato chips. Bake in 350° oven 35 minutes. Serve at once. Makes 8 servings.

Memo to Meal Planner: Sliced fresh tomatoes make an excellent accompaniment to this meat casserole with its crunchy potato chip top. Serve with rye bread or hot whole wheat rolls. Team your favorite tapioca pudding, well chilled, with brownies or chocolate chip cookies for a delightful, nutritious, make-ahead dessert.

ORIENTAL RICE SALAD

Top yellow rice with chopped red apples and mandarin oranges.

1¼ tsp. salt	2 unpeeled red apples, chopped
½ tsp. curry powder	1 (11 oz.) can mandarin
½ tsp. salad oil	oranges, drained
2 c. water	1 tblsp. chopped green onion
1 c. uncooked rice	and top
1½ c. cooked ham, cut in	⅓ c. French dressing
julienne strips	2 tblsp. sugar
1 c. sliced celery	2 tblsp. vinegar or lemon juice

Add salt, curry powder and salad oil to water; heat to boiling. Add rice; cover, lower heat and simmer 20 minutes. Remove from heat and let stand, covered, 10 minutes. Cool and chill.

Combine chilled rice, ham, celery, apples, orange sections and green onion.

Blend together French dressing, sugar and vinegar. Pour over rice mixture and toss gently. Makes 8 servings.

Memo to Meal Planner: As a main-dish salad for a women's lunch, served with hot rolls and tea, this beautiful salad bowl is a great success. Strips of ham add protein as well as flavor. Celery contributes crunchy texture. Apples and mandarin oranges provide a marvelous flavor contrast to the rice seasoned with a little curry powder. Serve the salad in individual bowls for a party luncheon. Served in a big bowl, the salad is a handsome touch to the buffet table. Then it takes a strictly salad role—a good companion for chicken.

HOT POTATO/FRANKFURTER SALAD

Garnish this main dish with sliced red radishes when in season.

6 c. sliced peeled potatoes	¼ c. sugar
4 slices bacon	1½ tsp. salt
¾ c. chopped onion	1 tsp. celery seeds
3 tblsp. flour	¼ tsp. pepper
1 c. water	1 lb. frankfurters, cut crosswise
¾ c. vinegar	in fourths

Cook potato slices in boiling salted water until tender; drain.

Meanwhile, fry bacon in large skillet until crisp; remove and set aside. Cook onion in bacon drippings until soft. Stir in flour. Add water and vinegar and cook, stirring, until mixture comes to a boil and is thickened. Stir in sugar, salt, celery seeds and pepper. Add frankfurter pieces. Cover and simmer 3 to 4 minutes, until heated. Add crumbled bacon and potatoes, tossing gently to cover with sauce. Heat thoroughly and serve hot. Makes 6 servings.

Memo to Meal Planner: If you can get bacon ends and pieces, they will cost less than sliced bacon. Serve this German-style potato salad with stewed tomatoes and corn, hot garlic bread and have a molded berry dessert. In summer serve sliced tomatoes and corn on the cob. Vanilla ice cream on cantaloupe slices happily ends the meal.

POTATO/HAM SALAD

Tempting main dish to serve for lunch or supper on warm days. It's a good idea to make salad in the cool morning and chill until mealtime.

4 c. cubed peeled cooked hot potatoes	3 c. cubed cooked ham
1 tsp. salt	1 c. chopped celery
¼ tsp. pepper	½ c. sliced green onions and tops
1 c. salad dressing	¼ c. chopped dill pickle
2 tblsp. sugar	¼ c. chopped fresh parsley
2 tblsp. vinegar	
1 to 2 tblsp. horseradish mustard	

Sprinkle hot potatoes with salt and pepper.

Blend together salad dressing, sugar, vinegar and mustard. Stir into potatoes. Cover and chill thoroughly.

Add ham, celery, green onions, pickle and parsley to potatoes; cover and chill at least 1 hour longer. Makes 6 servings.

Memo to Meal Planner: Make the most of summer's food gifts when you serve this salad. Line bowl with lettuce and garnish salad with tomato wedges. Round out meal with green beans, hot rolls and vanilla ice cream topped with sugared sliced peaches.

MAIN-DISH POTATO SALAD

Eggs and cheese convert potato salad into a tasty main dish.

4 c. diced peeled cooked warm potatoes	1 c. chopped celery
1 tsp. salt	2 tblsp. chopped onion
¼ tsp. pepper	1 c. mayonnaise or salad dressing
1 tblsp. vinegar	1 tblsp. sugar
4 hard-cooked eggs, chopped	2 tblsp. vinegar
2 c. diced Cheddar cheese (8 oz.)	3 slices luncheon meat, cut in julienne strips (optional)

Over warm potatoes in bowl sprinkle salt, pepper and 1 tblsp. vinegar. Chill. Add eggs, cheese, celery and onion.

Blend together mayonnaise, sugar and 2 tblsp. vinegar. Stir into potatoes. Garnish with luncheon meat. Chill. Makes about 2 quarts.

Memo to Meal Planner: Serve hearty salad with sliced tomatoes, hot buttered corn or green beans and crusty rolls or bread. The garnish of luncheon meat is optional, but many men who think of potato salad as a side dish know it is the main dish when they see the meal.

HOT MACARONI SALAD

German-style potato salad, popular in Pennsylvania Dutch areas and other places, inspired this hearty main-dish salad.

3 slices bacon, diced	½ c. water
½ c. chopped onion	1 (8 oz.) pkg. elbow macaroni, cooked and drained
2 tblsp. flour	1 c. sliced celery
2 tblsp. sugar	6 hard-cooked eggs, diced
1½ tsp. salt	½ c. mayonnaise or salad dressing
1 tsp. celery seeds	
⅛ tsp. pepper	
½ c. vinegar	

Cook bacon in skillet; drain on paper toweling and set aside. Cook onion in bacon drippings until soft, but do not brown.

Combine flour, sugar, salt, celery seeds and pepper. Blend in vinegar and water. Stir into onion in skillet and heat until bubbly.

Combine hot macaroni, celery, hard-cooked eggs and bacon. Add hot vinegar mixture and mayonnaise. Toss gently and serve at once. Makes 6 servings.

Memo to Meal Planner: Serve this all-season salad with crisp red radishes in the spring, sliced tomatoes in summer and chilled tomato juice the remainder of the year. If you have fresh parsley or chives, chop and sprinkle the herb over the salad to add color. Rye bread is an excellent accompaniment.

TUNA LUNCHEON SALAD

The popularity of this salad with people of all ages stems from the crunchiness of the potatoes—a new note. The appealing yellow-and-white egg garnish adds protein, making this an adequate main dish.

1 (7 oz.) can tuna, drained and flaked
1 c. shredded peeled carrots
1 c. chopped celery
2 tblsp. minced onion
2 tblsp. sweet pickle relish
¾ c. mayonnaise or salad dressing
1 (4 oz.) can shoestring potatoes
3 hard-cooked eggs, cut in wedges

Combine tuna, carrots, celery, onion and pickle relish in a large bowl. Gently stir in mayonnaise; chill. Just before serving, stir in potatoes. Garnish with egg wedges. Makes 6 servings.

Memo to Meal Planner: Serve this flavorful main dish with mugs of hot tomato soup or juice and toast or crackers. Cookies and milk make an ideal dessert.

TUNA/BEAN SALAD

Salad teamed with whole wheat bread makes great sandwiches.

1 (15½ oz.) can navy beans, drained and rinsed, or 2 c. cooked navy beans
1 (7 oz.) can tuna, drained
1 c. chopped celery
⅓ c. chopped onion
1 tblsp. parsley flakes
½ tsp. garlic salt
⅛ tsp. pepper
¼ c. salad oil
3 tblsp. lemon juice

Combine all ingredients and chill several hours. Makes 6 servings.

Memo to Meal Planner: If fresh tomatoes are in season, garnish salad with tomato wedges. Using the salad for a sandwich filling provides a change of pace, which children especially enjoy. Cupfuls of hot soup are excellent escorts for either the salad or sandwiches.

GREEN PEA/SALMON SALAD

Faint dill weed flavor is the special touch in this main-dish supper salad—serve with hot rolls or biscuits.

1 (1 lb.) can pink salmon	½ tsp. salt
1 (10 oz.) pkg. frozen peas, thawed	⅔ c. mayonnaise or salad dressing
6 hard-cooked eggs, chopped	2 tblsp. lemon juice
1 c. thinly sliced celery	1 tsp. dried dill weed
⅓ c. sliced green onions and tops	Lettuce
	Tomatoes (optional)

Drain salmon; remove and discard skin and bones. Combine with peas, eggs, celery and onions. Sprinkle with salt.

Mix together mayonnaise, lemon juice and dill weed. Stir into salmon mixture. Chill at least 1 hour before serving.

Serve in bowl lined with lettuce or on lettuce-lined salad plates. Garnish with tomato wedges when in season. Makes 6 servings.

Memo to Meal Planner: Made with red salmon, this salad is more colorful, but the delicate flavored pink fish costs less and tastes great.

Salads You Toss

Following are tossed salad recipes for all seasons, made with vegetables nearly always available. There are four economical cabbage salads—all different and all delicious. One tossed salad you can make one day for serving the next. Several are teamed with cottage cheese, a country kitchen favorite. For variety try the homemade salad dressings in this cookbook (see Index) with these salads.

TOSSED CARROT SALAD

With a toss of carrots, red apples and cottage cheese, you have a family-type, nutritive salad that brightens meals.

2 c. shredded peeled carrots	¼ tsp. salt
1 c. finely chopped unpeeled apples	2 tblsp. French dressing
1 c. creamed cottage cheese	Lettuce

Combine all ingredients in bowl. Toss to mix well. Serve on lettuce-lined plates. Makes 6 servings.

Memo to Meal Planner: For a simple, quick lunch, serve with hot tomato or other soup and peanut butter sandwiches or Open-face Burgers (see Index for recipe).

VEGETABLE/ORANGE SALAD

The best time to make the salad is when spinach leaves in gardens are young. That usually is when the cost of the ingredients is kindest to the pocketbook. Set a bowl of it on the buffet table and watch everyone admire.

2 qts. spinach, torn in bite-size pieces	1 (11 oz.) can mandarin oranges, chilled and drained
1 cucumber, sliced	¼ tsp. salt
½ medium onion, sliced and separated into rings	½ c. French dressing

Combine vegetables and orange sections in salad bowl. Sprinkle with salt. Add dressing and toss gently. Makes 8 servings.

Memo to Meal Planner: Serve this decorative salad with fish, but it's also good in meals featuring meat, chicken, cheese and egg dishes.

Cabbage/Cottage Cheese Salad

Cabbage is available the year around, and among the salad vegetables is one of the most economical. Meal planners depended on it for generations to provide crispness and a pleasing sweet-tart taste in the form of slaw. Seasonings came from staples in the kitchen, such as vinegar, sugar, celery seeds and salt, and sometimes sour cream.

Many thrifty women are turning once again to cabbage salads to make their meals more appetizing. New seasonings will keep the family from tiring of them.

CABBAGE/COTTAGE CHEESE SALAD

The rich, creamy flavor undertones come from the cottage cheese.

1 c. small curd creamed cottage cheese
½ c. mayonnaise or salad dressing
2 tblsp. vinegar

2 tblsp. sugar
1 tsp. celery seeds
½ tsp. salt
⅛ tsp. pepper
8 c. shredded cabbage

Blend together cottage cheese, mayonnaise, vinegar, sugar, celery seeds, salt and pepper. Add cabbage and toss. Makes 8 servings.

OCTOBER COLESLAW

The bright flash of a few cranberries and the intriguing honey-celery seed flavor transform a simple country coleslaw into a special-occasion salad. Cabbage is one of the less expensive salad vegetables most years. Shred it fine for best results. And use a sharp knife to retain the largest amount of vitamin C.

⅓ c. sliced fresh cranberries
1½ tblsp. honey
1 tsp. celery seeds
1 tsp. grated orange peel (optional)
⅓ c. mayonnaise or salad dressing

2 tsp. vinegar
4 c. shredded cabbage
¼ tsp. salt
Dash of pepper

Combine cranberries, honey, celery seeds and orange peel. Let stand 15 minutes. Stir in mayonnaise and vinegar.

Sprinkle cabbage with salt and pepper. Add cranberry mixture and toss lightly. Makes 6 servings.

APPLE COLESLAW

Marshmallows add a touch of sweetness many people enjoy.

4 c. shredded cabbage	1 tblsp. sugar
2 c. diced unpeeled apples	¼ tsp. salt
½ c. miniature marshmallows	1 tblsp. vinegar
½ c. mayonnaise or salad dressing	

Combine cabbage, apples and marshmallows in salad bowl.

Blend together mayonnaise, sugar, salt and vinegar. Add to cabbage mixture and toss. Makes 6 servings.

Memo to Meal Planner: For a sweeter salad, increase the measurement of marshmallows to 1 c. You can omit marshmallows entirely, however, if you prefer a tart slaw.

LEMON COLESLAW

Ideal salad to carry to covered dish suppers. Tightly covered, the salad keeps several days in the refrigerator. The vegetables soften slightly as they stand, which explains why the yield measures less than the ingredients used in making the salad. The surprise in this coleslaw is the pleasing lemon flavor, even though no lemon juice is added. The trick is lemon flavor gelatin, which also helps the vegetables retain much of their original crispness.

8 c. shredded cabbage	1 tsp. celery seeds
1 c. shredded peeled carrots	¼ tsp. pepper
⅔ c. finely chopped green pepper (or less)	¼ tsp. mustard seeds
⅓ c. grated onion	½ c. salad oil
½ c. sugar	¾ c. vinegar
1 tsp. salt	1 (3 oz.) pkg. lemon flavor gelatin

Combine cabbage, carrots, green pepper and onion in large bowl.

Combine sugar, salt, celery seeds, pepper and mustard seeds in saucepan. Add salad oil and vinegar; heat to a boil. Remove from heat and stir in gelatin; continue to stir until gelatin is dissolved. Cool, then pour over vegetables and toss gently. Cover and let stand overnight in refrigerator. Makes 1½ quarts.

OVERNIGHT TOSSED SALAD

Good tossed salads that will wait without wilting are rare. This chef's salad is a good example of one that will hold up for hours. The trick is to spread the dressing over the salad to exclude the air during the long chilling. If you wish to serve it in a buffet supper, bring the salad from the refrigerator at the last minute. Stand by it, and toss the salad when the first guest is ready to help himself.

6 c. chopped lettuce	½ c. sliced green onions and
½ tsp. salt	tops
½ tsp. sugar	½ c. sliced celery
⅛ tsp. pepper	2 c. shredded process Swiss
6 hard-cooked eggs, sliced	cheese (8 oz.)
1 (10 oz.) pkg. frozen peas,	1¼ c. mayonnaise or salad
thawed	dressing
½ lb. bacon ends and pieces or	
bacon, crisp-cooked and	
crumbled	

Place half the lettuce in a large bowl. Sprinkle with salt, sugar and pepper. Top with layer of eggs, then peas, bacon, remaining lettuce, green onion, celery and cheese.

Spread mayonnaise evenly over the top to cover. Place tight cover on bowl and refrigerate 24 hours. Toss just before serving. Makes 8 servings as a main dish, 12 as a side dish in a meal.

REFRIGERATOR VEGETABLE SALAD

American version of an Italian make-ahead mixed vegetable salad.

5 tblsp. salad oil	4 c. shredded cabbage
2 tblsp. wine vinegar	1 (1 lb.) can French-style
½ tsp. salt	green beans, drained
¼ tsp. pepper	1½ c. shredded peeled carrots
⅛ tsp. dried orégano leaves,	⅔ c. chopped green pepper
crushed	¼ c. finely chopped onion
1 clove garlic, cut in half	

Combine salad oil, vinegar, salt, pepper, orégano and garlic; let stand 15 minutes for flavors to blend. Discard garlic.

Meanwhile, combine vegetables in salad bowl. Stir dressing and pour over vegetables. Toss gently. Cover and chill at least 1 hour to mellow flavors. Makes 8 servings.

Memo to Meal Planner: This salad is a perfect escort for lasagne or macaroni and cheese.

Other Country Favorite Salads—and Dressings

Old-time favorites with new features . . . to serve with confidence for almost any occasion . . . that's what you'll find in the following group of recipes. You arrange some country favorite salads on individual plates. Peach Salad, with canned peach halves and red onion rings on salad greens, is a classic example. Some others you combine in a bowl and stir gently with a spoon to distribute the vegetables and salad dressing, such as the recipe for Broccoli Salad and those containing beans.

At the end of this chapter are five outstanding homemade salad dressings. They're quick and economical. Team them with the salad recipes that precede them; you'll like the results. Other salad dressing recipes appear in Chapter 2 (see Index for the recipes).

PEACH SALAD

Golden peach halves and red onion rings in a bright salad like this bring sunshine to the dining table.

1 (1 lb. 13 oz.) can peach   Salad greens
halves, drained   French Celery Seed Dressing
1 red onion, sliced and   (see Index)
separated into rings

Chill peaches. On each salad plate arrange 1 peach half and onion rings on salad greens. Spoon over French Celery Seed Dressing. Makes 6 or 7 servings, depending on number of peach halves in can.

Memo to Meal Planner: The salad tastes as good as it looks, and complements chicken dishes and many meats, from hamburgers to the aristocratic pork roast. You can substitute cubes of lime or raspberry flavor gelatin or jellied cranberry sauce for the onion rings if you like. Use home canned peaches if you have them.

COOL MINTED PEA SALAD

Serve this salad of bright green frozen peas, cucumbers and mint to help everyone forget hot, humid weather.

2 (10 oz.) pkgs. frozen peas,
   thawed and drained
1 medium cucumber, peeled
   and chopped
⅓ c. chopped celery
⅓ c. mayonnaise or salad
   dressing

1 tblsp. sugar
½ tsp. mint flakes
½ tsp. salt
1 tblsp. lemon juice

Combine peas, cucumber and celery in salad bowl.

Blend together mayonnaise, sugar, mint, salt and lemon juice. Stir gently into vegetables. Makes 6 servings.

Memo to Meal Planner: By all means, use fresh instead of dried mint if you have it in your garden. Use 3 tblsp. chopped leaves. The salad is wonderful with lamb and pleasing with chicken and pork dishes.

BROCCOLI SALAD

Switch from buttered broccoli to salad for a happy change. The distinctive, make-ahead salad is colorful and delicious—and travels well.

2 lbs. fresh broccoli
1 c. Italian salad dressing
¼ c. finely chopped dill pickle

¼ c. minced green pepper
1 tblsp. parsley flakes
2 hard-cooked eggs, diced

Trim ends of broccoli; peel stems if tough. Cook in boiling salted water until tender-crisp. Drain.

Mix together remaining ingredients; pour over broccoli. Chill several hours, or overnight. Stir occasionally. Makes 8 servings.

Memo to Meal Planner: You can use Homemade Italian Salad Dressing (in this chapter) when making this salad. Fried chicken is a good companion. In home meals serve it with pan-fried fish or crisp-coated fish cakes. Consider teaming the salad with Exceptional Tuna Patties (see Index).

COTTAGE CHEESE/VEGETABLE SALAD

Use odds and ends of vegetables you have to brighten cottage cheese.

2 c. small curd creamed cottage
  cheese
½ c. grated peeled carrot
1 tomato, peeled and chopped
⅓ c. diced cucumber

⅓ c. diced celery
2 tblsp. chopped green pepper
2 tblsp. chopped green onion
1 tsp. seasoned salt
Lettuce leaves (optional)

Combine cottage cheese, vegetables and seasoned salt. Serve in lettuce cups or in lettuce-lined salad bowl. Makes 6 servings.

FOUR-SEASON BEAN SALAD

You can keep most of the makings for this salad in your cupboard. Homemade Italian Salad Dressing imparts piquant accents that make the salad a good companion for almost all main dishes.

1 (1 lb.) can cut green beans,
  drained
1 (1 lb.) can cut wax beans,
  drained
½ c. chopped celery

2 tblsp. finely chopped onion
2 tblsp. chopped pimiento
Homemade Italian Salad
  Dressing (see Index)
Grated Parmesan cheese

Combine vegetables in salad bowl. Add Homemade Italian Salad Dressing and stir gently. Cover and chill several hours or overnight, stirring occasionally. Just before serving, drain off dressing and stir in cheese. Makes 6 to 8 servings.

CASSEROLE BEAN SALAD

They'll praise this casserole—it's filled with hot salad.

1 (1 lb.) can green beans,
  drained
1 (1 lb.) can wax beans,
  drained
1 (15 oz.) can kidney beans,
  drained and rinsed
⅓ c. chopped celery
¼ c. chopped green pepper

¼ c. chopped onion
½ c. mayonnaise or salad
  dressing
1 tblsp. sugar
¼ tsp. salt
⅛ tsp. pepper
2 tblsp. vinegar

Combine beans, celery, green pepper and onion.

Blend together mayonnaise, sugar, salt, pepper and vinegar. Stir into vegetable mixture. Turn into 1½-qt. casserole. Bake in 350° oven about 20 minutes, until hot. Makes 8 servings.

Memo to Meal Planner: Serve this new, different 3-bean salad with a platter of sliced cold chicken, turkey or meat, or with deviled eggs. In summer meals, add iced watermelon to the menu and you have a feast. Bring out piping hot corn on the cob if it's in season.

PICNIC ZUCCHINI/KIDNEY BEAN SALAD

Fresh zucchini appears in this salad that's a treat to eat and fine to serve both indoors and out since it carries well.

3 small zucchini, thinly sliced (about 1 lb.)
¾ c. chopped green pepper
½ c. chopped onion
1 (15 oz.) can kidney beans, drained and rinsed

¼ c. salad oil
3 tblsp. vinegar
1½ tsp. garlic salt
¼ tsp. pepper

Combine all ingredients in salad bowl. Cover and refrigerate at least 4 hours. Stir occasionally. Makes 8 servings.

Memo to Meal Planner: This distinctive salad is especially good with hamburgers and Italian-type dishes, such as Beef Lasagne and Beef/Noodle Casserole (see Index for recipes).

COTTAGE CHEESE SALAD DRESSING

Packed with cottage cheese and vegetables, the dressing is low in calories and boosts the protein and vitamin content of meals.

1½ c. creamed cottage cheese
1 (8 oz.) can tomato sauce
2 tblsp. lemon juice
1 tblsp. parsley flakes

½ tsp. salt
½ tsp. garlic salt
¼ tsp. instant minced onion
⅛ tsp. pepper

Combine all ingredients in blender container. Whirl until thoroughly blended. Chill at least 1 hour for flavors to blend. Makes 2 cups, enough for 12 servings over wedges of head lettuce.

Memo to Meal Planner: Make dressing with the style of cottage cheese you prefer. Spoon it over wedges of head lettuce.

FRENCH CELERY SEED SALAD DRESSING

Celery seed is returning to spice shelves in country kitchens. No rule prevents you from following our grandmothers' practice of scattering a few of the tiny seeds in potato and cabbage salads, cottage cheese and tomato juice, but with electric mixers and beaters, it is no chore to whip up marvelous salad dressing. This salad dressing is one example of how the spice is used today. It glorifies fruit salads.

⅓ c. sugar
½ tsp. dry mustard
½ tsp. paprika
½ tsp. celery seeds
⅛ tsp. salt

¼ c. vinegar
3 tblsp. honey
½ tsp. grated onion
½ c. salad oil

Combine sugar, mustard, paprika, celery seeds and salt in small bowl of mixer. Stir in vinegar, honey and onion. Pour in oil in a slow stream, beating constantly with electric mixer at high speed until thickened. Store in refrigerator. Makes 1 cup.

HOMEMADE ITALIAN SALAD DRESSING

You can shake up a jar of this dressing in 5 minutes from start to finish. It will cost less than Italian dressing you buy.

1 c. salad oil
⅓ c. wine vinegar
1 tsp. salt
1 tsp. sugar
¼ tsp. dried orégano leaves,
   crushed

¼ tsp. dry mustard
¼ tsp. paprika
⅛ tsp. pepper
1 clove garlic, minced

Combine all ingredients in jar; cover and shake to mix thoroughly. Let stand at least 2 hours to blend seasonings. Shake before using. Makes 1⅓ cups.

Memo to Meal Planner: Serve this dressing on lettuce and tossed green salads served with lasagne and other cheese main dishes.

THOUSAND ISLAND SALAD DRESSING

Tired of lettuce salads? Redeem them with this dressing.

1 c. mayonnaise or salad
   dressing
2 tblsp. ketchup
1 tblsp. chopped dill pickle

1 tsp. grated onion
1 hard-cooked egg, finely
   chopped

Combine all ingredients. Makes about 1⅓ cups.

Memo to Meal Planner: While Thousand Island Salad Dressing works wonders with vegetable salads, it gives sandwiches new subtle flavors that are delightful, too. Spread it on one slice of the buttered bread. Try it for cheese, chicken, meat and Reuben sandwiches.

RUSSIAN SALAD DRESSING

Make this salad dressing to save money and add variety to salads.

1 c. salad oil
½ c. ketchup
¼ c. vinegar
¼ c. grated onion
2 tsp. Worcestershire sauce

1½ tsp. celery seeds
½ tsp. salt
½ tsp. paprika
⅛ tsp. pepper
¼ c. light corn syrup

Combine all ingredients, except corn syrup, in bowl. Beat in corn syrup with rotary beater. Cover and refrigerate. Makes 2 cups.

Memo to Meal Planner: This salad dressing with faint sweet undertones is ideal for boosting flavor of plain lettuce and cabbage salads.

CHAPTER 9

Satisfying Simple Desserts

Baked Cherry Pudding, Rhubarb Cobbler, Lemon Crisp Supreme, Pink Grapefruit Pie . . . these are among the dessert recipes in this chapter.

Perhaps you're trying to serve fewer desserts to encourage members of your family to keep their weight down. (And to cut costs!) Have you thought of reducing the size of servings instead of eliminating them completely? A single cookie provides that final sweet taste at meal's end that so many people like. And it can do more. Oatmeal Drop Cookies, for example, enriched by the addition of soybean protein, add good nutrition as well as a sweet. Peanut Cookie Balls also contribute body-building protein.

You will find a variety of other recipes for desserts that contribute protein. If you crossed baked custards off your list because they cook slowly and must be removed from the oven at exactly the right stage, try our delicate Skillet Custards, and return the milk-and-egg dessert to your table. These custards cook in 15 minutes.

Economical "from-scratch" puddings can be delicious. You'll have trouble deciding between old-fashioned Perfect Rice Pudding and new-fashioned Orange County Rice Pudding, to which cottage cheese adds a faint tang.

Among the make-ahead specialties ideal to serve at women's luncheons and parties are Frosty Lemon Squares and Pink Lemonade Dessert. They are attractive and tasty, yet light enough to please the calorie watchers and inexpensive, too.

When fruits, berries and melons are bountiful, desserts are no problem in country kitchens. Most women manage to find time to treat their families and friends to luscious desserts made with fresh fruits—like Peach Crisp and Purple Plum Crunch.

In winter especially, recipes for oven desserts that bake alongside other foods are in demand. They save work and make economical use of oven heat. Notice how many of our puddings bake in a 350° oven, the same temperature required by many baked main dishes.

Any collection of "desserts" today should include sweet rolls and other breads. Country women long ago substituted them for the more costly and richer traditional desserts. They are rediscovering that homemade breads, accompanied by a beverage and perhaps fruit, never fail to win enthusiastic acceptance when served for dessert in meals and informal refreshments. The splurge of activity in bread baking has something to do with the trend.

Cut slices of Carrot Bread, a loaf made with whole wheat flour, for instance. Or our inexpensive Orange Quick Bread. You will appreciate why breads for dessert have caught on.

Every woman knows that desserts give the last impression, and often the lasting one, of meals. You can serve them and reduce the strain on the budget by using the thrifty recipes that follow. See also the chapter on Homemade Mixes for more superior desserts.

Old-fashioned Economy Puddings

Perhaps you were lucky enough to have a grandmother who made memorable milk-and-egg puddings. If you were, you probably also recall how often you found bright homemade jelly hidden under the meringue on bread pudding. And you remember the plump raisins in rice pudding. What you probably did not know was that these were economical desserts. Grandmother utilized and disguised leftover bread, often dry, in her puddings and she used inexpensive rice as a basis for dessert.

These desserts were born of necessity in pioneer kitchens when trips in town were not daily. Recipes were handed from mother to daughter. Our affluent society just about abandoned them, but it is time to bring them back in the name of good, nutritious—and economical—eating.

The two bread and rice pudding recipes that follow produce delicate, light puddings. Take advantage of their gold-tipped meringues and carry the pudding-filled casserole to the table and serve.

BREAD PUDDING DE LUXE

When making this pudding, notice that 2 of the eggs are separated to provide the egg whites used in the meringue.

4 c. bread cubes	1 tsp. vanilla
3 eggs	¼ c. currant, grape or apple
2 c. reconstituted nonfat dry	jelly
milk, scalded	¼ c. sugar
⅓ c. sugar	

Place bread cubes in ungreased 1½-qt. casserole.

Beat together 1 egg and 2 egg yolks; gradually beat in milk, ⅓ c. sugar and vanilla. Pour over bread cubes. Place casserole in pan of hot water. Bake in 350° oven 1 hour, or until knife inserted 1″ from edge of casserole comes out clean. Remove casserole from oven. Gently spread jelly over top.

Beat remaining 2 egg whites until frothy; gradually beat in ¼ c. sugar. Continue beating until stiff, dry peaks form. Spread over pudding, sealing to edge. Return to pan of hot water in oven and bake about 15 minutes, until meringue is lightly browned. Cool 30 minutes before serving faintly warm. Makes 6 servings.

PERFECT RICE PUDDING

Good way to encourage the family to enjoy milk and eggs.

½ c. uncooked rice	2 eggs, separated
1 c. water	2½ c. milk
½ c. sugar	1½ tsp. vanilla
1 tblsp. cornstarch	½ c. raisins
⅛ tsp. salt	¼ c. sugar

Combine rice and water in saucepan. Heat to boiling, stirring occasionally. Reduce heat, cover and simmer 14 minutes.

Meanwhile, blend together ½ c. sugar, cornstarch and salt. Beat egg yolks slightly; add along with milk to sugar-cornstarch mixture. Beat with rotary beater. Stir in rice, vanilla and raisins. Pour into ungreased 1½-qt. casserole. Place in pan of hot water. Bake in 350° oven 1½ hours, stirring occasionally, until pudding is creamy and most of liquid is absorbed. Remove casserole from oven.

Beat egg whites until foamy. Gradually beat in ¼ c. sugar; continue beating until stiff peaks form. Spread on pudding, sealing to edge. Return casserole to pan of hot water in oven. Continue baking about 15 minutes, until meringue is light golden brown. Makes 6 servings.

Memo to Meal Planner: Serve this pudding hot or cold, and if you like, pass a pitcher of milk to pour over it. You can make it with reconstituted nonfat dry milk.

BAKED CHERRY PUDDING

Old-fashioned country pudding with a new-fashioned topping.

1 (1 lb.) can tart pie cherries (water pack)	1 c. sugar
1 c. sifted flour	2 eggs
1 tsp. baking powder	1 envelope dessert topping mix
½ tsp. salt	Cherry Sauce
2 tblsp. butter or regular margarine	

Drain cherries, reserving juice. Set aside juice and all but 1 c. cherries for sauce.

Sift together flour, baking powder and salt.

Cream together butter and sugar. Add eggs and beat well. Blend in sifted dry ingredients. Stir in 1 c. drained cherries. Turn into well-greased 9″ square pan. Bake in 350° oven 35 to 40 minutes.

Meanwhile, prepare dessert topping by package directions, and make Cherry Sauce. Serve pudding topped with dessert topping and Cherry Sauce. Makes 9 servings.

Cherry Sauce: Combine ⅓ c. sugar, 1 tblsp. cornstarch, reserved cherry juice and remaining cherries. Cook, stirring constantly, until thick and clear. Blend in 2 to 4 drops red food color.

Memo to Meal Planner: This pudding has the texture of a chewy cake. The Cherry Sauce is on the scant side, but the whipped topping rounds it out beautifully. An ideal time to make this pudding is when you can tuck it in the oven to bake alongside a main dish. This might be Ham/Sweet Potato Bake (see Index for recipe). Complete the meal with buttered broccoli. If you have guests (or to please the family) add a relish tray.

APPLESAUCE BREAD PUDDING

The top of this fruited bread-egg-milk pudding is somewhat crusty. A good way to salvage dry bread if you have it. The dessert still will be a bargain in cost, good nutrition and taste.

8 slices dry white bread
2 c. applesauce
½ c. raisins
¼ c. brown sugar, firmly packed
½ tsp. ground cinnamon
2 eggs
2 c. reconstituted nonfat dry milk
½ c. brown sugar, firmly packed
½ tsp. vanilla
¼ tsp. salt
Dash of ground nutmeg

Arrange 4 slices bread in bottom of greased 9″ square pan, cutting off crusts if necessary to fit. (If necessary to dry bread, spread slices in 300° oven for 30 minutes.)

Combine applesauce, raisins, ¼ c. brown sugar and cinnamon. Spread over bread. Top with remaining bread slices.

Beat eggs; beat in milk, ½ c. brown sugar, vanilla and salt. Pour over bread. Sprinkle with nutmeg. Bake in 350° oven 55 to 60 minutes. Let stand 30 minutes before serving. Makes 9 servings.

CORN FLAKE/MOLASSES PUDDING

This dessert has a molasses taste reminiscent of Indian pudding.

2 eggs, slightly beaten
½ c. molasses
¼ c. sugar
1 tblsp. melted butter or regular margarine
½ tsp. ground cinnamon
¼ tsp. ground nutmeg
¼ tsp. salt
3 c. reconstituted nonfat dry milk
4 c. coarsely crushed corn flakes
Vanilla ice cream

Combine eggs, molasses, sugar, butter, cinnamon, nutmeg and salt in large bowl. Stir in milk and corn flake crumbs. Turn into greased 1½-qt. casserole. Set in pan of hot water. Bake in 350° oven about 1 hour, until knife inserted halfway between center and edge comes out clean. Serve warm topped with ice cream. Serves 6.

Memo to Meal Planner: Put Economy Pot Roast (see Index for recipe) and the pudding in the oven together. They will cook in about the same time. Serve with your favorite cabbage salad.

ORANGE COUNTY RICE PUDDING

Tasty, unusual rice pudding is a friend of budget watchers.

3 c. reconstituted nonfat dry milk	½ tsp. grated orange peel
	½ tsp. grated lemon peel
½ c. uncooked rice	1 tsp. vanilla
½ c. sugar	¾ c. creamed cottage cheese
¼ tsp. salt	Orange sections (optional)

Scald milk in top of double boiler. Stir in rice, sugar and salt. Cover and cook over boiling water for 1 hour, stirring 5 or 6 times. Uncover and cook 30 to 40 minutes, until thickened. Remove from heat and add orange and lemon peels and vanilla. Chill.

Beat cottage cheese. Mix into chilled pudding mixture. Serve garnished with orange sections, if desired. Makes 6 servings.

Old-fashioned Cottage Pudding, Rediscovered

Frontier women often brought cheer to their families and friends by serving them fluffy, cakelike cottage pudding made with ingredients usually on hand in their kitchens. Often on busy days they stirred up the batter at the last minute before dinner and hurried it into the oven. Recipes for the pudding varied little, if at all, but different sauces provided change. Those flavored with lemon and vanilla were the universal favorites.

Now their great-great-granddaughters, many of whom have no memory of tasting cottage pudding in their childhood, are discovering the easy, quick, economical and delicious dessert. They consider it one of their best "from-scratch" convenience foods. The recipes that follow, perfected through the years, are foolproof.

OLD-FASHIONED COTTAGE PUDDING

Speedy dessert that fits perfectly into many oven dinners.

1¾ c. sifted flour	¼ c. shortening
¾ c. sugar	1 egg
2 tsp. baking powder	¾ c. milk
½ tsp. salt	1 tsp. vanilla
⅛ tsp. ground mace	Lemon or Vanilla Sauce

Sift together flour, sugar, baking powder, salt and mace into bowl. Add shortening, egg, milk and vanilla, and beat until smooth. Spread into greased and floured 9″ square pan. Bake in 350° oven 30 to 35 minutes. Serve warm with Lemon Sauce. Makes 9 servings.

LEMON SAUCE

At its best when served hot over oven-warm cottage pudding.

1 c. sugar	1 tblsp. grated lemon peel
2 tblsp. cornstarch	¼ c. butter or regular margarine
⅛ tsp. salt	2 tblsp. lemon juice
2 c. water	

Combine sugar, cornstarch and salt in saucepan. Stir in water and lemon peel. Cook, stirring constantly, until mixture comes to a boil. Boil 1 minute, stirring constantly. Remove from heat and stir in butter and lemon juice. Makes about 2 cups.

Variation

Vanilla Sauce: Omit lemon peel and juice from the recipe for Lemon Sauce. Add 2 tsp. vanilla with the butter after removing from heat.

Memo to Meal Planner: Keep the sauces warm until serving time or reheat the cooked mixture and add the butter and lemon juice or vanilla just before serving. When provisions were low in frontier homes and the supply of lemons and vanilla was exhausted, 1½ to 2 tsp. grated nutmeg often were added with the butter.

SKILLET CUSTARDS

It takes no more than 15 minutes to cook these delicate custards. Caramel ice cream sauce adds marvelous flavor.

4 eggs	1 tsp. vanilla
⅓ c. sugar	⅛ tsp. salt
3 c. reconstituted nonfat dry milk	½ c. caramel ice cream sauce

Put eggs and sugar in blender; set at low speed and blend well. Add milk, vanilla and salt. Blend just until mixed. (Or blend ingredients by hand with rotary beater.) Place 1 tblsp. caramel sauce in the bottom of each 6-oz. custard cup. (You will need 8.) Fill with egg mixture.

Set 4 filled custard cups in each of 2 large skillets. Add water to within ½" of top of cups. Heat water just to the simmering point. Cover, reduce heat and simmer 10 to 15 minutes, until custards are set (do not boil). Immediately remove custard cups, cool and refrigerate until well chilled. Makes 8 servings.

Memo to Meal Planner: If you prefer a less sweet dessert, omit caramel sauce and sprinkle tops of egg mixture before simmering with ground or grated nutmeg. This egg-and-milk dessert is a good investment in nutrition. You can make it with whole milk, but using dry milk reduces costs and the number of calories.

PINEAPPLE RICE CUSTARD

Luscious way to make a small can of pineapple serve eight. You can substitute whipped dessert topping for the whipped cream to cut costs.

¾ c. sugar	Milk (about 1¾ c.)
¼ tsp. salt	2 eggs, slightly beaten
1 envelope unflavored gelatin	1½ to 2 c. cooled cooked rice
1 (8¼ oz.) can crushed pineapple	1 tsp. vanilla
	½ c. heavy cream, whipped

Combine sugar, salt and gelatin in saucepan.
Drain pineapple, reserving juice. Add enough milk to pineapple

juice to make 2 c. Stir liquid and eggs into mixture in saucepan, blending well. Cook and stir until mixture coats a spoon. Cool.

Fold in drained pineapple, saving out a little for garnish, rice and vanilla. Chill until mixture begins to thicken. Fold in whipped cream. Spoon into dessert dishes and chill. Garnish with reserved crushed pineapple. Makes 8 to 10 servings.

Cobblers—A Popular Country Dessert

Send the family away from the dinner table in a happy state of mind. This is the psychology of many country women who are good at holding down food costs. They find the last "course" largely determines how people feel about a meal. The man who would have preferred grilled porterhouse steak instead of the ground beef he got forgets about it when he is served a warm cherry cobbler. By dinner's end he experiences a well-fed satisfaction and that's what counts.

Cobblers can be made in great variety by using the different fruits *in season* when they are lowest in cost. Start with spring's slender pink rhubarb stalks, move on to summer's berries, cherries, peaches and then to faithful apples available many months. Canned cherry pie filling makes a fine winter cobbler.

Pass a pitcher of milk to pour over the dessert, if desired. It adds to good nutrition and often to the enjoyment of the homey country dessert.

RHUBARB COBBLER

Bake in spring when rhubarb is abundant, then try the variations.

1 c. sifted flour	1 to 1½ c. sugar
2 tblsp. sugar	2 tblsp. cornstarch
1½ tsp. baking powder	2 tblsp. water
¼ tsp. salt	4 c. rhubarb, cut in 1″ pieces
¼ c. butter or regular margarine	1 tblsp. butter or regular
1 egg, slightly beaten	margarine
¼ c. milk	

To make topping, sift together flour, 2 tblsp. sugar, baking powder and salt. Cut in ¼ c. butter until mixture resembles coarse crumbs.

Blend together egg and milk; add to dry ingredients. Stir just to moisten.

Combine 1 to 1½ c. sugar and cornstarch in saucepan. Stir in water and rhubarb. Cook, stirring, until mixture comes to a boil; boil 1 minute. Remove from heat and stir in 1 tblsp. butter. Place in greased 8″ square pan. Top immediately with 6 mounds of topping. Bake in 400° oven 20 to 25 minutes. Serve warm. Makes 6 servings.

Memo to Meal Planner: The amount of sugar for the filling depends on the tartness of the rhubarb. It is a good idea to start with 1¼ c. sugar for the early season rhubarb, which is tart. For a company dessert, top with scoops of vanilla ice cream at serving time.

Variations
Cherry Cobbler: Make this like Rhubarb Cobbler substituting cherry filling for the rhubarb filling. Heat 1 (1 lb. 5 oz.) can cherry pie filling with 1 tblsp. butter or regular margarine until bubbly.
Peach Cobbler: Make this like Rhubarb Cobbler, substituting peach filling for rhubarb filling. In saucepan combine ½ to ⅔ c. brown sugar, firmly packed, 1½ tblsp. cornstarch and ¼ tsp. ground cinnamon. Stir in ⅓ c. water and cook, stirring constantly, until mixture comes to a boil. Stir in 4 c. sliced peeled fresh peaches and simmer until peaches are thoroughly hot. Add 1 tblsp. butter or regular margarine.
Apple Cobbler: Make this like Rhubarb Cobbler substituting apple filling for rhubarb filling. In large saucepan combine 1 c. sugar, 1 tblsp. cornstarch and ½ tsp. ground cinnamon. Stir in 6 c. sliced peeled apples. Cook over low heat, stirring frequently, until apples are almost tender. Remove from heat and stir in 1 tblsp. butter or regular margarine.

WINTER FRUIT COBBLER

You can also use canned peaches, apricots, cherries or blueberries.

2 (16 to 17 oz.) cans blackberries	4 tsp. baking powder
	½ tsp. salt
½ c. butter or regular margarine	1 c. milk
1 c. sugar	1 tsp. vanilla
2 c. sifted flour	¼ c. sugar
½ tsp. ground cinnamon	Vanilla ice cream

Drain blackberries, reserving juice. Add water to make 2 c. juice.
Cream together butter and 1 c. sugar until light and fluffy.
Sift together flour, cinnamon, baking powder and salt.
Combine milk and vanilla.
Alternately add half of sifted dry ingredients and all of milk mixture to creamed sugar and butter. Add remaining half of dry ingredients and beat until batter is smooth. Pour into greased 13×9×2″ baking pan. Spoon blackberries over the top. Sprinkle with ¼ c. sugar; pour over the reserved fruit juice. Bake in 375° oven 55 to 60 minutes, or until done. Serve warm with ice cream on top. Makes 10 to 12 servings.

Memo to Meal Planner: The amount of sugar needed to sprinkle over fruit depends on the sweetness of the syrup in which it was canned. It varies from ¼ to ¾ c. sugar. If you use canned peaches or apricots, slice the fruit.

Economical Fruit Crisps

With a waste-not policy, farm women traditionally utilized the windfalls and imperfect fruit, vegetables or other food they could salvage. This economical custom returns to favor when high prices invade food budgets.

Fruit crisps were a way of using odds and ends in desserts other than conventional pies. They are easier and quicker to make. Instead of rolling the topping as you do pie crusts, you merely sprinkle it over the fruit and bake it. You can make many kinds as the gifts of the season come and go. Recipes for delicious crisps follow.

APPLE CRISP

Crunchy, cinnamon-spiced oatmeal topping on apple slices. Good traveling dessert to take to a co-operative supper.

¾ c. quick-cooking rolled oats	½ tsp. ground cinnamon
¾ c. brown sugar, firmly packed	½ c. butter or regular margarine
½ c. flour	4 c. sliced peeled apples

Combine rolled oats, brown sugar, flour and cinnamon. Cut in butter until thoroughly mixed.

Place apples in greased 8" square pan. Sprinkle oat mixture evenly over top. Bake in 375° oven 30 to 35 minutes. Serve hot or cold. Makes 6 servings.

Variations
Peach Crisp: Make like Apple Crisp, but substitute 5 c. sliced peeled fresh peaches, combined with ¼ c. white sugar and 3 tblsp. flour, for the apples.

Cherry Crisp: Make like Apple Crisp but substitute cherry filling for the apples. To make filling, combine 1 (1 lb.) can pitted tart red cherries (water pack) with ½ c. white sugar, 4 tsp. quick-cooking tapioca and a few drops of red food color. Let stand 5 minutes. Cook and stir until mixture is thickened. Pour into greased 8" square pan. Cool before adding topping. Bake as directed.

Extra-Easy Cherry Crisp: Make like Apple Crisp but substitute 1 (1 lb. 5 oz.) can cherry pie filling for the apples.

Memo to Meal Planner: Serve crisps with ice cream or ice milk or whipped topping, if you like. If you wish to bake the crisp ahead, but want to serve it fairly warm, reheat it in a low oven at mealtime.

LEMON CRISP SUPREME

Add a few drops of yellow food color to the lemon mixture to make this refreshing, delicious dessert prettier.

6 tblsp. butter or regular margarine	⅓ c. shredded coconut
¾ c. brown sugar, firmly packed	¾ c. sugar
	2 tblsp. cornstarch
1 c. sifted flour	¼ tsp. salt
½ tsp. baking soda	1 c. hot water
½ tsp. salt	1 egg, beaten
¾ c. cracker crumbs	½ tsp. grated lemon peel
	½ c. lemon juice

Cream together butter and brown sugar.

Sift together flour, soda and ½ tsp. salt. Stir into creamed mixture along with cracker crumbs and coconut. Press half of mixture into an 8" square pan. Bake in 350° oven 10 minutes.

Meanwhile, combine white sugar, cornstarch and ¼ tsp. salt in saucepan. Blend in hot water. Cook, stirring constantly, until mixture is clear and bubbly. Remove from heat. Stir a small amount of hot

mixture into egg; return to saucepan. Cook, stirring, until mixture
boils. Remove from heat and stir in lemon peel and juice. Pour over
baked crust in pan; sprinkle reserved half of crumb mixture over top.
Bake in 350° oven 30 minutes. Makes 6 servings.

PURPLE PLUM CRUNCH

*This plum-good dessert is to late summer and early autumn what
strawberry shortcake is to months home-grown berries are ripe. It's a
country kitchen rule to use fruits in season.*

5 c. quartered and pitted fresh
  purple plums
¼ c. brown sugar, firmly
  packed
1 c. sifted flour
½ c. sugar
½ c. brown sugar, firmly
  packed

½ tsp. salt
½ tsp. ground cinnamon
1 egg, beaten
½ c. melted butter or regular
  margarine
Vanilla ice cream or whipped
  dessert topping (optional)

Toss together plums and ¼ c. brown sugar. Place in greased
11×7×1½″ baking pan.

Stir together flour, white sugar, ½ c. brown sugar, salt and cinnamon. Add egg, tossing with a fork until mixture is crumbly.
Sprinkle over plums. Drizzle melted butter over top. Bake in 375°
oven 45 minutes. Serve warm with ice cream. Makes 8 servings.

Homemade Sweet Rolls

Some meal planners depend on homemade yeast breads for trumps.
Homemade rolls and loaves will rescue economical meals from the
ordinary. By using fresh or reconstituted nonfat dry milk for the
liquid in making bread, the protein content is stepped up with a
negligible cost increase.

The revival of the old-time baking day is here. Farm women often
go on a baking spree to build up a supply of breads in their freezers.
"It is good work for stormy days," one country woman says. "With
sweet rolls on hand," she adds, "I need not worry what to have for
dessert. My family prefers them to many rich, overly sweet and
more expensive desserts."

By dividing the recipe for Basic Oatmeal Sweet Yeast Dough in half you can bake two kinds of rolls just about as easily as one. They help keep variety in meals with little extra expenditure of time or money, and are an ideal accompaniment for coffee when you entertain friends.

BASIC OATMEAL SWEET YEAST DOUGH

Divide dough in half and make two kinds of sweet rolls.

1 pkg. active dry yeast	1 tsp. salt
¼ c. warm water (110 to 115°)	1 c. milk, scalded and cooled
4 to 4½ c. flour	to lukewarm
1 c. quick-cooking rolled oats	½ c. butter or regular margarine
½ c. brown sugar, firmly	2 eggs
packed	

Sprinkle yeast on warm water; stir to dissolve. Combine with 1 c. flour, rolled oats, brown sugar, salt, milk, butter and eggs in large mixer bowl. Beat until mixture is well blended. Stir in enough of remaining flour to make a soft dough. Turn onto lightly floured surface; knead until smooth and elastic, about 5 minutes. Place in greased bowl; turn dough over to grease top. Let rise in warm place until double, about 1½ hours. Punch down dough. Divide in half. Make Caramel Cinnamon Rolls and Orange Stickies as directed.

CARAMEL CINNAMON ROLLS

Oats in the dough give rolls a delightful, different taste.

½ Basic Oatmeal Sweet	⅓ c. brown sugar,
Yeast Dough	firmly packed
2 tblsp. melted butter	1 tsp. ground cinnamon
or regular margarine	

Roll dough into 12×9″ rectangle. Brush with butter.

Combine brown sugar and cinnamon. Sprinkle over dough. Roll up from long side, as for jelly roll; seal edge. Cut in twelve 1″ slices. Place in greased muffin-pan cups. Let rise in warm place until double, about 30 minutes. Bake in 375° oven 20 minutes. Makes 12.

ORANGE STICKIES

Spooning orange syrup over partly baked rolls is the trick.

½ Basic Oatmeal Sweet Yeast
   Dough
3 tblsp. melted butter or regular
   margarine
½ c. brown sugar, firmly
   packed

1 tsp. grated orange peel
⅔ c. sugar
⅔ c. orange juice
2 tblsp. butter or regular
   margarine

Roll dough into 15×9″ rectangle. Brush with 3 tblsp. melted butter. Combine brown sugar and orange peel; sprinkle over dough. Roll up from long side, as for jelly roll; seal edge. Cut in fifteen 1″ slices. Place cut side down in greased 13×9×2″ baking pan. Let rise in warm place until double, about 30 minutes.

Meanwhile, combine white sugar and ⅓ c. orange juice in saucepan. Bring to a boil; reduce heat and simmer 5 minutes. Remove from heat and stir in 2 tblsp. butter and remaining ⅓ c. orange juice.

Bake rolls in 375° oven 15 minutes. Spoon orange syrup over rolls. Return to oven and bake 15 minutes longer. Invert while hot over tray or platter. Makes 15 rolls.

ECONOMICAL COFFEE CAKE

Serve warm from oven with coffee or tea for morning or afternoon refreshments or in any of the day's three meals. Keep this recipe handy to make the three tempting variations—one topped with apples, another containing a spicy sugar-nut filling and the third wearing a crisp crunchy oat topping.

¾ c. sugar
¼ c. shortening
1 egg
½ c. milk
1½ c. sifted flour

2 tsp. baking powder
½ tsp. salt
⅓ c. brown sugar, firmly
   packed
1 tsp. ground cinnamon

Beat together white sugar, shortening and egg to mix thoroughly. Blend in milk.

Sift together flour, baking powder and salt; stir into beaten mixture. Spread in greased 9″ square pan.

Combine brown sugar and cinnamon and sprinkle over top of batter. Bake in 375° oven 25 to 35 minutes. Makes 9 servings.

Variations

Quick Apple Coffee Cake: Spread batter for Economical Coffee Cake in greased 9" square pan. Arrange 2 thinly sliced unpeeled apples over top of batter. Combine ⅓ c. brown sugar, firmly packed, and ½ tsp. ground cinnamon; sprinkle over top of apples. Bake in 375° oven 40 to 45 minutes.

Filled Quick Coffee Cake: Spread half of batter for Economical Coffee Cake in greased 9" square pan. Combine ½ c. brown sugar, firmly packed, 2 tblsp. flour, 1 tsp. ground cinnamon, 2 tblsp. melted butter or regular margarine and ⅓ c. finely chopped nuts. Sprinkle over batter in pan. Spread remaining half of batter evenly over top. Bake in 375° oven 30 minutes.

Cinnamon/Oat Coffee Cake: Spread batter for Economical Coffee Cake in greased 9" square pan. Combine ½ c. quick-cooking rolled oats, ½ c. brown sugar, firmly packed, and 1 tsp. ground cinnamon. Sprinkle over top of batter. Bake in 375° oven 30 minutes.

Orange Quick Bread—A Hostess Favorite

How to entertain friends often and serve them really good refreshments without wrecking the food budget requires planning. One Missouri woman invites neighborhood friends, a few at a time, to stop in for a cup of coffee or tea. With the beverage she serves one delicious accompaniment considerate of her pocketbook.

Orange Quick Bread is one of her favorites—also a favorite of her friends. Her family delights in the share of the loaf she saves for them. She flavors the bread with orange peel, which is otherwise wasted. Frequently, she adds the orange itself to fruit cup or salad for dinner or supper. Other times she twists plastic wrap around the fruit and refrigerates it to serve for breakfast the next day.

ORANGE QUICK BREAD

Hostess and guests recommend this simple economical bread.

1 tblsp. finely shredded orange peel	½ c. sugar
	3 tsp. baking powder
½ c. sugar	½ tsp. salt
½ c. water	1 egg, beaten
Milk	1 tblsp. melted shortening
2 c. sifted flour	Orange Glaze (optional)

In small saucepan simmer orange peel with ½ c. sugar and water until peel is tender and translucent. Pour into measuring cup and add enough milk to make 1 cup.

Sift together flour, ½ c. sugar, baking powder and salt.

Combine egg, milk mixture and shortening. Add all at once to flour mixture; stir just until mixture is blended. Do not overblend.

Turn into greased 8½ ×4½ ×2½" loaf pan. Bake in 350° oven 40 to 50 minutes. Let cool on rack 10 minutes. Spoon Orange Glaze on loaf, if desired. Cool and refrigerate before slicing. Makes 1 loaf.

Orange Glaze: Combine 1 c. sifted confectioners sugar with 1 tblsp. orange juice and blend until smooth. (This is a heavy glaze. For a lighter glaze, use ¾ c. confectioners sugar.)

APPLE/ORANGE COFFEE BREAD

You will have better luck slicing this loaf neatly if you first refrigerate it. Makes wonderful bread-and-butter sandwiches.

½ c. butter or regular margarine	⅓ c. orange juice
1 c. sugar	1 c. finely chopped unpeeled apples
2 eggs	
2 c. sifted flour	⅓ c. chopped nuts
1 tsp. baking soda	1 tsp. grated orange peel
½ tsp. salt	

Cream together butter and sugar. Add eggs and beat until mixture is light and fluffy.

Sift together dry ingredients. Add alternately with orange juice to creamed mixture. Fold in apples, nuts and orange peel.

Turn into greased 9×5×3" loaf pan. Bake in 350° oven 50 to 55 minutes. Cool. Makes 1 loaf.

CARROT BREAD

"The most delicious whole wheat bread I ever tasted!" That's what guests say when they are served this carrot-nut loaf.

1½ c. sifted flour
1½ tsp. baking powder
1 tsp. baking soda
1 tsp. salt
½ tsp. ground cinnamon
1 c. whole wheat flour
⅔ c. brown sugar, firmly
   packed

2 eggs, beaten
1 c. milk
¼ c. melted butter or regular
   margarine
1 c. grated peeled carrots
½ c. chopped nuts

Sift together white flour, baking powder, baking soda, salt and cinnamon into a bowl.

Stir whole wheat flour and measure. Stir into dry ingredients along with brown sugar.

Combine eggs, milk and butter. Add to dry ingredients and stir just until ingredients are blended; do not overmix. Fold in carrots and nuts. Turn into well-greased 8½ × 4½ × 2½" loaf pan. Bake in 350° oven 45 to 50 minutes. Cool. Makes 1 loaf.

VERSATILE BLUEBERRY KUCHEN

If you are lucky enough to live in blueberry country, near it or any other place where you can pick up a bargain in the frosty-blue berries, try this simple country dessert. The magic of this recipe is the way it stretches 2 cups blueberries to make 6 to 8 servings. The kuchen is a cross between a dessert and a coffee bread.

1 egg
½ c. sugar
¼ c. melted butter or regular
   margarine
¼ c. milk
1½ c. sifted flour

2½ tsp. baking powder
¼ tsp. salt
2 c. blueberries
1 tblsp. lemon juice
3 tblsp. sugar
½ tsp. ground cinnamon

Beat egg with ½ c. sugar until blended; stir in butter and milk.

Sift together flour, baking powder and salt. Stir into liquid ingredients until smooth. Spread batter in greased 8" square pan.

Mix blueberries and lemon juice. Sprinkle evenly over top of batter in pan. Mix 3 tblsp. sugar and cinnamon; sprinkle over berries.

Bake in 350° oven 45 to 50 minutes. Serve warm as is, or top with ice cream or whipped dessert topping. Makes 6 to 8 servings.

FRUIT PUDDING CAKE

Good inexpensive dessert. You can use leftover fruits instead of the fruit cocktail. Use 1½ c. fruit and ½ to ⅔ c. of their juice.

1 (1 lb. 1 oz.) can fruit
  cocktail
1 egg, beaten
1 tsp. vanilla
1½ c. sifted flour
1 c. sugar

1 tsp. salt
1 tsp. baking soda
½ c. brown sugar, firmly
  packed
½ c. chopped walnuts
Whipped dessert topping

Place fruit and juice in mixing bowl; add egg and vanilla. Sift flour, white sugar, salt and baking soda over it. Beat with spoon until smooth. Pour into greased 13×9×2″ baking pan. Sprinkle on brown sugar and nuts. Bake in 325° oven 40 to 45 minutes, or until pudding begins to pull away from sides of pan. Cut in squares and serve with whipped dessert topping. Makes 9 servings.

APPLE UPSIDE-DOWN CAKE

Easy, quick and tasty dessert to bake on busy days.

2 tart red apples
⅓ c. melted butter or regular
  margarine
½ c. brown sugar, firmly packed

¼ c. chopped nuts
1 pkg. spice cake mix (for
  1-layer cake)
Whipped dessert topping

Slice unpeeled apples thinly. Spread melted butter in 8″ square baking pan. Arrange apple slices in rows over butter. Cook over medium heat 3 minutes; remove from heat. Sprinkle with brown sugar and nuts.

Prepare cake mix according to package directions. Spread evenly over apples. Bake in 350° oven 30 to 35 minutes. Remove from oven and turn cake upside down over serving dish; let stand 3 minutes, then remove pan. Serve warm with whipped dessert topping. Makes 6 servings.

Memo to Meal Planner: Consider this dessert for a meal featuring baked beans or a substantial soup, such as Hoosier Bean or Pork/Lentil Soup, for the main dish (see Index for recipes).

CHOCOLATE OATMEAL CAKE

For a coffee accompaniment or for dessert in a guest or family meal, this homespun moist cake is a marvelous choice. Easy to make, and it's kind to the food budget.

1¼ c. boiling water
1 c. quick-cooking rolled oats
½ c. butter or regular margarine
1 (4 oz.) bar sweet cooking chocolate, broken in pieces
1½ c. sifted flour
1 c. sugar

1 tsp. baking soda
½ tsp. salt
1 c. brown sugar, firmly packed
3 eggs
1 tsp. vanilla
Coconut Topping

Pour boiling water over oats; add butter and chocolate. Let stand 20 minutes; stir until blended.

In large mixer bowl sift together flour, white sugar, soda and salt. Stir in brown sugar. Add eggs, vanilla and oatmeal mixture; beat at low speed just to combine well. Spread in greased 13×9×2″ pan.

Bake in 350° oven 35 to 40 minutes. Let stand in pan 10 minutes. Spread Coconut Topping over cake and broil 4 to 5″ from heat about 1 minute, until bubbly. Serve warm or cool. Serves 15.

Coconut Topping: In small saucepan combine ⅓ c. butter or regular margarine, ¼ c. milk and ¾ c. brown sugar, firmly packed. Cook and stir until mixture boils. Reduce heat and simmer 2 to 3 minutes, stirring frequently. Stir in 1 c. shredded coconut.

CHOCOLATE/BANANA UPSIDE-DOWN CAKE

This recipe makes two desserts at the same time—upside-down cake for one day, right-side-up cake for the next.

¼ c. butter or regular margarine
½ c. brown sugar, firmly packed
2 large bananas, peeled and cut in ½″ slices

¼ c. chopped nuts
1 pkg. chocolate cake mix (for 2-layer cake)
Whipped dessert topping or ice cream (optional)

Melt butter over low heat in 8 or 9″ square pan. Sprinkle brown sugar over butter. Arrange bananas over brown sugar and sprinkle nuts between banana slices.

Prepare cake batter by package directions. Pour half of batter over bananas. (Use other half to make Right-Side-Up Cake.) Bake in 350° oven 35 to 45 minutes. Invert cake immediately on plate; leave pan over cake a few minutes before removing. Serve warm with whipped dessert topping, if desired. Makes 9 servings.

Right-Side-Up Cake: Pour remaining half of batter in greased and floured 8 or 9″ square pan. Bake as directed on package. Cool, wrap and freeze or serve the next day, frosted as desired.

COTTAGE CHEESE CUPCAKES

For a special treat, lemon-glazed cupcakes are hard to beat. It is easy to find a less expensive dessert than these little spice cakes, but difficult to find one equally good packed with the top-quality protein cottage cheese provides.

1½ c. creamed cottage cheese	½ tsp. baking soda
¼ c. butter or regular margarine	½ tsp. salt
1 c. brown sugar, firmly packed	½ tsp. ground cinnamon
1 egg	¼ tsp. ground ginger
2 tsp. grated lemon peel	¼ tsp. ground nutmeg
½ c. sugar	¾ c. raisins
1½ c. sifted flour	Lemon Glaze

Put cottage cheese through sieve or strainer.

Cream together butter and brown sugar until light and fluffy. Beat in egg and lemon peel. Beat in cottage cheese and sugar.

Sift together flour, soda, salt and spices. Mix into cottage cheese mixture. Fold in raisins. Fill 18 greased muffin-pan cups (or cups with paper liners) two thirds full. Bake in 350° oven 30 to 35 minutes. Cool and spread tops with Lemon Glaze. Makes 18 cupcakes.

Lemon Glaze: Mix 2 tblsp. lemon juice into 1½ c. sifted confectioners sugar until smooth and of spreading consistency.

Memo to Meal Planner: You can use chopped dates for the raisins. Compare costs of the two dried fruits when you plan to bake the cakes. And you can omit the glaze, although it is the crowning glory. It makes the cakes taste wonderful.

PEANUT COOKIE BALLS

Peanuts are the something new in these rich, tiny cookies that resemble the famous Mexican wedding cakes. They contain good protein and add bits of crispness and flavor.

⅔ c. shortening	2½ c. sifted flour
½ c. peanut butter	¾ c. finely chopped salted
½ tsp. salt	peanuts
½ c. sifted confectioners sugar	Sifted confectioners sugar
1½ tsp. vanilla	

Cream together shortening, peanut butter and salt until mixture is light and fluffy. Gradually add ½ c. confectioners sugar. Blend in vanilla, then flour. Mix in peanuts.

Shape dough into balls. Place 1½″ apart on ungreased baking sheet. Bake in 375° oven about 12 minutes, until golden brown. Cool 5 minutes. Roll in confectioners sugar. Makes 4 dozen.

Memo to Meal Planner: These small cookies are the perfect accompaniment for baked apples or applesauce. You will find that peanuts cost less than other nuts, but use what you have on hand.

OATMEAL DROP COOKIES

They taste like any good oatmeal cookie with raisins, but they contain extra protein from soybeans. Serve with fruit for dessert.

¾ c. shortening	1 tsp. ground cinnamon
1 c. brown sugar, firmly packed	½ tsp. baking soda
½ c. sugar	¼ to ½ tsp. ground cloves
1 egg	1½ c. quick-cooking rolled oats
¼ c. water	1½ c. textured vegetable protein
1 tsp. vanilla	¾ c. raisins
1 c. sifted flour	½ c. chopped nuts
1 tsp. salt	

Beat together shortening, sugars, egg, water and vanilla until mixture is light and fluffy.

Sift together flour, salt, cinnamon, soda and cloves. Stir into beaten mixture along with remaining ingredients.

Drop by rounded teaspoonfuls onto greased baking sheet. Bake in

350° oven 12 to 15 minutes or until almost no imprint remains when touched with finger. Remove immediately from baking sheet to wire racks. Makes 6 dozen.

SCOTIA OAT SQUARES

This is a large recipe for crisp, rolled oatmeal cookies. A FARM JOURNAL *food scout, while visiting in Nova Scotia, tasted these cookies. She liked them so much that she asked how they were made. Returning to her California home, she duplicated the north-of-the-border cookies in her kitchen. Once you make them you will understand her enthusiasm. Oatmeal is a whole grain cereal with excellent nutritional qualifications.*

2 c. shortening	3 c. flour
1½ c. sugar	6 c. quick-cooking rolled oats
1 tsp. vanilla	Water
½ tsp. baking soda	Graham flour
1 tsp. salt	

Cream together shortening, sugar and vanilla until light and fluffy.

Sift together soda, salt and flour three times. Gradually add to creamed mixture, and blend. Stir in oats until well distributed. Add enough water (about 2 tblsp.) to make a dough that holds together when rolling.

Sprinkle graham flour on breadboard and on top of dough. Divide dough in thirds or fourths; carefully roll each piece to make a rectangle about ⅛″ thick. Cut in 2½″ squares; place on greased baking sheet. Bake in 375° oven 18 to 20 minutes. Cool on racks. Makes about 8 dozen.

Cottage Cheese Pancakes for Dessert

For dessert in an otherwise light meal have cottage cheese pancakes. Serve them hot with butter or margarine and cinnamon sugar (3 tblsp. sugar to ½ tsp. ground cinnamon) or jelly, jam or fruit preserves. Bake them on the electric grill at the table, if you like, and deliver really hot cakes. This dessert takes advantage of the increasing importance of cottage cheese, an excellent protein food, as an ingredient in cooking.

COTTAGE CHEESE DESSERT PANCAKES

Great, off-the-grill dessert to make at the last minute.

1 c. sifted flour
1 tsp. baking powder
1 tsp. salt
2 c. small curd creamed cottage
   cheese

4 eggs, well beaten
⅓ c. milk

Sift together flour, baking powder and salt; combine with cottage cheese. Add eggs and milk and mix thoroughly. Bake on lightly greased griddle, using ¼ c. batter per pancake. Makes about 14.

Memo to Meal Planner: These unusual and delicious pancakes make an ideal dessert for a soup and salad meal. Or serve them for informal evening refreshments with coffee.

PEACH-PUDDING PARFAIT

Handsome, new version of peaches and cream costs less.

1 (3 or 3¼ oz.) pkg. vanilla
   pudding and pie filling
1½ c. milk

½ c. dairy sour cream
2 c. diced peeled fresh peaches

Combine pudding and pie filling mix and milk in medium saucepan. Cook over medium heat, stirring constantly, until mixture thickens and bubbles. Remove from heat; stir in sour cream. Cool.

Arrange alternate layers of peaches and pudding in parfait glasses, ending with pudding layer that completely covers fruit. Chill until serving time. Makes 6 servings.

Memo to Meal Planner: If presenting the parfait to guests, you may want to serve a small crisp cookie as an accompaniment. After summer's fresh peaches disappear, use frozen and canned peaches. Other fruits, such as strawberries, fresh and frozen, make great stand-ins.

FROSTY LEMON SQUARES

If you are looking for a delicious and refreshing light dessert, this one fills the bill. It's easy to make. Tastes like a richer, more expensive dessert; and in comparison to most, it is low in calories.

1 c. graham cracker crumbs	⅓ c. lemon juice
2 tblsp. butter or regular margarine	⅔ c. sugar
	Dash of salt
2 eggs, separated	⅔ c. nonfat dry milk
1½ tsp. grated lemon peel	⅔ c. water

Toss together graham cracker crumbs and butter. Sprinkle about three fourths crumb mixture over bottom of 9″ square pan.

Beat together egg yolks, lemon peel and juice, sugar and salt until blended.

Combine egg whites, dry milk and water in large mixer bowl. Beat at high speed about 5 to 6 minutes, until stiff peaks form. At low speed beat in egg yolk-lemon mixture just until blended. Pour over crumbs in pan. Sprinkle remaining crumbs evenly over top. Freeze.

To serve, dip bottom of pan briefly in warm water. Cut in squares. Makes 9 servings.

FRUITED PINK WHIP

When you need a make-ahead dessert, try this light, fluffy treat. It's the "pink of perfection" in looks and taste. Part of its superior flavor comes from the blending of pineapple and banana flavors.

1 (13¼ oz.) can crushed pineapple	1 (6 oz.) can evaporated milk, thoroughly chilled
Water	2 bananas
1 (3 oz.) pkg. cherry flavor gelatin	1 c. vanilla wafer crumbs
⅓ c. water	¼ c. melted butter or regular margarine

Drain pineapple, reserving syrup. Set pineapple aside. Add enough water to syrup to make 1 c. Heat to boiling. Dissolve gelatin in boiling syrup; add ⅓ c. water. Chill until mixture is the consistency of egg whites.

Pour well-chilled evaporated milk into small mixer bowl that has been chilled; whip at high speed until milk stands in soft peaks.

Turn whipped milk into large mixer bowl. Whip at medium speed 3 to 4 minutes, while gradually adding thickened gelatin.

Cut peeled bananas in halves lengthwise, then slice. Fold bananas and crushed pineapple into whipped mixture.

Combine vanilla wafer crumbs and butter. Spread half of crumbs in the bottom of 8″ square pan. Pour in the gelatin mixture. Sprinkle remaining crumbs over the top. Chill until set. Makes 8 or 9 servings.

PINK LEMONADE DESSERT

Easy, pretty bridge club dessert that women rave about.

1 (14 oz.) can sweetened condensed milk	1 (9 oz.) carton frozen whipped topping
1 (6 oz.) can frozen pink lemonade concentrate, thawed	1½ c. graham cracker crumbs

Thoroughly blend together sweetened condensed milk (not evaporated) and lemonade concentrate. Fold in whipped topping.

Sprinkle half of crumbs in bottom of greased 9″ square pan. Spread whipped mixture over crumbs. Sprinkle remaining crumbs over top. Chill. Makes 9 servings.

PINK GRAPEFRUIT PIE

When you find a bargain in grapefruit, make this new pie.

2 baked 10″ pie shells	Few drops red food color
2 large pink grapefruit	1 (14½ oz.) can evaporated milk, chilled
1 c. grapefruit juice	¼ c. lemon juice
1 envelope unflavored gelatin	2 egg whites
2 egg yolks, beaten	¼ tsp. cream of tartar
½ c. sugar	¼ c. sugar
¼ tsp. salt	
½ tsp. grated lemon peel	

Cut peel and white membrane from grapefruit. Lift out sections and drain well, reserving juice. Add water, if necessary, to make 1 c. juice. Soften gelatin in ½ c. grapefruit juice.

Combine egg yolks with ½ c. sugar, salt, lemon peel and remaining ½ c. grapefruit juice. Cook over low heat, stirring constantly, until mixture thickens and coats the back of a spoon. Remove from heat, add softened gelatin and stir until it is dissolved. Add a few drops of food color to tint a delicate pink. Add grapefruit sections and chill until mixture mounds when a little is dropped from a spoon.

Beat thoroughly chilled evaporated milk in chilled bowl until it begins to thicken. Add lemon juice and beat until mixture resembles whipped cream.

Beat egg whites until foamy; add cream of tartar, and continue beating. Gradually add ¼ c. sugar, beating until soft peaks form.

Combine thickened egg yolk mixture with whipped evaporated milk. Fold in egg whites and spoon evenly into baked pie shells. Refrigerate at least 2 to 3 hours. Makes 2 pies.

Memo to Meal Planner: There are two ways to include this exciting pie in menus. One is to feature it as the dessert in an otherwise ordinary meal. The other approach is to serve the pie in a special-occasion meal when all the food from start to finish is exceptionally delicious and distinctive. It "fits both shoes." The California hostess who shares the recipe, sometimes uses white instead of pink grapefruit, if she can buy it at the better price.

CHERRY/CHEESE TORTE

An easy-to-fix, make-ahead dessert with delightful flavor and eye appeal.

1½ c. graham cracker crumbs	1 c. sifted confectioners sugar
1 envelope dessert topping mix	1 (1 lb. 5 oz.) can cherry pie
1 (8 oz.) pkg. cream cheese, softened	filling

Place crumbs in bottom of greased 12×7½×2″ baking dish.

Prepare dessert topping mix by package directions.

Cream together cream cheese and confectioners sugar until light and fluffy; fold in whipped topping. Gently spread over the crumbs. Top with cherry pie filling. Chill at least 2 hours. Makes 12 servings.

INDEX

* RETAIL CUTS OF BEEF—WHERE THEY COME FROM AND HOW TO COOK THEM

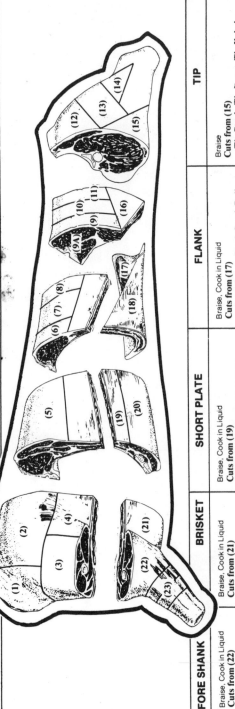

CHUCK
Roast, Broil, Panfry

Braise, Cook in Liquid
Cuts from (1)
Beef for Stew, Ground Chuck
Cuts from (2)
Boneless Chuck Eye Roast, Blade Roast or Steak
Cuts from (3)
Chuck Short Ribs, Arm Pot-Roast or Steak, Boneless Shoulder Pot-Roast or Steak
Cuts from (4)
Chuck Short Ribs, Cross Rib Pot-Roast

RIB
Roast, Broil, Panfry

Cuts from (5)
Rib Roast, Rib Steak, Boneless Rib Steak, Rib Eye (Delmonico) Roast or Steak

SHORT LOIN
Roast, Broil, Panfry

Cuts fom (6)
Steaks: Top Loin, Boneless Top Loin
Cuts from (7)
Steaks: Top Loin, T-Bone, Boneless Top Loin, Tenderloin (Filet Mignon); Tenderloin Roast (also from (9A))
Cuts from (8)
Steaks: Porterhouse, Top Loin, Boneless Top Loin, Tenderloin; Tenderloin Roast

SIRLOIN
Broil, Panfry

Cuts from (9)
Pin Bone Sirloin Steak, Boneless Sirloin Steak
Cuts from (10)
Flat Bone Sirloin Steak, Boneless Sirloin Steak
Cuts from (11)
Wedge Bone Sirloin Steak, Boneless Sirloin Steak.

ROUND

Braise, Cook in Liquid
Cuts from (12)
Rolled Rump
Cuts from (13)
Round Steak, Top Round Steak, Cube Steak, Bottom Round Roast or Steak, Eye of Round
Cuts from (14)
Heel of Round, Ground Round

TIP

Braise
Cuts from (15)
Tip Steak, Tip Roast, Tip Kabobs
Cuts from (16)
Tip Roast, Tip Steak, Tip Kabobs

FORE SHANK

Braise, Cook in Liquid
Cuts from (22)
Beef for Stew
Cuts from (23)
Shank Cross Cuts

BRISKET

Braise, Cook in Liquid
Cuts from (21)
Fresh Brisket, Corned Brisket

SHORT PLATE

Braise, Cook in Liquid
Cuts from (19)
Short Ribs, Skirt Steak Rolls
Cuts from (20)
Skirt Steak Rolls, Beef for Stew

FLANK

Braise, Cook in Liquid
Cuts from (17)
Flank Steak, Flank Steak Rolls
Cuts from (18)
Ground Beef, Beef Patties